PEACE BE
STILL

MUSIC IN AMERICAN LIFE

PEACE BE
STILL

HOW
JAMES CLEVELAND
AND THE
ANGELIC CHOIR
CREATED A
GOSPEL CLASSIC

ROBERT M. MAROVICH

UNIVERSITY OF
ILLINOIS PRESS
Urbana, Chicago, and Springfield

Library of Congress Cataloging-in-Publication Data
Names: Marovich, Robert M., author.
Title: Peace be still : how James Cleveland and the
    Angelic Choir created a gospel classic / Robert M.
    Marovich.
Description: Urbana : University of Illinois Press,
    2021. | Series: Music in American life | Includes
    bibliographical references and index.
Identifiers: LCCN 2021008762 (print) | LCCN
    2021008763 (ebook) | ISBN 9780252044113
    (cloth) | ISBN 9780252086168 (paperback) | ISBN
    9780252053054 (ebook)
Subjects: LCSH: Cleveland, James. Peace be still. |
    Gospel music—History and criticism. | Gospel
    music—New Jersey—History and criticism. |
    Angelic Choir.
Classification: LCC ML410.C66 M37 2021 (print) | LCC
    ML410.C66 (ebook) | DDC 782.25/4—dc23
LC record available at https://lccn.loc.gov/2021008762
LC ebook record available at https://lccn.loc.gov/
    2021008763

For Laurel Delaney, with all my love;

and

For all Angelic Choir members, living and departed.

I just had Mary, Jane, and John Doe from up the street, down the street, and around the corner. But I knew if you put them in the church atmosphere, we would do well.

—Reverend Lawrence C. Roberts

True history tells of everyday people who do extraordinary things quietly, not even realizing that they have left their mark.

—Margo Lee Williams

Contents

Acknowledgments

This book was birthed from a dream I had one night in 2013, while preparing to produce a one-hour radio special honoring the fiftieth anniversary of the recording of *Peace Be Still*.

I dreamt that I traveled back to September 1963, to the church where the *Peace Be Still* recording was taking place. There I was, a visitor from the future, sitting in on the live session, writing down what was happening. At one point, I introduced myself to the Reverend James Cleveland—he wasn't *Reverend* James Cleveland then—and said I was a Chicago boy. He liked that. I said I was from Rogers Park, and he knew where that was. I said I knew the South Side and shouted, "35th and South Parkway!" I went to give him a fist bump and he lurched back. His reaction startled me at first, then I remembered—nobody was giving fist bumps in 1963!

Later in the dream, while Cleveland was at the piano, working on one of the songs, I wished him good luck. Smiling like the Cheshire cat, I told him I believed the record would be one of the best-selling gospel albums in history. He turned around, looked straight into my eyes, and replied, "Boy, don't put that kind of pressure on me!"

I shared my dream with the Reverend Doctor Stefanie Minatee, a longtime member of the Angelic Choir community, and she suggested I write a book about the album. She even offered to gather some Angelic Choir alumni for me to interview. That group interview took place one Sunday in October 2013. I was awestruck to be sitting in Nutley's historic First Baptist Church, interviewing those members who were present from the very beginning of the Angelic Choir as well as those who had joined along the way. Their insights anchor this book. But without Reverend Minatee's encouragement and support, I doubt this book would ever have come to pass. I am eternally thankful to her and grateful she has successfully overcome the health issues that plagued her not long after that interview. She is a warrior in every respect.

Still, to my mind, there was one important hurdle to overcome for the book to become a reality. I needed the blessing and participation of Dolores "Bootsy" Roberts, the Reverend Lawrence Roberts's widow. She graciously offered both. I thank her for her willingness to be interviewed and to read through a draft of the full manuscript and make important suggestions. Thanks also to Phyllis Morris and Yvonne Walls Wislow for gathering Angelic Choir alumni for follow-up telephone interviews, and to the Reverend Brian Z. Evans, Kimberly Johnson, and the First Baptist Church of Nutley, New Jersey, for welcoming me to the church every time I visited to conduct research. Sister Kim's assistance and encouragement have been a particular source of inspiration. Thanks to Robert Logan for sharing memories and photos and answering last-minute questions. He is a wealth of knowledge. Many thanks to Dennis Bines for his memories and insights and for providing me with a copy of the Angelic Choir Reunion DVD he produced. Thanks to Joe Peay for his reminiscences and for introducing me to Melodi Ewell Lovely, who shared the largely untold story of her father's role in the reintroduction of "Peace Be Still." To Carol Hobbs, once again a lifesaver with her accurate and efficient transcription work. And thanks to my wife, Laurel Delaney, for her steadfast support of my writing career and for being an inspiration to me every day.

I also want to single out several individuals and institutions who took the time to make critical contributions to this book: The American Guild of Organists, especially James Kennerley and Eric Birk; Tom Ankner and the Newark Public Library; Will Boone; Rebecca "Betty" Brooks; Isaac Brown; Jay Bruder; Reverend Doctor Malcolm Byrd; Vivian Carroll; Dan Cherry; Robert Darden; Glenn G. Geisheimer (oldnewark.com); Gloria Givens; Grey Roots Museum and Archives Collection, Owen Sound, Ontario; Jennifer Griffith; Bernadine Hankerson; Janet Harper, formerly librarian at the Center for Black Music Research, Columbia College Chicago; Linwood Heath;

Anthony Heilbut; the late Gertrude Deadwyler Hicks; the late JaVan Hicks; Sylvia Hicks; Eli Husock; A. Jeffrey LaValley; Melodi Ewell Lovely; Eric Majette Jr. and the Living Testimony Foundation; the Malaco Music Group, especially Rosetta Anderson, Louise Black, Melissa Brown, Tommy Couch Sr., Tommy Couch Jr., Darrell Luster, Stewart Madison, James Robinson, and Wolf Stevenson; Derek Mikel May; Pastor Norman K. Miles Sr. and Trinity Temple Seventh-day Adventist Church, Newark; the late Raymond Murphy; Brenda Nelson-Strauss and the Archives of African American Music and Culture at Indiana University, Bloomington; Doug Oxenhorn and the New Jersey Historical Society; Etta Jean Nunnally; Brenda O'Neal; Kevan Peabody; Monica Pege; Bob Porter; Inez Reid; the late Reverend Doctor Lawrence C. Roberts; Robert Rogers; Percy Spencer; Lorraine Stancil; Nellie Suggs; Elizabeth Surles and the Institute for Jazz Studies at Rutgers University; Annette May Thomas; Nick Van Dorn and the Nutley Public Library; Geraldine Griffin Watlington; Jacqui Watts-Greadington; Marcel West; Harry L. Williams; Keith Van Williams; and Margo Lee Williams.

I express my appreciation to the anonymous peer reviewers whose excellent recommendations improved the manuscript greatly. And to anyone I have forgotten to mention here, I apologize. Please charge it to my head and not my heart. I will thank you personally.

Finally, I am grateful to the team of dedicated professionals at the University of Illinois Press, and especially to Director Laurie Matheson. Laurie's faith in me and my work for the past eight years affirmed my decision to leave a long career in nonprofit fund development to pursue writing for a living. I've been a fan of the University of Illinois Press's Music in American Life Series since the early 1980s. To make a second appearance in the catalog, alongside the award-winning authors and acknowledged experts I admire, is humbling.

PEACE BE
STILL

Introduction

Producing the third volume of the James Cleveland and the Angelic Choir series of live in-service albums was turning out to be more complicated than anticipated.

For one thing, the First Baptist Church of Nutley, New Jersey, where James Cleveland and the Angelic Choir recorded the first two volumes of their live Sunday Service collaboration, was no longer standing. Where the little wooden church once stood was the foundation for a larger and more modern worship facility. In a gesture of ecumenical goodwill, Trinity Temple Seventh-day Adventist Church in Newark, a quick drive south of Nutley, invited the First Baptist congregation to use its sanctuary until the new building was completed. The location change meant that the Savoy Records engineer had to recalibrate what he learned from wiring First Baptist Church to meet the acoustic challenges of Trinity Temple.

Then there was the problem of musicians. This time, James Cleveland was going to have to work without organist Billy Preston and choir director Thurston Frazier, both critical contributors to the first two volumes of the Cleveland–Angelic Choir collaboration. Their replacements, albeit skilled players, had not yet worked with the Angelic Choir in a live recording setting. And although the previous two volumes of the Sunday Service series had literally been recorded on Sundays, when the spiritual residue of a morning of soul-stirring worship could bleed into the afternoon's recording session, for reasons lost to time, this one would take place on a Thursday evening.

On top of everything else, the senses of the nation were deadened by an explosion that had occurred earlier that week. On Sunday morning, September 15, 1963, segregationists planted dynamite beneath the stairs of a Baptist church in Birmingham, Alabama. The blast killed four young women and injured seventeen others. Was even the church, the epicenter of African American religious and community life, no longer safe? And here was the Angelic Choir, just four days later, fellow Baptists gathered in a church that wasn't theirs with musicians they hadn't worked with, in a city with its own history of racial tensions, recording a Sunday-morning service on a Thursday night. By all accounts, neither was the Birmingham tragedy on the minds of the choristers that evening, nor did it deter them from the work at hand. Still, if there was a recipe for a soul-stirring, hand-clapping, foot-patting live recording session, this wasn't it.

What the Angelic Choir did have, however, was the energetic presence of James Cleveland. The Chicago-born singer, songwriter, arranger, pianist, choir director, and all-around religious music entrepreneur had a God-given gift for directing a recording session. His deft orchestration of the evening's activities and the resilience of the choristers and their leader, the Reverend Lawrence Roberts, as well as a resilience forged in the crucible of daily struggles that came with being black in America, were revealed in the singing that evening.

Hours later, the final notes having rung off the walls of Trinity Temple and the last *amen* uttered, a peace fell on the assembly. The Savoy Records engineer left Trinity Temple, boxes of tape reels tucked under his arms. In the days to come, Roberts and Savoy's gospel music producer Fred Mendelsohn would transform those tapes into volume 3 of the Sunday Service series, best known by its subtitle, *Peace Be Still*.

The first two Cleveland–Angelic Choir Sunday Service volumes received glowing praise in the trade press, but Savoy didn't appear, at first, to have much faith in volume 3. Perhaps it was the absence of Frazier and Preston that most concerned Savoy, or perhaps they felt the novelty had worn off. Whatever the reason, while the liner notes to volumes 1 and 2 treated the albums like historic releases, recognizing the key participants with brief biographies, the back cover of volume 3 contained little more than generic platitudes. Savoy placed scant media advertising for volume 3. The company submitted the standard pressing order of three thousand copies and mailed copies of the album to gospel radio announcers. The announcers placed the opening track, a new arrangement of a long-overlooked eighteenth-century hymn called "Peace Be Still," on their turntables, set the needle a quarter-turn behind the lead-in groove, started the disc spinning, turned up the on-air volume, and watched, in wonder, as their phones lit up.

Both *Peace Be Still* and its title track entered *Billboard*'s Top Spirituals charts in early 1964 and remained there for nearly two years. Sales significantly exceeded Savoy's curiously low expectations. Quickly exhausting the initial run of three thousand copies, the album sold—sources vary—between four hundred fifty and eight hundred thousand copies.[1] This at a time when gospel album success meant selling fifty thousand copies at best. Moreover, the title track is cited by some of today's most prominent gospel singers, songwriters, and musicians as having had a profound influence on their artistic development. Historian Tom Fisher considers *Peace Be Still* "the major founding effort of the modern black gospel chorus sound."[2] It was generally considered to be the best-selling African American gospel album until 1972, when Aretha Franklin's two-disc *Amazing Grace* (also featuring James Cleveland, this time with his Southern California Community Choir), assumed the title. *Amazing Grace*, however, appealed to secular and sacred music enthusiasts alike, and particularly to Franklin's sizable multicultural fan base, but *Peace Be Still* was purchased primarily by African American churchgoers who heard it played over local religious radio broadcasts, at the local religious book and record store, and in the living rooms of family and friends. Recognizing a hit, music ministers began teaching "Peace Be Still" to their church choirs. Professional gospel soloists, choirs, and groups placed the song on their set list. Dozens recorded their own versions. An eighteenth-century hymn gathering dust in the hymnbook was brought back to life.

But why was *Peace Be Still* more popular than other contemporary gospel albums? Did the title track grab listeners with its dramatic arrangement, its evocative lyrics, or both? Did the album communicate a 1960s African American religious worldview with more spiritual lucidity than other religious releases of the day?

Despite the commercial success of *Peace Be Still* and its lasting impact on generations of gospel singers, musicians, and enthusiasts, even the most basic production information has been frustratingly difficult to ascertain. Who were the musicians? Who did the writing and arranging? Who were the soloists? Why wasn't there more publicity in the trade magazines? Was Thursday, September 19, the date of the recording, as the Savoy files indicate, or was it Sunday, September 15, the same day as the Birmingham bombing, as some have suggested? And who was Harvey, the enigmatic artist whose painting adorned the album's front cover? This book is an attempt to solve the mysteries, and debunk some assumptions, surrounding the album and its participants.

Peace Be Still remains the most recognizable title in the nine-volume Sunday Service collaboration between James Cleveland, Lawrence Roberts, and the Angelic Choir—the first multivolume collection, in fact, in the history of recorded gospel music. Effective in its employment of biblical metaphor, thrilling in its evocation of eternal life, and groundbreaking in its choral arrangements, *Peace Be Still* was among the earliest inductees into the Library of Congress National Registry of Historic Sound Collections, which preserves "culturally, historically, or aesthetically important" sound recordings. In 1999 it was inducted into the Grammy Hall of Fame. "Peace Be Still" remains a popular selection to sing at funerals and other important religious occasions—a gospel chestnut that soothes the sorrowful and encourages the discouraged. Churchgoers rejoice upon hearing the first few familiar notes of the song's iconic piano introduction.

"Peace Be Still" and other album cuts have become cultural touchstones, their sound symbolic of a tumultuous era in U.S. history. For example, "Peace Be Still" and another album selection, "I Will Wear a Crown," can be heard emanating from a kitchen radio in the 2016 film adaptation of August Wilson's stage play *Fences*. "Peace Be Still" is sung at the conclusion of *Detroit*, Kathryn Bigelow's 2017 film about the 1967 Detroit riots. Malaco Music Group, which purchased the Savoy gospel catalog from Prelude Records in late 1986, reports that *Peace Be Still*, now available as a compact disc and in downloadable formats, still sells, sixty years on.

Although it was not the first African American gospel recording to be produced in a church and in front of a live audience or congregation, *Peace Be Still* is frequently credited as having given birth to the live recording era in African American gospel music because it was the first such album to achieve stupendous sales figures. Today, many African American gospel artists prefer to record in a live worship setting with an enthusiastic congregation for their audience. No studio can replicate the symbiosis between a gospel artist and a church audience. Some gospel vocalists depend so deeply on the interactive exchange with an audience that a recording studio, lacking the instantaneous feedback of live worship, constrains their art.

Eking every ounce of utility from the album's unanticipated success, Savoy Records became, for more than two decades, the undisputed frontrunner in the production and sales of live gospel choir recordings. Savoy became as synonymous with choirs as Peacock Records of Houston, Texas, was with quartets. Sales figures for *Peace Be Still* and subsequent Cleveland–Angelic Choir releases confirmed that the African American marketplace particularly, though not exclusively, was willing to pay for a recording of a live in-service experience that it could enjoy anytime, anyplace, anywhere. So much so that soon after the Cleveland-Angelic Choir Sunday Service partnership ended, Savoy launched a *James Cleveland Presents* series of albums, many made by church and community choirs singing in front of packed churches. Like *Peace Be Still*, these albums also brought the worship experience into the home. They were particularly effective as the soundtrack to the Sunday morning ritual of preparing for church. They also introduced the effervescence of African American church music ministries to those who might never step inside a church.

Peace Be Still even altered the way record companies conceptualized long-playing gospel albums. No longer were they haphazardly programmed collections of radio singles and fillers—they were developed deliberately to disseminate a live in-service experience that could transcend denominational, cultural, and spatial boundaries. In the 1970s, as gospel albums surpassed singles in popularity, it was not unusual for releases featuring gospel choirs—including the Angelic Choir—to contain songs that ran as long as ten minutes—far longer than radio announcers were accustomed to programming.

Not only did *Peace Be Still* cement James Cleveland's star status in the gospel music industry, it converted the Angelic Choir, composed largely of amateur singers, from a church ensemble into a national touring choir not unlike professional prewar African American choruses such as the Hall Johnson Choir, the Eva Jessye Singers, and Wings over Jordan. But whereas these latter groups focused mostly on preservation of the folk spiritual, the

Angelic Choir introduced audiences to the latest gospel songs and gospelized hymns, often containing vocal and instrumental techniques drawn from R&B, rock 'n' roll, and soul. With Roberts's religious declamations replacing Cleveland's own, the Angelic Choir gave African American churchgoers a revival experience wherever they appeared. For those unable to travel to First Baptist Church in Nutley, New Jersey, First Baptist Church came to them in the form of Roberts and the choir.

Besides its contribution to gospel music, the Angelic Choir also served as a musical model of the American spirit of individualism. The rugged individualist is portrayed in American history, literature, and mythology as an ordinary person who musters the courage and cunning to overcome extraordinary odds and accomplish extraordinary things. Whether it is Huckleberry Finn challenging the tradition of chattel servitude to save his friend Jim, Captain Ahab battling a whale of enormous proportions, or John Henry and Casey Jones defying death, the Angelic Choir, whom the Reverend Lawrence Roberts once described as "Mary, Jane, and John Doe from up the street, down the street, and around the corner," surmounted their modest status to become something akin to "America's gospel choir" during the 1960s and early 1970s. Not that they might have become famous without ample direction from James Cleveland, whose instincts for present-ing a gospel song was without parallel in his era. But Cleveland, too, was a rugged individualist, his economically impoverished migrant parents barely teenagers when they gave birth to their famous son. A gospel gadfly with an unquenchable desire for success, Cleveland used streetwise hustle to assert himself into the good graces of the music mainstream—a particularly dif-ficult thing to do in Chicago, where the genre's first generation of leaders reigned as a seemingly intractable hierarchy. It was a frustration with this glass ceiling, as well as a commitment to educating hundreds of thousands of lesser-known but no less talented church singers and musicians, most of them young, that led Cleveland to adopt for his Gospel Music Workshop of America the egalitarian motto "Where Everybody Is Somebody."

For centuries, black sacred music, and particularly the folk spiritual, contained coded expressions of protest against the status quo. During the Reverend Doctor Martin Luther King Jr.'s campaign of nonviolent resis-tance, protesters railed against a resistant white majority not with fists and weapons but with prayer and song. Spirituals and gospel hymns such as "Ain't Gonna Let Nobody Turn Me Around," "We Shall Overcome," and "This Little Light of Mine" were sung zestfully by protesters. Singing gave them the courage to face unknown dangers. But nobody sang "Peace Be Still" on the front lines of freedom. It was not a freedom song or a protest song, at least in the conventional sense. It worked on a different plane of consciousness, as we shall explore in this book.

No matter that "Peace Be Still" was from another century—what Savoy Records captured in a Seventh-day Adventist church in Newark that Thursday evening in September 1963 was the transcendent spirituality of a choir of young, cosmopolitan Baptists singing their troubles over as a believing community. They sang not from a feeling of helplessness or victimhood, the kind implicit in the lyrics of gospel songs from an earlier era, but from the 1960s standpoint of hopefulness. Not from the passive "Lord, have mercy, if you please," as articulated in the hymn "Let Us Break Bread Together," but from an optimistic outlook of overcoming. Not *if*, but *when*. This was gospel music in the era of Dr. King and President Kennedy. Endowing the hymn with the energy of human desire, the Angelic Choir seized it, like a sword and shield, and carried it into spiritual battle against evil forces known and unknown. "One of the most vital ways we sustain ourselves," scholar bell hooks wrote, "is by building communities of resistance, places where we know we are not alone."[3] Using its collective voice to represent the broader believing community, the Angelic Choir sang of a resistance and resilience that no oppressor could overpower.

On the other hand, by evaluating recorded versions of "Peace Be Still" from 1963 to the present, one discovers that, like black music in general, the song evolved from a coded statement of resilience into an explicit call for direct action. Even James Cleveland would come to use it to communicate his own perspective on the state of race relations in America. As recently as February 2020, African American activists in St. Louis, Missouri, and East St. Louis, Illinois, called their anticrime marches Peace Be Still.[4] Gospel singer Yolanda "Yoli" DeBerry explains why she included "Peace Be Still" on her August 2020 EP, *My Worship Playlist*: "It was the Sunday after something extremely violent happened in our country. Spiritually, I was just sick of it all. I shut everything out and for a moment, I just asked God to bring peace to the world. We need everyone to put these guns down, put these prejudices down, put down everything that is causing the world to turn in a crazy way."[5]

Protesters may still turn to the freedom songs of the 1960s for inspiration, but in churches, whenever "Peace Be Still" is sung, it reminds everyone that a superhuman force has the ultimate authority to quiet the storms of discrimination and disenfranchisement and heal emotional wounds. Just as freedom songs or repurposed folk spirituals prepared the marching people to confront violence and even death with steely resolve, the gospel songs and hymns of *Peace Be Still* encouraged the church, irrespective of its appetite for direct social action, to prevail by placing its destiny in the capable hands of Jesus, assured in the belief that it will not only survive the winds and the waves but emerge victorious.

1

The Reverend Lawrence C. Roberts and the First Baptist Church of Nutley

The township of Nutley sits serenely near the Passaic River in Essex County, New Jersey, about eight miles north of Newark and sixteen miles west of New York City. Incorporated in 1902, Nutley has a slightly rolling topography, a picturesque business district with a decidedly Italian American flavor, and a civic pride in being happily anonymous. "George Washington never slept in any beds here," joked the March 3, 1939, edition of the *Nutley Sun*.

Perhaps the first president of the United States never slumbered in Nutley, but the township is not as anonymous as it claims. It has, in fact, been home to a number of notables, among them Annie Oakley, Buffalo Bill's Wild West show performer and inspiration for the MGM musical *Annie Get Your Gun*. Illustrator Frederick Dana Marsh, homemaking queen Martha Stewart, and members of first lady Jaqueline Kennedy Onassis's extended family have lived in Nutley. And from 1961 to 2005, Nutley was home to one of the nation's most celebrated gospel choruses, the Angelic Choir. It was the main ensemble in the music ministry of the First Baptist Church, the township's first African American church and one of only two that served the area's black population during the first few decades of the twentieth century.

Not that Nutley ever had a particularly sizable black population. Before 1902, when Nutley was still called Franklin Township, only a handful of African Americans resided there. The demographics changed around 1916 as blacks began migrating from the American South to the Northeast as part of the first wave of the Great Migration. One of the most significant demographic shifts in twentieth-century America, the Great Migration lasted from 1915 to 1970. According to Pulitzer Prize–winning journalist Isabel Wilkerson, whose epic *The Warmth of Other Suns* is a remarkable history of the movement, millions of African Americans departed the South for northern urban areas so they could make a better life for themselves and their families. Jobs were available in cities such as Newark, where manufacturing fed the insatiable appetite of World War I for supplies but lacked the manpower to keep up with demand. Eastern seaboard railways made New York City and Newark (and Nutley, by extension) popular ports of entry for African American migrants traveling from Florida, Georgia, and the Carolinas.

It didn't take long for southern migrants to discover that the "Promised Land" of the North was not prepared to accommodate them. According to a February 17, 1917, *Nutley Sun* article,

> The problem of caring for the Southern negroes [*sic*] who have been emigrating to the North for the last year in expectation of making their fortunes has presented itself in Nutley, as in most other towns and cities hereabouts. Three negro families, numbering in all eleven persons are now being cared for by the Social Service Bureau. They came north after hearing stories of the high wages to be made but on arrival were unable to secure work and soon were destitute. The Bureau has given them clothing and financial aid.[1]

Although as late as the 1950 US Census, only 2 percent of Nutley's population, or 453 people, was non-white, even a tiny community needed a convenient house of worship.[2]

The Rising Mount Zion Baptist Church

Whether its edifice be austere or modest, stone cathedral or repurposed storefront, the most important institution in the African American community is the church. Historically denied access to, and membership in, mainstream political, economic, and civic associations, African Americans turn to the church for more than worship. The church also functions as a community center, a social service agency, an employment center, a youth fellowship hall, and a vehicle for building leadership skills and community status by holding positions of authority, such as on the Trustee Board, the Deacon Board, the Mothers Board, the Nurse Ministry, the Department of Christian Education, the Music Ministry, and the Usher Board. "For the Negro," writes Kenneth Clark, "his church is his instrument of escape, his weapon of protest, his protective fortress behind which he seeks to withstand the assaults of a hostile world and within which he plans his strategies of defiance, harassment, and, at times, his frontal attacks against racial barriers."[3] For the few hundred African Americans who settled in or around Nutley during the era of the Great Migration, their "protective fortress" was Rising Mount Zion Baptist Church.

Rising Mount Zion was established in Nutley in 1889 as a prayer group by early migrants William Robinson, born in North Carolina around 1867, and his wife Nannie, born in Virginia around 1870.[4] The young Robinson couple held the prayer group's initial services in their Chestnut Street residence, but by 1890, the Rising Mount Zion membership outgrew the Robinson home and secured more spacious quarters at Nutley Town Hall. Around this same time, Nannie remarried and her new husband, the Reverend George Moon, assumed the church's spiritual leadership. Moon moved the congregation from Nutley Town Hall to a spot on Passaic Avenue. Rising Mount Zion remained on Passaic until 1907, when the congregation purchased two hilly plots at 13 and 15 Harrison Street in Nutley. There they erected a humble white wooden frame edifice, the quintessential little wooden church on a hill.[5]

Of an array of pastors leading Rising Mount Zion prior to 1959, the Reverend George B. Riley appears to have made the most significant contribution to the church's growth. Elected pastor in 1936, Riley modernized the wooden church by purchasing an organ, expanding and enlarging the building, and overseeing a name change. On April 11, 1939, Rising Mount Zion Baptist Church was officially rechristened First Baptist Church of Nutley. When Riley died in 1949, he was succeeded by the Reverend Joseph J. Napier, born around 1911 in Dooley County, Georgia. Napier led the church from 1950 to 1959 while also holding a job with the Union Building Construction Company in nearby Passaic. But by the end of the 1950s, the First Baptist congregation had dwindled to just a handful of members.[6] Its future uncertain, the church sought a pastor with vision and youthful vigor to lead it into the next decade. They would select the Reverend Lawrence Roberts.

Lawrence Curtis Roberts

In many ways, the life story of Lawrence Roberts is a history, in microcosm, of African American gospel music in Essex County, New Jersey, for which the county seat is Newark. For nearly thirty years, the pianist, singer, song-writer, choir director, record company executive, talent scout, and church leader was an integral member of the county's professional, semiprofes-sional, and amateur gospel artists. This community benefited first from his musical talent and, later, his ability to secure for them record deals and public appearances.

Lawrence Curtis Roberts was born in Newark on August 12, 1936, to James and Estelle Holmes Roberts.[7] Growing up, Lawrence never knew his father. He told gospel historian Eric Majette Jr. in 2004 that

> My father, I never really knew. Further down the line, when I was working for Savoy Record Company the phone rang one day, and the gentleman asked my coworker, Mr. Fred Mendelsohn, could he speak to me? He told Mr. Mendelsohn he was my father. I was grown at the time and had three children of my own. I was actually floored. I went to the phone. He asked me about my grandparents, et cetera, so I knew it was legit. He told me he was going to be in town for the weekend and he wanted to see me. And I graciously consented to see him. He came over to our home. At that time I was living in Newark, and unfortunately prior to leaving, he asked me, could I let him have seventy-five dollars? A man that I had never seen, a man that I grew up totally without any efforts on his part to help me. He left, and that following Friday, I received a phone call that he was dead.[8]

Absent his father, Roberts was raised by his mother and maternal grandpar-ents, George and Annabelle Holmes, at 42 Boyd Street in Newark's Central Ward.[9] George Holmes, born in Smithfield, Georgia, on October 10, 1894, was a farmer (probably a sharecropper) for a Mrs. W. E. Bryant.[10] By 1917, George had married Annabelle (born in Georgia, circa 1901) and they had an infant son, William. Daughter Estelle, Roberts's mother, was born about a year later. Sometime prior to 1930, the Holmes family gathered their be-longings and migrated north. They settled in Newark, first at 81 Tichenor Street and then moved about two miles northwest, to 42 Boyd Street.[11]

By the time the Holmes family arrived in Newark, the city's black popu-lation was 5 percent of the total census, or approximately 26,000, having swelled from 4,477 a half-century earlier.[12] The majority of blacks lived in the city's Central Ward because in Newark, as in other major northern cities, African Americans, regardless of their financial and class status, were barred from living in better-appointed white-majority communities. Gospel singer and noted background vocalist Emily "Cissy" Houston said her father, Nitcholas "Nitch" Drinkard, aptly summarized the difference between racism as practiced in the North and the South: "Don't tell me how bad the South was. . . . It's the same up here; you don't have to be a Ku Klux Klanner in a white robe; you could just as well be wearing a business suit and work at City Hall."[13]

Indeed, although Newark offered more freedoms than were available in the South, African American migrants still found themselves relegated to lower-paying jobs. For men, that meant unskilled factory work or employment as janitors, servants, and porters. Female migrants took in laundry and served as domestics for white families.[14] George Holmes made his living at the Swift slaughterhouse in nearby Kearny, New Jersey.[15] Around the time of his birth, Lawrence's mother Estelle was a seamstress for the WPA Sewing Project, darning clothes and creating new garments to be given away to financially struggling families like her own.[16]

But if decent-paying jobs were limited and housing was suboptimal, newcomers to the Central Ward could at least function within what African American novelist Richard Wright dubbed the "fluid folk life of the South." Newark's housing restrictions inadvertently offered transplanted southerners the freedom to replicate their familiar southern folkways within their new community. And since this community contained dry-goods stores, grocers, taverns, restaurants, beauty salons, barber shops, schools, pharmacies, and churches, Newarker African Americans could avoid interacting with the unfriendly world around them as much as possible. Growing up in nearby Paterson, New Jersey, future Angelic Choir member and gospel soloist Lorraine Stancil recalled that

> It was a different time. Families were very, very close-knit. My mom [a migrant from Greensboro, North Carolina] had four children and all we knew was walking up Governor Street, which was the street we lived on. Walking—we didn't have a car. [Mom] would put her flat shoes in a paper bag and walk us to church during the week and of course all day on Sunday. We didn't even have a telephone. We had to use the neighbor's phone, they had one. The neighborhoods protected the children. A neighborhood child would do something wrong and [neighbors] were able to chastise that child and then speak to the parents, and the parents would take it even further once you got home.[17]

Young Lawrence Roberts attended Eighteenth Avenue Elementary School and Cleveland Junior High. Around age nine, he accepted Christ as his personal savior, was baptized, and joined Little Mount Calvary Baptist Church at 123 Prince Street, the former location of Newark's landmark Metropolitan Baptist Church. Taking a few formal piano lessons but spending more time at gospel musicales studying the techniques of gospel pianists, Roberts began accompanying some of the services at Little Mount Calvary.[18]

Roberts became sufficiently proficient on piano to audition successfully for entrance to Newark's School of Fine and Industrial Arts. The multicultural high school known as Arts High was founded in September 1931, with a mission to place art and drama on the same plane as mathematics, science, and language. Jazz stars Sarah Vaughan and Wayne Shorter, R&B singer Melba Moore, and pop starlet Connie Francis are among the school's alumni.[19] At Arts High, Roberts learned to read music. He learned vocal techniques, such as breathing from the diaphragm when singing, which he himself employed and taught others throughout his music career. He also took full advantage of the school's many extracurricular offerings, such as joining a music trio with Connie Francis and jazz vocalist Andy Bey, singing the part of Rodolfo in the school's production of Puccini's *La Bohème*, and captaining the school's track team.[20] Beneath Roberts's photo in the 1954 Arts High yearbook, which noted his football and basketball proclivities, was the note "Although he is undecided about his future career, he will most likely have the best of luck in any field he enters, because of his very genial personality."[21]

But despite his piano proclivities, the young Roberts really wanted to play saxophone. "I thought I was going to be a jazz musician," he recalled in an August 2006 interview, "but my grandmother [Annabelle Holmes] had other plans for me. Back then, it wasn't what *we* wanted to do, we did what our parents *desired* us to do. And going to church regularly with her, I acquired a great love for [gospel music]. Before I knew it, I was stuck with it."[22]

One gospel group in particular that had a profound influence on young Roberts was the Roberta Martin Singers.[23] A pioneering gospel music ensemble, the Roberta Martin Singers was organized in 1933 by Chicago-based singer, pianist, songwriter/arranger, and music publisher Roberta Martin (1907–69). By the early 1950s, when Roberts was in high school, the Martins had transitioned from being an all-male group to a mixed-voice ensemble, with outstanding female vocalists Delois Barrett Campbell, Bessie Folk, and Gloria Griffin. Their immense popularity, fueled by personal appearances and popular singles on Apollo and Savoy Records, kept them on the road nine months of the year. One stop on their national tour was Newark's Metropolitan Baptist Church, where the group sang for a two-week revival every year.[24] "When [the Roberta Martin Singers] came to town," First Baptist Church musician Robert Logan reflected, "it was like Billy Graham coming to Newark or some other famous evangelist. The churches were always packed. Everyone was interested in the new style of singing called gospel."[25] Roberts found opportunities to assist in the planning of the Martin Singers' annual visit to Metropolitan.

Besides attending school and church, Roberts worked at Louis Krupnick's drugstore at 205 Court Street in Newark,[26] making ice-cream sundaes and doing whatever needed to be done, then at the S. S. Kresge Department Store at 508 Broadway. Roberts told music educator Dr. Birdie (Byerte) Wilson Johnson (1926–2019) that his first job at Kresge was as an errand boy for owner Sebastian S. Kresge, "who had a luxurious apartment on the top floor of the store." Kresge was sufficiently impressed with Roberts that he gave him a job in the store's lampshade department.[27]

One Sunday during Roberts's teenage years, he was invited by a friend named Jesse "Mickey" Jones to visit his church, Zion Hill Baptist Church. Jones figured that Roberts would enjoy Zion Hill's youth and adult choruses.[28] Located at 22 Nicholson Street in Newark and led by the Reverend James A. Pullins, Zion Hill was known for its home quartet, the L&N Gospel Singers, named for the Louisville & Nashville Railroad line that brought southern migrants north.[29] Ernest Nunnally, a member of the L&N Gospel Singers, would go on to play a significant role in Roberts's ministerial and music career.[30] But there was a far more important reason Roberts was eager to visit the church—a young female member who had captured his fancy. Dolores Roberts filled in the details:

> One of the fellows that was a member of my church, Mickey Jones, he and my husband were friends. Well, my husband had interest in this girl named Dolly. He said, "I want to meet Dolly. I've been seeing her and I want to meet Dolly." So [Mickey] said, "Well, she'll be singing Sunday, or she may be in church Sunday, so come to church with me." So [Lawrence] came to church. He was sitting up in the balcony and I was singing in the junior choir, and he said to Mickey, "Who's that little girl right there with the long hair?" Mickey said, "That's Bootsy." He said, "Wow, I want to meet her." [Mickey] said, "I thought you wanted to see Dolly." "No, I want to see *her*!"[31]

Born Dolores Pigford in Newark on February 4, 1937, "Bootsy" was given her nickname by the family's next-door neighbor while she was still a newborn. Like Roberts's grandparents, Bootsy's parents were Georgia migrants who arrived in Newark in the 1920s. But instead of moving to the Central Ward, they settled in the city's Hill District. "We were poor but we didn't know we were poor," Bootsy recalled. "We had everything everybody in the neighborhood had. We had enough food to eat, we had clothes, shoes when we needed them." At the same time, they saw how the other half lived. "Right next to my house was an opera theater," Bootsy said. "We used to sit on the fire escape and we'd see the white people come in with their long chauffeured limousines. They had a red carpet out on the street. They'd walk into the opera, and we'd sit on the fire escape to listen and see them go in with their fine clothes."[32]

Bootsy was drawn to other music styles besides the arias she heard while sitting on the theater fire escape. She admired the singing of gospel star Clara Ward of Philadelphia's famous Ward Singers as well as the jazz stylings of Arts High alumna Sarah Vaughan, at the time one of the nation's most popular vocalists. Bootsy was also inspired by two local family groups, the Drinkard Singers and the Pitts Sisters:

> I lived around the corner from Cissy [Drinkard] Houston and her family [the Drinkards]. Cissy and her family lived on Charlton Street and I lived on Montgomery. The Drinkard Singers used to sing around the various churches. [So did] Connie Pitts and her sisters. Connie Pitts's father had a church right around the corner from their house, and so all the children in the neighborhood would attend his church. We went to [Zion Hill], but [Pitts's father] would give different little programs and we'd go to the programs at his church.[33]

For their part, Bootsy and her sisters harmonized while doing housework and eventually reckoned they were good enough to become a full-fledged vocal group like the Drinkards or the Pitts sisters. They called themselves the Pigford Singers. "People started hearing us sing all the time," she said, "and they used to call us for programs in different churches. We appeared in the small churches around our neighborhood."[34]

Lawrence Roberts joined Zion Hill out of his growing affection for Bootsy, but also he hoped to accompany its Young People's Choir, which at the time was directed by the pastor's daughter, Ruth Martin. In time, he received his wish and eventually succeeded Martin as the Young People's Choir director.[35] According to Robert Logan, Zion Hill had just embraced gospel music when Roberts joined. "Zion Hill Baptist Church was very staunch for a Baptist church," he explained. "At one time in the Baptist church, everything was mostly hymns. There were some that didn't want gospel music, some still wanted to sing the hymns in the hymnbook, but there were others who wanted the new style of music called gospel. . . . Back then we had a lot of young people. The music was changing during that period, so they had the senior choir, they had an inspirational choir, they had a gospel choir, and a youth choir."[36]

Around this time, Roberts formed the Voices of Faith, a 125-voice community choir composed of youth and young adults from Zion Hill and other local churches. Community choirs like the Voices of Faith provided wholesome musical outlets for youth and fellowship with their peers from churches throughout the region. Logan was among the Zion Hill youth who joined the Voices of Faith. "We used to travel to all the different churches around Newark," he said. "Every Friday, Saturday, or Sunday, there was a program going on somewhere. They'd invite you in, and the choir would come and fill the church up—just the choir alone would fill the church!"[37]

In the midst of all this activity, Lawrence and Bootsy, eighteen and seventeen years old, respectively, married in a house ceremony on October 24, 1954.[38] In the coming years, they would give birth to three children: Derrick, Vanessa, and Renee.[39]

2

Gospel Music in Newark

When it came to forming a music ministry for First Baptist Church, Roberts didn't have to look very far. Newark in the mid-twentieth century was a wellspring of professional, semiprofessional, and amateur gospel singers and musicians who could, and often did, compete head-to-head with groups from New York City, its larger neighbor across the bay.

As gospel historian Ray Funk has observed, Newark's introduction to gospel music, like most metropolitan areas, came through local male jubilee quartets such as the Southern Sons, the Silver Echo Quartet, and the Coleman Brothers. Among the city's earliest professional and semiprofessional gospel artists, these quartets emulated the tight harmonies and percussive rhythms of the nationally popular Golden Gate Quartet and the Selah Jubilee Singers of New York City.[1] During the 1950s, these troupes, as well as other local quartets such as the Afro Quintette (also known as the Afro Jubilees) and the Hightower Brothers, began to adopt the rawer and more aggressively sung gospel quartet style popularized by the Soul Stirrers and the Blue Jay Singers of Birmingham, Alabama. Migrating to Newark from Florida, the Hightower Brothers was a family group whose secret weapon was its lead singer, the preteen Robert "Sugar" Hightower.[2] His exuberant presence on gospel programs was a harbinger of child soul stars such as "Little" Stevie Wonder and Michael Jackson.

The Coleman Brothers are fascinating not only for their singing but for how they, as members of Newark's African American migrant community, adapted to discrimination in employment by embracing entrepreneurship. In 1925, during the first wave of the Great Migration, three brothers, Lander, Melvin, and Russell Coleman, moved from Kenbridge, Virginia, to Montclair, New Jersey. They formed Coleman Records in 1944. Located at 59 Court Street in Newark, Coleman Records boasted a recording studio to capture the sounds of local and visiting gospel and secular talent. The Five Blind Boys of Alabama, the Original Blind Boys of Mississippi, and gospel crooner Charles Watkins were on the Coleman roster, as were R&B units such as the Ray-O-Vacs. The studio also enabled the Coleman Brothers quartet to broadcast every Sunday over Newark's WHBI-AM. Songs they sang included Lander's composition "Milky White Way," a 1947 hit for the Trumpeteers gospel quartet that Elvis Presley covered in 1960. The brothers eventually purchased the building they occupied and converted it into the Coleman Hotel, a seventy-two-room inn that provided much-needed accommodations for out-of-town African Americans. Touring actors, musicians, and singers—from Ruth Brown and Billie Holiday to Big Maybelle—found lodging at the Coleman Hotel when other inns would not provide them with accommodations.[3]

A Newark singing dynasty worthy of a book-length biography, the Drinkard Singers (also known as the Drinkard Jubilairs) were organized by family patriarch Nitcholas "Nitch" Drinkard. Nitch and Delia Mae Drinkard migrated from Blakely, Georgia, to Newark in 1923, bringing son William and daughters Lee and Marie ("Reebie") with them. By 1933, they had added five more children to the family: Hank, Anne, Nicholas ("Nicky"), Larry, and Emily ("Cissy"). Settling into an apartment on Court Street, Nitch worked in road repair and Delia worked at the Singer sewing machine factory in Elizabeth, New Jersey.[4] Around 1938, a fire ravaged their apartment building, forcing the family to move. Settling into a new Newark neighborhood, they began attending St. Luke's AME Church, where the pastor was the Reverend Elzae Warrick. It was at St. Luke's where they began singing as a family group.[5]

Initially a mixed-voice quartet composed of Cissy, Larry, and Nicky,[6] the Drinkard Singers expanded to include daughter Lee Drinkard Warrick (Lee married Pastor Elzae's son, Mancel), who became the group's manager.

Reebie Drinkard Epps taught the ensemble songs to sing and ran rehearsals.[7] Anne Drinkard Moss joined the lineup in the 1950s. When Anne departed the ensemble, they replaced her with Lee's adopted daughter, Judy Guions. Meanwhile, Lee's biological daughters, Dionne and Dee Dee Warrick (they would change their surname to Warwick for professional purposes), parlayed their experience as background singers into careers as popular solo recording artists. So did Guions, who adopted Judy Clay as her stage name.

Pastor Warrick left St. Luke's around 1949, and by 1954, the Drinkards also departed St. Luke's, shifting their affiliation to New Hope Baptist Church in Newark. Cissy, who directed the New Hope Choir and later organized its Radio Choir,[8] would go on to form a trio of background singers called the Sweet Inspirations. The Sweet Inspirations backed top-selling artists from Aretha Franklin to Elvis Presley while also singing and recording as a unit. Born in Newark on August 9, 1963, Cissy's daughter Whitney ("Nippy") Houston became one of the best-selling popular music artists of all time. Her death at age forty-eight on February 11, 2012, was mourned by millions worldwide.

Harry Freeman Johnson was another local singer drawn into the Drinkard music dynasty and Roberts's music galaxy. A native Newarker and member of the city's Wells Cathedral Church of God in Christ, Freeman Johnson sang with his brothers and, with Larry and Nicky Drinkard, in a vocal harmony group called the Four Bells.[9] Military service temporarily interrupted Johnson's musical pursuits, but he returned to singing upon his discharge. Johnson's raspy baritone—a dead ringer for James Cleveland's gruff delivery—made him the Angelic Choir's in-house substitute for Cleveland when the latter was unavailable.[10]

The Drinkard Singers noted Roberts's own vocal proclivities at a gospel presentation held at Bishop Alvin A. Childs's Faith Temple Church of God in Christ in New York, where the Youth Cavalcade Choir was on the program.[11] Roberts tells the story to gospel historian Eric Majette Jr.:

> In the audience that night was the Drinkard Family. . . . The fellow who had been singing with them had been drafted into the service. I did a song with Bernice Bass's Youth Cavalcade Choir, and when it was over, they sang, and I was floored by their style and their originality. I went to Miss Warrick and asked her, "Could I become a part of your group?" She said, "Well, let me pray about it." But they heard me. They consented to let me become a member of the Drinkard Singers, and that was my initial induction into what I think of as professional gospel singing. I stayed with them two or three years.[12]

Other Newark gospel notables whom Roberts befriended while they were members of Bass's Youth Cavalcade Choir were Constance "Connie" Pitts of the Pitts Sisters (she also soloed for True Love Baptist Church in Newark),[13] organist Robert Banks, and pianist Leon Lumpkins (1934–2007).[14] Robert Banks (b. February 3, 1930) went on to a storied career as a singer, accompanist, songwriter, producer, and recording artist in the jazz, R&B, and gospel fields. He was a stalwart recording artist and studio musician for Savoy Records before recording his own projects for Verve. Throughout his career, he worked with artists representing a broad range of styles, including the blues of Willie Hightower and the soul stylings of Solomon Burke as well as the contemporary gospel of Myrna Summers and the Interdenominational Choir. (He produced their 1970 album *Tell It Like It Is* for Cotillion, a subsidiary of Atlantic Records.) Greater Abyssinian Baptist Church minister of music Leon Lumpkins organized the Gospel Clefs, a piano- and organ-led male gospel group with high harmonies and unusual melodies and arrangements that emulated the highly charged, flamboyant style of female groups such as the Davis Sisters and the Ward Singers. Among Lumpkins's many compositions for the Gospel Clefs was the exquisite 1958 "Open Our Eyes," a prayer pleading for peace and brotherhood. Chicago disk jockey Herb "Cool Gent" Kent was so moved by its message that he concluded his radio broadcasts over WVON-AM by playing the song.[15] The song crossed over into the pop world when it was covered in 1973 by Earth, Wind and Fire.

The Newark-based Unique Gospel Singers would ultimately contribute one of its vocalists, Pearl Tucker Minatee, to Roberts's music ministry. Minatee was born on April 11, 1931, in Newark's East Ward, the oldest of seven children of Henry Fogie Tucker and Hattie Mollie Dixon Tucker. The Tuckers were southern migrants who met and married in Newark. Pearl attended East Side High School, sang alto in the All State Choir, and was offered a scholarship to study voice at Shaw University, but she stayed home to help her family make ends meet. She attended Mount Zion Baptist Church and sang in its choir alongside her friend, Sarah Vaughan. With the Unique Gospel Singers, Pearl sang locally as well as on Anna Tuell's New York–based religious radio program. Despite their local popularity, the Uniques recorded only eight sides for Savoy, of which four were released: "Jesus Wonderful Jesus" / "Strength and Courage" in 1954 and "I Had to Tell It" / "I Wonder Where Would You Be" in 1958.[16] The Reverend Doctor Stefanie Minatee, Pearl's daughter and the leader of the acclaimed New Jersey gospel choir

Jubilation, suspects that her mother met Roberts during the period when she was in the Uniques.[17]

In addition to the Youth Cavalcade Choir, other popular African American choirs in 1950s Newark included the Abyssinian Baptist Church Gospel Choir, led by Alex Bradford and Leon Lumpkins; the Abyssinian Young People's Choir, which featured lead vocals by a young Kenneth Glover; and the Back Home Choir, organized by brothers Charles and Jeff Banks. According to gospel promoter Joe Bostic, the Back Home Choir, organized around 1955, took its name from the Banks Brothers' monthly songfest called "The Back Home Hour." The songfest was the brainchild of southern settlers in Newark who wanted to participate in local "singing get-togethers" that reminded them of their southern worship experience. Charles amassed the Back Home Choir out of this assembly.[18] The choir's successful appearance at the 1957 Newport Jazz Festival was captured by Verve Records. So was the Drinkard Singers set. Both ensembles parlayed their appearances into a record contract with RCA Victor.

Besides the Abyssinian Baptist Church Gospel Choir with Leon Lumpkins, Bootsy recalled two other choral ensembles particularly popular with black Newarkers: "The churches that were quite popular, and famous with the choirs, at that time were Zion Hill with Lawrence Roberts at the organ and choir director, and at New Hope, it was Cissy [Drinkard] Houston and her brother Nicky Drinkard. So whenever other churches had choir anniversaries, they would always hold the three choirs to the end because they knew we were going to turn it out. [There were] maybe about fifteen church choirs [in Newark], but the three choirs the people wanted to hear were our three choirs."[19]

This pool of talent in Newark did not go unnoticed by the community of East Coast independent record companies, or "indies," that emerged during and immediately after World War II. After Apollo Records in New York hit pay dirt in 1948 with Mahalia Jackson's two-sided hit, "Move On up a Little Higher," labels began investigating the commercial potential of the gospel choirs and groups in their own backyards. The Drinkard Singers, the Afro Quintette, the Lucille Parks Singers, the Unique Gospel Singers, the Gospel Clefs, and, later, the Back Home Choir, signed with Newark-based Savoy Records. This hometown imprint would figure prominently in the local gospel community and, with Roberts's assistance, become one of the most important gospel record labels of all time.

Savoy Records

Record-man-turned-historian Arnold Shaw dubbed Savoy Records, founded by Herman Lubinsky in the first week of November 1942, "the first R&B label of consequence, in terms of both the artists it developed and its longevity."[20] Shaw's recollection of Lubinsky, born Hyman Lubinsky to Russian émigrés in Branford, Connecticut, on August 30, 1896, was as an "alert and hard-working entrepreneur," "energetic," and a "loud talker."[21] Indie record company expert John Broven called Lubinsky the "quintessential loudmouth, overweight, cigar-smoking record man with little apparent charm or saving graces" but added that, "for all his failings, he was a brilliant record man."[22]

Lubinsky was also a pioneering radio man. A profile in the January 1923 issue of the *Radio Dealer* called Lubinsky "perhaps the greatest contributor to radio progress," noting that his decision to make the new medium a career began when he was about eight years old.[23] Indeed, the story goes, a fifteen-year-old Lubinsky happened to be serving as a wireless operator on the *SS Carpathia* when, on April 14, 1912, he heard and copied down distress signals coming from the *RMS Titanic* after it struck an iceberg and proceeded to sink. The *Carpathia* came to the aid of the ship's survivors. At the outbreak of World War I, Lubinsky served as a naval radio operator and taught radio to Army men at New Haven High School. Later, he taught electrical theory and practice at the Essex County Vocational School for Boys. He contributed technical articles to electronics journals. After the war, he worked as a federal revenue agent and, by 1922, operated the Standard Electric Company in Newark. Better known as the Radio Record Shop of Newark, the business was located at 77 Elizabeth Street.[24]

Lubinsky founded New Jersey radio station WRAZ in June 1923. The station's call letters changed to WCBX in April 1924 and on October 15 of that year received the right to change its call letters to WNJ (for Wireless New Jersey). Listed variously as located in Newark's Hotel St. Francis at 22–24 Park Street and in the Lubinsky home at 89 Lehigh Avenue, WNJ was known as the Voice of Newark because of its ethnic programming for a city teeming with eastern and southern European immigrants and African American migrants. Around 1933, a tussle with the Federal Communications Commission over signal range resulted in Lubinsky's inability to renew his station's FCC license. Exiting broadcasting, Lubinsky focused on his Radio Record Shop, now at 58 Market Street, where he sold radios, radio parts, and phonograph records. Music enthusiasts could dive into a bin of nineteen-cent disks and preview the latest singles in private listening booths.[25] On November 7, 1942, Lubinsky expanded his empire by opening Savoy Records in offices just above the Radio Record Shop. The company name was probably derived from Harlem's popular Savoy Ballroom, nicknamed The Home of Happy Feet.[26] Savoy's earliest releases were by modern jazz artists who were not being courted by major labels.

But it was challenging to open a new diskery in November 1942. Four months earlier, the increasing popularity of jukeboxes and radio broadcasts of phonograph records prompted the American Federation of Musicians (AFM), led by its authoritarian president, James Caesar Petrillo, to strike over its members' loss of live performance revenue. The AFM demanded that royalties from each record sold be placed in a musicians' compensation fund for the benefit of the membership.[27] Musicians recording in violation of the ban were in danger of incurring severe consequences from the AFM.

On the other hand, the strike gave shoestring independent record companies like Savoy a chance to gain a foothold in an industry hitherto dominated by deep-pocketed major companies like Victor, Columbia, and Decca. "The Petrillo-enforced hiatus in the record industry," noted *Billboard* in January 1943, "has provided an open door for many of the lesser known labels to come to light."[28] To provide new product to consumers without breaking the ban, some record companies, including Savoy, rereleased prewar recordings or previously unissued sides. Although Savoy brazenly advertised its first issues in *Billboard* as "not pre-war materials,"[29] jazz discographers believe that Savoy's first four sides, all instrumentals, were previously unissued audition sessions Lubinsky cut in 1939 of the Dictators, a jazz combo formed by pianist Clement "Clem" Moorman.[30] Two of these initial sides, "Rhythm and Bugs" and "Tricks," were released the week of December 1, 1942, on Savoy 100 as by the *Savoy* Dictators.[31]

The fledgling Savoy hit pay dirt with its subsequent releases on a combo called the Picadilly Pipers, featuring Moorman on piano, and recording under the recording ban–busting nom de plume of the Bunny Banks Trio.[32] The trio's "Don't Stop Now," with vocals by Bonnie Davis, entered *Billboard*'s Harlem Hit Parade chart at number eight on January 30, 1943, and made it to number one by April 10 of that year.[33] Former Savoy employee Bob Porter told researchers Robert Cherry and Jennifer Griffith that although Lubinsky, like other independent record company owners, toyed with a variety of music styles at the start, his entrepreneurial instincts suggested that black music was the most direct route to profitability.[34]

Lubinsky did not tarry when it came to squeezing every ounce of opportunity out of the local African American music community. In 1943 he dipped into the font of black religious music by forming the King Solomon subsidiary. The first King Solomon artist was the Kings of Harmony, an a cappella quartet from New York City that sang in the style of fellow New Yorkers the Selah Jubilee Singers.[35] By spring 1948, Savoy was releasing gospel sides on its flagship label, assigning them to a new 4000-numbered religious series. The two initial sides in the 4000 series were by the Progressive Four, a male gospel quartet that, like the artists released on King Solomon and the pioneering Newark quartets, sang in the unaccompanied jubilee style. According to music historian Jay Bruder, at least three of the first six singles on Savoy's newly established 4000 gospel series were leased from Lillian Claiborne and Haskell Davis's DC diskery. The sides arrived from Gotham Records owner Ivin Ballin, who was handling DC's pressing and distribution at that time.[36]

Savoy signaled its shift to the emerging piano- and organ-led gospel group sound in January 1949, when it shuttered King Solomon and signed the Ward Singers of Philadelphia to its flagship label. As the Consecrated Gospel Singers, Gertrude Ward and her daughters Willarene (Willa) and Clara appeared for the first time in public as a singing trio in 1934. The trio's appearance at the 1943 National Baptist Convention in Chicago was so well received that they began receiving invitations to sing at churches throughout the nation. Their first record, an independently pressed rendition of Mary Lou Coleman Parker's "Jesus" (performed by Gertrude Ward and Daughters) led to a recording contract with Savoy. The single paved the way for the Wards' more-than-decade-long string of Savoy hits. With the acquisition of Marion Williams, Frances Steadman, Henrietta Waddy, Kitty Parham, and Esther Ford, the Ward Singers evolved into an effervescent, handclapping, shouting, falsetto-note-hitting, aisle-walking, and nattily coiffed female gospel super group.

If Lubinsky was, as Shaw suggests, "more of a wheeler-dealer than a creative record man," he also acknowledges that "either by accident or intuition, he employed a series of extremely good record producers."[37] Starting in 1945, it was Teddy Reig (1918–84) who steered to Savoy some of New York's most sophisticated jazz and bebop artists, among them Charlie Parker, Lester

Young, and Dizzy Gillespie.[38] Savoy's first R&B artists and its earliest flag-ship label gospel releases came courtesy of career record man Ralph Bass (1911–97), who worked for Lubinsky from 1948 to 1951.[39] When Lee Magid (1926–2007) joined Savoy in November 1950, he not only sustained the la-bel's share of R&B and religious artists, but he also stepped up production of sides by emerging vocal harmony groups such as the Four Buddies.[40] Fred Mendelsohn climbed aboard in 1951 after Bass departed Savoy to run King Records' new Federal imprint.[41]

Fred Mendelsohn would play a significant role in the growth and sustain-ability of Savoy's religious series. Born May 16, 1917, Mendelsohn was raised on Manhattan's Lower East Side. His initial exposure to black music was as a teenager working in a drugstore in a predominantly African American sec-tion of Brooklyn.[42] In 1944 he became the music director for New York radio station WBNX[43] and started Regent Records three years later. Mendelsohn entered Savoy's orbit in mid-June 1948 when he sold a portion of Regent to Lubinsky, who became the company's treasurer and general sales manager while Mendelsohn remained president and artists and repertoire chief.[44] By 1949, Regent and Savoy were sharing offices in Lubinsky's 58 Market Street location. Between Magid, whom Broven called "the hustler with the staccato speech to match"[45] and Mendelsohn, whom Shaw remembered as "husky but gentle,"[46] Savoy became a major force among independents recording and selling popular and religious black music.

Another of Lubinsky's inspired hires was Oscar "Ozzie" Cadena. Born in Oklahoma City in 1924 and raised in Newark, Cadena started as an em-ployee of Lubinsky's Radio Record Shop. He produced jazz and gospel for Savoy Records between 1954 and 1959,[47] frequently using the New Jersey studio of audio engineer Rudy Van Gelder for his projects. Considered one of the most important recording engineers in jazz, Van Gelder (November 2, 1924–August 25, 2016) began his professional life as an optometrist. By 1959 he had moved into full-time recording engineering, working with Savoy and other important jazz labels such as Blue Note, Prestige, and Impulse. He was known for his fair fees and almost compulsive preparedness. Peter Keepnews, writing in the *New York Times*, noted that Van Gelder "was not in charge of the sessions he recorded; he did not hire the musicians or play any role in choosing the repertoire. But he had the final say in what the records sounded like, and he was, in the view of countless producers, musi-cians and listeners, better at that than anyone."[48] Skilled in capturing the musical intricacies of postwar jazz and bebop, Van Gelder's engineering and Cadena's production gave Savoy gospel music a crispness rarely captured on disk prior to this time.

Mendelsohn and Magid enlarged Savoy's gospel roster significantly by signing the Davis Sisters of Philadelphia away from Gotham in 1955 and the Roberta Martin Singers away from Apollo two years later, in late January 1957.[49] Whether it foresaw the rise in popularity of piano- and organ-led gospel groups, helped fuel it, or both, Savoy Records became the premier label for this fast-growing style of gospel music. In turn, gospel music became the company's priority after the payola scandal of 1960 ruined the careers of disk jockeys such as Alan Freed and put some small record labels out of business. Savoy gradually dropped its popular line and by the early 1960s focused almost exclusively on religious music, eventually amassing what became, according to Shaw, "one of the largest catalogues of gospel records" in the country.[50]

Lawrence Roberts's relationship with the record business in general and Savoy Records in particular began in October 1957, when he decided to form a small gospel group. "Just out of a whim of seeing other folks get started," he recalled, "I picked girls from the [Zion Hill Young People's] choir and started my own group. And it was a success."[51] His group, the Gospel Chordettes, consisted of Bernadine Greene Hankerson (formerly of Philadelphia), Delores "Amy" Best (formerly of Detroit), Marjorie Raines, Freda Roberts (no relation, originally from Jacksonville, Florida), and Gertrude Deadwyler Hicks (Brooklyn, New York).[52] Sandy Miller Osborne recalled childhood days sitting on the porch of her family's home on Sherman Avenue in Newark, listening to the Gospel Chordettes rehearsing around the upright piano in their living room. She remembered how, much to her mother's dismay, Roberts's heavy-handed piano playing left the upright in constant need of tuning.[53] The Gospel Chordettes sang in and around Newark initially and then expanded its territory to New York City when Bishop A. A. Childs invited them to sing for the congregation at his Faith Temple Church of God in Christ.[54]

One of the Gospel Chordettes' most popular songs in performance was the Roberts-composed "I Can't Believe It," a cheerfully but pointedly critical editorial on the social ills of the world at midcentury. It reminds the listener of the headshaking critiques Sister Rosetta Tharpe chronicled in her 1946 hit, "Strange Things Happening Every Day." In a hoarse, declamatory tone, Roberts led the Gospel Chordettes on the spunky chorus: "Fighting on the land, trouble everyplace / And just the other day they sent a *Sputnik* into space."

Invoking *Sputnik* gave "I Can't Believe It" novelty potential—an astute move at a time when novelty singles, especially those about outer space, science fiction, intergalactic creatures, and B-movie themes, had the potential to become radio hits.[55] But referring to the Soviet satellite was also a commentary on US anxiety during the late 1950s. When the Soviets launched *Sputnik* on October 4, 1957, the ever-present threat of nuclear annihilation brought on by deteriorated political relations between the United States and the Soviet Union came into sharper focus. Americans gazed nervously into the sky, wondering whether *Sputnik*'s surveillance capability was a prelude to World War III.[56]

Ward Singers matriarch Gertrude Ward heard the Gospel Chordettes sing "I Can't Believe It" on a program the two groups shared and thought the young people might have a hit on their hands. She suggested Roberts contact Herman Lubinsky at Savoy and ask him to record the song.[57] It didn't take much convincing. Several of Roberts's colleagues in the Newark gospel community, likely some of the same "folks" he saw "get started," had already released singles on Savoy. In fact, it seemed as if everybody Roberts knew had a deal with Savoy. Besides the Gospel Clefs, the Unique Gospel Singers, the Afro Quintette, the Lucille Parks Singers, and the Drinkard Singers, the Greater Abyssinian Baptist Church Youth Choir and Jeff and Charles Banks of Greater Harvest Baptist Church were also on the Savoy roster. Alex Bradford, serving as minister of music for Abyssinian Baptist Church under the church's pastor, Reverend Raphus P. Means, a Spartanburg, South Carolina, native, recorded for Savoy's new Gospel subsidiary.

Years later, Roberts recalled that "I went down to Savoy [at 58 Market Street]. I had written some songs, and a very dear friend of mine, Professor Robert Banks, was working for Mr. Lubinsky at the time. I let Mr. Lubinsky hear my music and find out if it had any commercial value. One of the songs I had written at the time was called 'I Can't Believe It.' And he liked it, wanted to record it, and that's how I got started."[58] On March 3, 1958, the Gospel Chordettes entered New York's City's Beltone Studios to cut five sides, including "I Can't Believe It." Roberts's pal Robert Banks accompanied on organ and an uncredited drummer, possibly either Bobby Donaldson or Joe Marshall, provided the song's hard-charging backbeat.[59]

Shortly thereafter, Savoy pressed and shipped "I Can't Believe It," backed with the Freda Roberts-led "He's Got the Whole World in His Arms." Savoy's advertisement in the March 24, 1958, issue of *Billboard* played up the novelty component of "I Can't Believe It" by referring to it as "the Sputnik song."[60] A week later, *Billboard* featured the single in its Review Spotlight column, calling it "exuberant" and "powerful" and that it "should click with lovers of spiritual themes." Although there was no mention of *Sputnik* in the magazine's Review Spotlight, a separate critique of both sides on the following page cited the song's "excellent lyrics tied in with 'sputnick' [sic]."[61] Lubinsky boasted to *Billboard* that the song was even garnering pop spins. The single's popularity placed the Gospel Chordettes on the stage of the Apollo Theater for a weeklong appearance in May 1958 as part of Fred Barr and Doc Wheeler's Gospel Caravan. They sang alongside the Davis Sisters, the Soul Stirrers, the Mighty Skylights, Raymond Rasberry Singers, and New York organist and group leader Professor Herman Stevens.[62] Decades later, Gertrude Hicks was still thrilled to have gone from rehearsals at the Millers to the stage of the legendary Apollo. "Oh, I thought I was somebody, oh yes!" she exclaimed.[63]

Satisfied with the success of "I Can't Believe It," Savoy arranged for the Gospel Chordettes to record again on June 23, 1958, this time at New York's Bell Sound Studio.[64] Employing the era's formula of cutting a follow-up single with a similar sound and theme, Savoy released "If You Make It to the Moon." This Roberts original with novelty potential featured Bobby Donaldson on drums and Banks on organ. Banks's eerie organ glissando on the introduction evokes 1950s science fiction matinees much as "Moon" sustains the space-age sentiment of "I Can't Believe It." On this piece, however, the focus was not the perceived terror of *Sputnik* but pushback on the prospect of putting an astronaut on the moon. "If you make it to the moon, tell me what you gonna look for?" Freda Roberts asks pointedly. Then engaging in a playful call-and-response with her fellow singers, Freda follows with "If you are looking for joy [on the moon]," the group responds, "we've got that here." Does the moon offer love and peace, Freda wonders? The group's answer is the same: "We've got that here." As with "I Can't Believe It," the speed of technological and social change in modern secular society was not always viewed as a positive development by socially conservative Christians.

When the follow-up single was pressed, it was credited not to the Gospel Chordettes but to the Lawrence Roberts Singers. "After ['I Can't Believe It'] was released," Roberts explained, "there was a group doing secular music called the Chordettes.[65] And they wrote Mr. Lubinsky a letter stating that their name was copyrighted and we couldn't use it. So I said, 'Well, I'll use a name I know they can't sue me about: Lawrence Roberts!' And that's how [the Gospel Chordettes] became the Lawrence Roberts Singers."[66]

"I Can't Believe It" and "If You Make it to the Moon" were indicative of Roberts's playfulness when it came to gospel music and his exposure to, and affection for, other music styles absorbed during his Arts High days. So did two more Lawrence Roberts Singers recordings, "Walk through the Valley" and "When the Lord Saved Me." Both are taken at a breakneck pace, with Roberts hammering the piano keys with such vigor at the outset of "Saved" that the opening chord contains a dissonant note; one can see how he could knock the Miller family's piano out of tune. Taken as a group, these selections are rollicking reminders of the sometimes negligible distance between the sacred and secular. Roberts's gospel-rock sensibility would color some of his later work, including one song during the forthcoming *Peace Be Still* session.

In his autobiography, *The Gospel Truth*, Roberts stated that the Gospel Chordettes / Lawrence Roberts Singers received no payment for their initial Savoy sides. They were just enjoying the opportunity to record and be heard on the radio. But after Savoy labelmate Alex Bradford told Roberts that one of their singles, probably "I Can't Believe It," was a hit in Chicago, St. Louis, and Alabama, Roberts confronted Lubinsky about the matter of compensation. Of his first lesson in the street hustle of the independent record business, Roberts reported, "I was then informed by Mr. Lubinsky that he was not aware (much to my surprise) that I had not been receiving any monies. We discovered that one of his employees had put an infant son's name on our record [as composer credit], and as a consequence was reaping the benefit of finances that we should have gained."[67]

But two days later, as the story goes, Lubinsky asked Roberts to substitute for Robert Banks on a recording session that Banks was unable to fulfill. Roberts agreed to play but only if Lubinsky would reconcile the royalty snafu. The company owner did so, and Roberts fulfilled his part of the bargain by playing organ on the session.[68] Recognizing Roberts's keyboard skills, his knack for writing gospel hits, and his connections to the regional gospel music community, Lubinsky hired him to be Savoy's gospel music producer.[69] Although flattered, Roberts told Lubinsky he was concerned he could not fulfill the requirements of the position because he knew nothing about the record business. Lubinsky assured him that if he took the job, he would personally show him the basics—from recording to distribution.[70]

The most important lessons he learned from Lubinsky, Roberts recalled, were the fundamentals of recording and editing technology. "He showed me how to edit, how to mark the tape, where to cut the tape, how to put it back together, how to take out the parts I didn't want or wouldn't make things happen, how to get the music so it flowed in sequence for the next chord coming." Lubinsky also gave his young protégé a crash course in sound balance. Lubinsky taught Roberts "how to not let a guitar and a piano clash. . . . not to let the organ override the piano, how not [to] let a soloist become a part of the background."[71]

Roberts absorbed his lessons well and quickly, but not without mistakes along the way. He recalled a harrowing experience during the production of a Meditation Singers session:

> If you took the tape off the machine, you had to do it very carefully because it was a large disc of tape and not covered on [one] side—just a bottom plate but not a top plate—and if you didn't handle it gently, it would fall apart and you'd have tape all over the floor. [And] I abruptly—I don't know what I was thinking about—got up, took it off, and dropped it. For four or five hours, I was in the room reeling tape on manually and trying to keep it straight. There is a God in heaven! I got it back on. And when it was all in order, I played it and nothing was damaged.[72]

Back in those days, Roberts said, "we really had just a three-man [gospel division]. It was Mr. Lubinsky, who always reminded us he signed the checks, Fred Mendelsohn, and myself. [A]nyone that was anybody during the '40s, '50s, '60s, '70s, they were on our label: the Gospel Clefs, Gospel Harmonettes, the Ward Singers, the Roberta Martin Singers, the Davis Sisters, the Gospel Chimes, James Cleveland, Albertina Walker and the Caravans—we had everybody!"[73] Roberts also credited the quality of Savoy's gospel product to its community of session musicians, notably Herman Stevens on organ, jazz talents Bernard Purdie and Joe Marshall on drums, Leonard Caston on bass, and Earl Hines Orchestra alumnus Clifton "Skeeter" Best on lead guitar.[74]

"The only thing [Lubinsky] was unfair with, and I should not really even be mad at him for that, and that was money," Roberts said. "I was underpaid, but I saw the country; I met the people, and this was one of my great interests."[75]

By 1959, the twenty-three-year-old Roberts was juggling multiple responsibilities. He was a new husband and father, a choir director, a gospel production and talent scout for Savoy Records, and manager of the Lawrence Roberts Singers. And his group was doing well. They were busy performing throughout the region and Savoy invited them back to record another single. That next disk, a November 1958 coupling of "When the Lord Saved Me" and "I'm a-Rollin'," received an enthusiastic review in *Billboard*, which called it a "first rate waxing" and the group "a fine one."[76] Roberts's expressive baritone lead, sung at full volume, on "I'm a-Rollin'," evokes Leon Lumpkins's equally passionate delivery on "Open Our Eyes," recorded just a month earlier.

On the heels of their continued success, the Lawrence Roberts Singers were invited to participate in radio station WCIN-AM's November 1959 fund-raiser to be held at the Cincinnati Gardens in Cincinnati, Ohio. Probably patterned after the successful annual Goodwill Revue, held by Memphis's WDIA to benefit local charities, the WCIN Goodwill Spectacular was, according to its publicity, "expected to be the largest show ever staged for Negro charities in the U.S." In addition to the Lawrence Roberts Singers, gospel stars such as Brother Joe May, Madame Edna Gallmon Cooke, the Rasberry Singers, and the Reverend Morgan Babb and his Philco Singers were slated to appear on the November 6, 1959, benefit musicale.[77] To top it off, in 1957, Zion Hill's pastor, Doctor John R. Stanford, had ordained Roberts a Baptist minister, and he was ready to embark on a ministerial career. What more could Lawrence Roberts take on?

3

The Birth of the Angelic Choir

For reasons lost to history, the Reverend Joseph J. Napier resigned from the pastorate of the First Baptist Church of Nutley after ten years of service. No sooner had the church inaugurated a search for a new pastor than a member named Birdell Malloy Smith tendered Roberts's name for consideration. She had known him since his days with the Drinkard Singers and could vouch for his singing, directing, keyboard accompaniment, and leadership skills. But could he preach? She invited the newly ordained Roberts to visit First Baptist to preach one Sunday. Roberts's oratory won the congregation over. Smith formally recommended that the church board install the young man as their new pastor.[1]

But there was one problem: Mount Zion Baptist Church in Westwood, New Jersey, also was courting Roberts for its pastorate. In the end, Roberts declined the Mount Zion offer because First Baptist was closer to his home and growing family. He also reasoned that First Baptist would be "a greater challenge for me and would prove my ability to pastor."[2] So, on July 24, 1960, with a starting salary of $15 per week, the Reverend Lawrence Roberts was installed as pastor of First Baptist Church. At twenty-four, he was the youngest Baptist pastor in New Jersey.[3]

The pastor took stock of his new assignment. Membership under Napier had dwindled to twelve. Although the wooden church structure was only fifty years old, it appeared to have outlived its usefulness.[4] To Roberts, it was nothing more than "a log cabin with a potbellied stove for our heat."[5] Robert Logan recalled that the church could fit about one hundred congregants.[6] Erecting a modern facility was essential for expanding the church's membership and ministry, but building a church from the ground up meant raising a substantial sum of money. A fund-raising campaign of this magnitude would require the financial support of more than twelve members. There was plenty of work ahead. Meanwhile, Roberts began ministering to the twelve.

At first, First Baptist was literally a mom-and-pop enterprise. Lawrence and Bootsy Roberts handled everything themselves, including running the music department. "When we went to First Baptist, we didn't have a choir," Bootsy recalled, "so my husband would play and sing a solo. [Or] he would play and I would sing a solo, and we would do a duet together. That was our music."[7]

But as much as the membership may have appreciated the Robertses' musical talents, the church really needed a choir. With only twelve members, a choir would have to be brought in from the outside. This was not uncommon for new churches or those in transition and with insufficient members to form a sizable singing ensemble. Roberts invited members of his Voices of Faith community choir to sing one Sunday a month at First Baptist. Among those who complied were Pearl Minatee and her sister Lillian (Pearl would eventually bring her whole family to First Baptist), Ernest Nunnally, Tommy Johnson, Freeman Johnson, and organist Robert Logan. All joined First Baptist. Gertrude Deadwyler Hicks was so eager to participate that she spent "the better part of an hour" taking the bus from Jersey City to Newark, and then waiting "on that [bus number] 13 to Nutley."[8] She also became a member of the church.

Hicks, a member of the Lawrence Roberts Singers and the Voices of Faith, would figure prominently in Roberts's music ministry in the years to come. Born March 9, 1938, to Georgiana and Arvie Deadwyler in Brooklyn, New York, Gertrude and her missionary parents left Brooklyn to establish the Mount Olive Pentecostal Faith Church in Jersey City, New Jersey. As her parents managed the myriad details of church operations, Gertrude learned to play classical piano under the tutelage of a Miss Thompson. In elementary school, Gertrude performed for school programs and eventually added singing to her musical toolkit.[9] Like many of Roberts's singers and musicians, she first met Roberts at Zion Hill.

Lawrence Roberts put Freda Roberts in charge of leading songs and named Ernest Nunnally the choir's first director.[10] Ernest Lee Nunnally Jr. was born on October 22, 1916, to Ernest Sr. and Sandy Robinson Nunnally in Blakely, Georgia, also the hometown of Nitch and Delia Mae Drinkard.[11] Ernest Jr. moved with his family to Newark around 1945, where they joined Zion Hill. Although he and his brother Archie were members of the L&N Gospel Singers, Ernest also joined the Voices of Faith.[12] Ernest's daughter, Etta Jean Nunnally, said her father took Roberts under his wing and "nurtured and taught [Roberts] a lot about gospel music."[13] Since Nunnally was twenty years older than Roberts and familiar with syncopated rhythm from working with the L&N Gospel Singers at Zion Hill, his tutelage was a huge help to the young pastor-musician.

Though he would eventually transition to organ, Robert Logan was the Voices of Faith's piano accompanist when they appeared at First Baptist. Born December 12, 1938, in Carteret, New Jersey, Logan began playing piano publicly around the age of twelve at Mount Sinai Fire Baptized Holiness Church, a Newark church his father, the Reverend Robert Logan Sr., pastored. "I'm self-taught by the anointing of the Holy Ghost," Logan said. "My mother [Rebecca Logan] laid hands on me and I started playing what they were singing right in the service."[14] As with Roberts, it was the hopeful pursuit of a young lady that brought Logan to Zion Hill, where he heard Roberts playing organ and leading the Young People's Choir. It didn't take much persuasion for him to join the Voices of Faith and even less to follow Roberts to First Baptist.

Of the musical instruments bequeathed to Roberts by First Baptist when he took over the church's leadership, Logan recalled there being "a piano, an organ, and one of the original speakers. Reverend Roberts, maybe a month later, decided to upgrade [the organ] because he was very good at what he wanted to hear. God blessed him to hear good music and good sounds, and the three- and four-part harmony required with groups and all that."[15]

Although not a member of Zion Hill, Raymond Murphy was another Voices of Faith chorister who assisted First Baptist Church's newly reconstituted music ministry. He first heard the Voices when they participated in a service at Pastor Warrick's New Hope Baptist Church:

I was actually an Episcopalian, and someone asked me to come to [New Hope one] Sunday morning. I sat up in the balcony, and I can remember that

Sunday just as plain as day. I'll never forget it. Five hundred folk dressed in black marched down the aisle singing "Lord, This Is a Mean Old World." And that was New Hope's choir, and the Voices of Faith marched in behind. I had never heard all this before. And then [Roberts] preached the Twenty-Third Psalm, and the day that he preached, it gave me a new meaning of what the Twenty-Third Psalm really meant. And that's when I started following him. I found out you had to be eighteen to join the Voices of Faith. I was only sixteen. I lied and I said I was eighteen and I joined the Voices of Faith. And they took me in. [Roberts] baptized me.[16]

The Voices of Faith sang for First Baptist's service every fourth Sunday, with Lawrence and Bootsy providing music for the other Sundays. "Eventually numerous Voices of Faith [members] started joining the church," Bootsy recalled. "When they joined the church, then we had enough members to form a choir."[17]

If First Baptist was to increase its membership and raise the funds to build a new church, it had to be modern and that meant having gospel songs in its repertory. That was, of course, not a problem for Roberts. By 1960, when the Voices of Faith became First Baptist's choir, gospel songs and gospel singing had become de rigueur in African American Protestant churches. But prior to 1933, when the National Convention of Gospel Choirs and Choruses, under the leadership of Thomas Andrew Dorsey, initiated a national campaign to organize gospel choruses in African American Protestant churches, the repertory of mainline Protestant church choirs in northern cities such as Newark and Nutley consisted of concert spirituals, hymns, anthems, and classical choral literature. Pastors disdained the hand-clapping and foot-patting religious music of Dorsey because of its musical proximity to jazz and blues, genres that, to them, represented nightclubs and the vice and immorality associated with those social institutions. Gospel music also reminded pastors of the unfettered worship of the southern folk church. The physicality and improvisation of the folk church ran counter to the button-down rules of conduct that bespoke middle-class respectability. And for many northern pastors and congregations, middle-class respectability meant performing the staid hymns and anthems of the western European tradition.

The attitude began to change when African Americans who moved north during the Great Migration brought their appetite for soul-stirring southern folk church practices with them. Their practices included physically and aurally demonstrative worship and zesty congregational singing of traditional spirituals, evangelical hymns, long- and short-meter hymns, and new gospel songs written by African American composers such as Charles A. Tindley ("Stand by Me"), Lucie E. Campbell ("Touch Me Lord Jesus"), Charles Price Jones ("I'm Happy with Jesus Alone"), and Dorsey ("If You See My Savior"). A direct descendant of West African music, which accompanied daily life, worship, and other ceremonies, gospel music encouraged hand clapping, foot patting, improvisation, lyric repetition, and communal participation in the singing. Migrants heard echoes of southern-style worship in Dorsey's gospel music and sought it out, even if that meant stealing away to a local Pentecostal, Spiritual, or Holiness church, where gospel music and folk church practices were not only welcome but essential components of the worship experience.

Thanks to gospel music evangelists such as Dorsey, his colleagues in the National Convention of Gospel Choirs and Choruses like Sallie Martin and Magnolia Lewis Butts, and singers such as Mahalia Jackson and the Ward Singers, one city after another fell sway to gospel music and gospel choirs in the 1930s and 1940s. Midwestern cities such as Chicago, Detroit, Cleveland, St. Louis, and Cincinnati were among the first to organize gospel choruses, with cities on the West and East Coasts, including Newark, following suit. Ultimately, it was the economic reality of operating a church in African American urban communities that prompted pastors to accept gospel music and gospel choruses. The sustainability of their ministry depended on a sizable tithing membership, and if the adage was true, that music brings people into the church and preaching keeps them there, avoiding gospel music meant potentially losing out on a steady flow of membership from the thousands of newly arrived southern migrants.

But despite their growing primacy as interpreters of the new gospel songs, African American church choirs rarely caught the attention of record companies prior to 1947. Those that did, as did the Nazarene Congregational Church Choir of New York City in 1926, were recorded singing spirituals and hymns in the staider northern style. Perhaps choirs were considered, at the time, too closely associated with the religious worship experience to be exploitable for Christian entertainment. On the other hand, the techniques of gospel soloists, quartets, groups, and musicians were imitated by secular groups, making the sounds of Saturday night and Sunday morning almost undistinguishable outside the lyric content. It wasn't until the mid- to late-1940s that commercial recordings of African American choirs singing newly composed gospel songs first appeared. And these were made not by church choirs but by professional touring troupes such as J. Garfield Wilson's Camp Meeting Choir of Charlotte, North Carolina ("Don't Wonder about Him," 1946) and Cleveland's Wings over Jordan Choir (Lucie Campbell's "He'll Understand and Say 'Well Done,'" 1948). Of the more than three hundred sides that Savoy Records had in its gospel catalog by 1960, only two were by church choirs. These disks were cut in November 1958 by the Young People's Choir of Newark's Abyssinian Baptist Church, probably produced at the recommendation of the church's music minister and Savoy recording artist Alex Bradford.[18]

The first known African American church choir to release a series of commercial singles of gospel songs from the pens of Dorsey and others, and to render them in the vigorous manner of the new aesthetic, was the Echoes of Eden of St. Paul Baptist Church of Los Angeles, California. St. Paul's newly elected pastor, the Reverend J. H. Branham, commissioned the formation of the Echoes of Eden to provide his Los Angeles congregation and radio listenership with the Dorsey-trained gospel choral style he enjoyed back home in Chicago. To direct the choir, Branham retained J. Earle Hines, a featured vocalist for the National Baptist Convention. In its earliest years, the Echoes of Eden featured vocally powerful lead singers such as Erie Gladney, Sallie Martin, and child singer Jamesetta Hawkins (later to become R&B star Etta James). Capitol Records, Johnny Mercer's five-year-old label, signed the chorus in 1947. Among their earliest recordings were songs featured by National Convention of Gospel Choirs and Choruses conventions such as Dorsey's "We Sure Do Need Him Now" and "I'm So Glad Jesus Lifted Me," a song credited to the Chicago Spiritual Church leader Reverend Clarence H. Cobbs.

Other African American church choirs that recorded gospel songs in the late 1940s and early 1950s released their music on local independent labels such as Black and White (St. Paul COGIC Choir of Chicago), Faith (Voices of Hope, with Thurston Frazier), Songs of the Cross (Hope Mission Choir), and Modern (Trinity Baptist Church, with Ineze Caston). That the Voices of Hope, Hope Mission Choir, and the Trinity Baptist Church were all Los Angeles enterprises demonstrates the dual influence of Hollywood's commercial record industry and the Echoes of Eden, whose regular radio broadcast on KOWL was a staple in African American households in southern California.

Savoy Records officially entered the business of recording church choirs when Lawrence Roberts persuaded Herman Lubinsky and Fred Mendelsohn to cut some singles of his Voices of Faith. By now a fairly experienced producer, Roberts nevertheless felt a thrill when the Voices of Faith entered a New York studio on Thursday, June 8, 1961. "When I came in to the studio and I saw all those people gathered around the microphones, I thought, this is my baby," he told Birdie Wilson Johnson in August 2000. "These are my children and this was the group I had made, I had started, I had named, I had taught."[19] But the group he "had named" was about to change its name. According to Raymond Murphy, it was after the Voices of Faith completed its first recording for Savoy that Roberts renamed them the Angelic Choir.[20]

The June 8 session produced six sides, including the choir's first single, "He Will" / "A Little Too Close to Be Afraid."[21] Written by James Cleveland, "He Will" was first recorded in 1960 by Detroit's Voices of Tabernacle under Cleveland's direction and with the brilliant soprano Hulah Gene Dunklin Hurley as lead singer. Cleveland also cut a version of the song for HOB Records with his vocal group, the Gospel Chimes. Marjorie Raines of the Lawrence Roberts Singers assumed Hurley's role for the Angelic Choir version.[22] "A Little Too Close" features a shouting lead by Roberts. The single earned four stars from *Billboard*, the magazine's highest rating for singles, indicating that it had high probability of achieving radio play.[23]

The single sold sufficiently well and received enough radio play for Savoy to authorize another Angelic Choir recording session for November 10, 1961. One song from the session, "It's the Holy Ghost," was a clever sendup of "Hit the Road Jack," the Percy Mayfield composition that Ray Charles and his Raelettes turned into a number one pop and R&B hit earlier that year. The Angelic Choir replaced the Raelettes' finger-wagging chorus, "Hit the road Jack / Don't you come back no more, no more, no more, no more" with "It's the Holy Ghost / Makes me feel all right, all right, all right, all right." As with "I Can't Believe It" and "If You Make It to the Moon," "It's the Holy Ghost" exemplified Roberts's instinct for giving gospel music a pop sensibility so it would appeal to a younger generation. "'Hit the Road Jack' was popular with everybody," Roberts told Birdie Wilson Johnson. "So I thought it would hark [sic] that popularity into the gospel field . . . which it did."[24] Indeed, "It's the Holy Ghost" earned a four-star rating in the January 13, 1962, issue of *Billboard*.

The flip, "I Know the Lord," also recorded on November 10, likewise received four stars from *Billboard*, in no small part to the choir's unbridled reading of the spiritual "I Know the Lord Laid His Hands on Me," with remarkable steel guitar accompaniment from Sam Windham. A Baptist musician from New York City whom Roberts and the Ward Singers employed for live and studio performances, Windham could make his steel guitar squeal and shriek like a soul succumbing to spirit possession. His high notes mimicked Marion Williams's stave-topping soprano flights. Although gospel vocal recordings of the period typically avoided extended instrumental solos, Windham's virtuosity was given full rein on "I Know the Lord."[25]

Ten of the thirteen sides the Angelic Choir recorded in June and November were compiled into the choir's eponymous debut album (Savoy MG-14049) and released in spring 1962. In addition to "It's the Holy Ghost" and "I Know the Lord," the album featured "Mercy Lord," a rereading of Dorsey's "Little Wooden Church on the Hill," complete with rocking piano, organ, drums, and Windham's blazing steel guitar. And whenever the studio musicians sped up the tempo, as on the Ernest Nunnally–led "Mercy Lord" and "No Weeping," they chugged along like Cameo-Parkway's house band, the Applejacks. Other religious chestnuts on the album are Charles A. Tindley's "We'll Understand It Better By and By," and a variation on Robert Lowry's 1876 "Nothing but the Blood," simply titled "The Blood." Both songs evoke the unconventional arrangements of Roberts's pal Leon Lumpkins and the Gospel Clefs. *Billboard* gave the album three stars in its May 19, 1962, issue, indicating moderate sales potential.[26]

Their slightly unconventional arrangements and rocking rhythm section notwithstanding, what the Angelic Choir lacked in studio experience they more than made up for in unbridled passion. They sound thrilled to be together in a recording studio, most for the first time, and confident in the hands of their capable leader. Indeed, it may well have been the choir's youthful everyman enthusiasm that appealed initially to listeners. It was no affectation. There was no audition process. All one had to do to join the Angelic Choir was become an adult member of the First Baptist Church of Nutley and receive Roberts's permission.

According to Raymond Murphy, part of the Angelic Choir's early success was also a result of Roberts's penchant for identifying and spotlighting the group's most vocally gifted members: "Reverend [Roberts] had to get leaders in the choir who could carry the sound, such as Gertrude [Hicks], Bernadine [Hankerson], Freeman [Johnson] . . . and one young lady, Margie [Raines]. When he heard Margie sing "Christ Is the Answer," it just blew him away!"[27] It helped, too, that Hicks, Hankerson, and Raines had already tallied a few years of experience singing, touring, and recording as the Lawrence Roberts Singers.

But success was also the product of rigorous rehearsal. With the exception of the week prior to a recording, when rehearsals were held nightly, Angelic Choir rehearsals occurred every Thursday or Friday. Bootsy recalled that her husband ran a serious rehearsal. "No lollygagging. We would have time to laugh, but when he was serious, he was serious, and if he had to yell at somebody, most of the time he was yelling at *me*! Everybody else could laugh and talk, and if I said one word, he used me for an example. 'This is no time to be laughing and talking, Bootsy.' I said, 'Well, everybody else is talking and laughing, but you have to call me out!' I guess they felt like if he'll pick on his wife, he'll get on me!"[28] Murphy concurred that "even though we were all grown and whatnot, [Roberts would] have no problem dressing us down and dressing us up again if it was called for. But rehearsals were just as serious as Sunday morning service. It wasn't taken lightly at all."[29]

Nevertheless, the banter between "Uncle" Lawrence and "Aunt" Bootsy, as they came to be known affectionately by the choir and the First Baptist congregation, provided moments of levity to counteract the serious work of learning new songs and perfecting others. Lorraine Stancil, who joined the Angelic Choir later, recalled an instance during a tour when Bootsy teasingly turned the tables on Lawrence, and he turned them right back on her: "We were about to take a tour of the mountain, [and] I heard Aunt Bootsy tell Uncle Lawrence, sort of jokingly, 'Lawrence, be quiet!' She asked him a question two minutes later, 'Is that right, Lawrence?' and he said, 'Uh-uh, you told me to be quiet!'"[30]

Despite the hard work, rehearsal felt like being with family. The Reverend Doctor Stefanie R. Minatee, daughter of Pearl Minatee and herself a future Angelic Choir member, recalled that "The Angelic Choir was like a big family. Everybody was friends with everybody."[31] Phyllis Morris, who joined the Angelic Choir in 1979, likened rehearsals to a worship service. "In rehearsal," Morris said, "the spirit was so high at times you didn't have to have a church service. We had our service just singing gospel music."[32]

Yvonne Walls, another chorister, had a similar recollection: "Sometimes the rehearsals were better than the recordings!" JaVan Hicks, who joined the choir around 1964, was pleased to discover that First Baptist Church had the type of soul-stirring services he enjoyed as a youth in Greensboro, North Carolina: "Growing up in the church in the South, being at First Baptist was a joy."[33]

The Angelic Choir's emerging popularity as a nationally recognized church choir augmented Savoy's already solid leadership in gospel music. "The field for gospel and spiritual product—and exposure to same—is increasing," Herman Lubinsky boasted to *Billboard* in early 1962. In response, his company expanded its release schedule to offer gospel not only on its flagship Savoy and Gospel subsidiary labels, but also on the Sharp, World Wide, and Regent subsidiaries. Lubinsky estimated that sixty new single releases would follow at the rate of a dozen a month—including material by Lawrence Roberts and the Angelic Choir.[34] Lubinsky's was no idle boast; Savoy had recently signed James Cleveland, an artist with the experience, visibility, and ambition to solidify the company's leadership position in commercial gospel music.

4

The Arrival of James Cleveland

On Friday, May 20, 1960, when James Cleveland walked up the steps at 58 Market Street and entered the Savoy Records office to sign his recording contract with the label, he encountered more than the company's usual chaotic clutter of desks, tables, and aisles "jammed with boxes and piles of circulars."[1] The company's employees were emotionally shaken. That morning, they arrived at the office to discover that marauders had entered the building, rifled through the file cabinets, helped themselves to $100 from the safe, and fled. Although Lubinsky told *Billboard* no files had been stolen, it was an unsettling start to what would become a nearly lifelong partnership between Savoy and Cleveland.[2] For the twenty-eight-year-old, signing an exclusive contract with Savoy Records must have felt like reaching the pinnacle of accomplishment, one he had been climbing toward for years. Indeed, just the week before, he appeared on the stage of the legendary Apollo Theater on a gospel program alongside iconic singer-guitarist and recording artist Sister Rosetta Tharpe.[3] Perhaps his time had come.

James Edward Cleveland was born in Chicago, Illinois, on December 5, 1931, to teenagers Ben L. Cleveland and Rosie Lee Brooks. All told, James had three sisters and two half-brothers. Rebecca "Betty" Brooks, Marion McCoy, and James were children of Ben and Rosie; Victoria "Vickie," Gerald, and Ben Jr. were children of Ben and a different mother.[4] According to US Census records, by 1940, James was living not with his parents but with his grandmother, a forty-five-year-old widow named Anna Ellis, and her sister, Irma Richardson, at 308 East Thirty-Third Street. Ellis attended Pilgrim Baptist Church at Thirty-Third Street and Indiana Avenue, a short walk from their apartment, and was a member of Pilgrim's relatively new gospel chorus, under Thomas A. Dorsey's direction. Young James accompanied his grandmother to choir rehearsals and, to counteract boredom, sometimes sang along with the choir. One day Dorsey overheard James's clear boy soprano, perched him atop a box, and had him render "All I Need Is Jesus" for the Pilgrim Baptist congregation. It was Cleveland's first public church solo.[5]

Solo performance notwithstanding, the young Cleveland's true desire was to play piano. He studied the semiclassical piano technique of gospel songwriter and group leader Roberta Martin. Cleveland's parents encouraged their son's musical ambition, but they were unable to afford a piano, so the young boy improvised. "I used to practice each night right there on the windowsill," he told author and historian Anthony Heilbut. "I took those wedges and crevices and made me black and white keys. And, baby, I played just like Roberta [Martin]."[6]

Cleveland soaked up Martin's piano style, but he also studied the singing techniques of her Roberta Martin Singers vocal ensemble. He was especially moved by group members and soloists Myrtle Scott, Eugene Smith, and Robert Anderson. One of the most prominent male soloists in gospel music during the 1940s and early 1950s, Anderson (1919–95) would go on to serve as one of Cleveland's informal musical mentors.[7] Moreover, Cleveland would adopt Eugene Smith's narrative preamble prior to a song performance. Cleveland was equally enthralled by Mahalia Jackson, who lived on Indiana Avenue a few blocks south of the Ellis household. Delivering the Queen of Gospel's newspaper to her stoop, Cleveland cupped his ear to her front door in hopes of hearing her singing.

By the 1940s, Cleveland had joined Thorne's Gospel Crusaders, a fifty-member youth chorus sponsored by a Mrs. Thorne who operated a music studio at 3305 South Michigan.[8] It was during his tenure as a Gospel Crusader that Cleveland's voice shifted from unblemished boy soprano to raspy baritone—a sound Cleveland himself described as "like a foghorn."[9] While a student at Wendell Phillips High School, Cleveland met Imogene Greene (1930–82), a budding gospel music vocalist, and served as her accompanist.[10] Floriene Watson Willis, a Phillips pupil and also a gospel singer, remembered that Cleveland played piano for the school's annual spring gospel music festival.[11]

Sometime in the 1940s, Cleveland and Greene joined the Lux Singers, a mixed-voice gospel group organized by local beautician and salon owner Beatrice Lux. In an era of gospel singing characterized by the tempered passion of the Roberta Martin Singers and Sallie Martin's Singers of Joy, the Lux Singers were just the opposite—spontaneous and sanctified. In addition to Cleveland, the Lux Singers ensemble included a young Clay Evans. The future pastor and civil-rights leader was newly arrived in Chicago from Brownsville, Tennessee, when he joined the Lux Singers. Decades later, Evans remembered Cleveland as "not big enough to get up on the piano stool but he had a lot of showmanship."[12]

Flush with experience from the Gospel Crusaders and the Lux Singers, and seeing the burgeoning success of other local gospel groups, Cleveland invited Norsalus McKissick and Bessie Folk, two members of the Roberta Martin Singers, to join him in a trio called the Gospelaires. According to Bessie's son, Eugene Folk, the nineteen-year-old Cleveland was living with his family at the time. "James was ambitious and eager to try new things," Folk said. "Norsalus was a close friend to my mother, and James knew that, so he asked them to help start his own group. Miss [Roberta] Martin agreed because the music was published by her, therefore the music remained 'in the family'."[13]

The Gospelaires cut six sides in October 1950 and January 1951.[14] The sessions, recorded in New York and released on Apollo Records, likely came to fruition through Martin's influence, since the Roberta Martin Singers were on Apollo at the time. However they got to New York, the Gospelaires were, like the Martin Singers, a paradigmatic example of the emerging organ- and piano-accompanied group that would soon compete successfully with soloists and quartets in the gospel music marketplace. "Oh What a Time," recorded during the Gospelaires' January 1951 Apollo Records session, constitutes Cleveland's first commercially recorded solo. His voice is a thin shadow of what was to come, but if you listen closely, you can hear the emergence of Cleveland's tear-stained rasp.

A short period of live performances by the Gospelaires followed, but by 1952, McKissick and Folk returned to the Roberta Martin Singers full time, and the Gospelaires were no more. Nevertheless, the experience whetted Cleveland's appetite and helped further his reputation in the industry as an up-and-coming singer, accompanist, and recording artist.

Cleveland was also a budding songwriter. The Roberta Martin Studio of Music published one of his first compositions, 1948's "Grace Is Sufficient."

Since Martin published only compositions her singers performed, Cleveland was all but guaranteed that his piece would be used in live programs and on recordings. "I sold all of [my] tunes to Miss Martin for little or nothing," Cleveland remarked ruefully later. "Of course, she made fabulous sums of money off of them, but that wasn't my interest at the time. My mother was still doing day work for eight hours a day and sometimes she would come home and I'd have the money there in my hand—more money than she was making as a grown woman—and it was a big deal."[15]

Cleveland tried every trick in his singular pursuit of gospel stardom. "I'd stand around by the door and hope somebody's musician didn't show up," Cleveland once said. "Then I'd offer to play for them."[16] Lorenza Brown Porter, manager of the Argo Singers, recalled receiving a note at one of the Argo's programs, asking her to invite James Cleveland to sing. It turned out Cleveland had written the note himself and had it passed forward to Porter.[17]

Cleveland's next artistic collaboration was with the Meditation Singers. Organized in Detroit in 1947 by Ernestine Rundless, the group was composed of members of the Voices of Meditation Choir at New Liberty Baptist Church, where Ernestine's husband (and former member of the Soul Stirrers), the Reverend E. A. Rundless, was pastor. In addition to Ernestine, the Meditation Singers featured Marie Waters, Herbert Carson, and a teenaged Delloreese Early. Early left the group in 1954 to pursue solo stardom as R&B chanteuse Della Reese.[18] Cleveland's piano accompaniment can be heard on the group's first two singles, recorded in late 1952 by Detroit producer and record-store owner Joe Von Battle.[19] From there, Cleveland and his high school pal Imogene Greene collaborated with Ella Mitchell, Rose Hines, and Dorothy Bates, who were known as the New York–based Gospel All-Stars. The group, featuring Cleveland on piano and Herman Stevens on organ, waxed six sides for Apollo in 1957.[20] One, the rollicking "That's Why I Love Him So," is alleged to have been inspired by Ray Charles's "Hallelujah, I Love Her So." But it is Cleveland's poignant duet with Greene on "Remember Me" that demonstrates the remarkable vocal timing the young man had already mastered.

Next for Cleveland was the Caravans, a female gospel group organized by Robert Anderson in the late 1940s to supply background vocals for his recordings and public appearances. Initially known as the Good Shepherd Singers, the Caravans supported Anderson until April 1952, when in the midst of a Chicago recording session they parted ways with their founder and used the time remaining on the session to launch their own recording career. Their sudden success was a mixed blessing. Nearly all of the original Caravans had families to care for and could not sustain the heightened travel schedule. One by one, they dropped out. That included the Caravans' piano accompanist Charlotte Nelson. When she departed the group in 1954, the ladies were in urgent need of a keyboard player—one with the flexibility to travel.

Albertina Walker, now serving as the Caravans' manager, happened to run into Cleveland hanging out at Mahalia Jackson's home. She offered him the position of chief musician for the Caravans. He joined the group at its October 5, 1954, session at Chicago's Universal Studio to record "What Kind of Man Is This" and "This Man Jesus."[21] "The record company didn't want to record James because they didn't think he could sing!" Walker reported years later. "But I told the record man [probably Leonard Allen or Lew Simpkins, owners of United and States Records] that I wasn't going to record until he recorded James. . . . The record company people still protested, they insisted that we were a female group and shouldn't use a male voice. But I insisted that they record James."[22]

It worked. Cleveland went on to make additional singles with the Caravans, and their popularity secured them entry on a package tour arranged by Specialty Records. Specialty owner Art Rupe recorded the Caravans and Cleveland singing "What Kind of Man Is This" at a July 22, 1955, stop at Los Angeles's Shrine Auditorium. Thanks to this recording, listeners can witness a twenty-three-year-old Cleveland in live performance, singing alongside the Caravans and pounding the piano into humble submission.

Cleveland supplemented the revenue he earned from recording, touring, accompanying, and composing by working with a variety of church choirs in Chicago and by serving as minister of music for the Reverend B. F. Paxton's True Light Baptist Church on Chicago's South Side. He held the True Light position until the late 1950s, when he departed once again for Detroit, this time to direct the choir at the Reverend C. L. Franklin's New Bethel Baptist Church.[23] While residing with the Franklins, Cleveland taught the Reverend C. L.'s teenaged daughter Aretha to play piano after her first instructor scared the girl so badly she went into hiding. James "showed me some real nice chords and I liked his deep, deep sound," Aretha told journalist Phyl Garland for an October 1967 issue of *Ebony*. She also praised his singing. "There's a whole lot of earthiness in the way he sings, and what he was feelin', I was feelin', but I just didn't know how to put it across. The more I watched him, the more I got out of it." Cleveland also helped organize a gospel group consisting of Aretha, her sister Erma, and two other girls. The group sang for local churches but broke up after eight months. "We were too busy fussin' and fightin'," Aretha acknowledged.[24]

When in 1958 the Reverend Charles Craig resigned as music minister of the Reverend James Lofton's Church of Our Prayer to organize Prayer Tabernacle Spiritual Church in Detroit, he hired Cleveland to be his minister of music. The task included directing the church's house choir, the Voices of Tabernacle. Just as some Zion Hill members followed the newly ordained Lawrence Roberts to First Baptist, participants in the Church of Our Prayer music ministry, among them soprano soloist Hulah Gene Dunklin Hurley and organist Frances Chandler, followed Craig to Prayer Tabernacle and became part of the Voices of Tabernacle.

The Voices of Tabernacle was a disruptive force in gospel music. Decades later, choir director and accompanist Charles Clency recalled vividly his first encounter with the Voices of Tabernacle. It was during a 1959 program on Chicago's South Side:

> Charles Craig and James Cleveland came out with a completely brand new idea of all kinds of contemporary chords, extended chords, chord altera-tions. I heard sounds I never heard before in gospel. I could not believe what I was hearing; none of us could. Alfred Bolden was on the organ, and Herbert "Pee Wee" Pickard was on the piano. . . . The organ and piano were unbelievable in terms of balance, quality, expertise, dynamics, soft, loud, spirituals, gospels, anthems. . . . James Cleveland always had soulfulness. He was the Ray Charles of gospel. But Charles Craig had the innovation and the musicianship.[25]

Clency and his fellow music ministers were not the only ones moved by the Voices of Tabernacle. So was Detroit beautician and entrepreneur Carmen Caver Murphy. Murphy's House of Beauty salon had been a successful Mo-tor City enterprise since its establishment in 1947. In the late 1950s, she formed a record label called HOB (House of Beauty) to capitalize on the plethora of local music talent. Initially releasing singles of pop music and rock-and-roll, Murphy entered the gospel field after Detroit deejay Jack Surrell, her unofficial artists and repertoire man, called to tell her about an amateur recording he had made of the Voices of Tabernacle. Surrell put the phone receiver next to his tape player and let Murphy hear "Calvary," led by Hulah Gene Dunklin Hurley.[26]

The timing could not have been better. Murphy's father, Bishop Henry L. Caver of Chicago's Christ Temple Church, had passed away and she wanted to honor him. Thinking that a recording of religious music might be the kind of tribute her father would have liked, Murphy cobbled together the funds to record the Voices of Tabernacle on HOB's first full-length album.

The Love of God by the Voices of Tabernacle, and the album's title track, a Cleveland-led arrangement of Leroy Crume's Soul Stirrers hit from 1958, exceeded Murphy's and Surrell's expectations. *Billboard* called the 125-voice choir "one of the great spiritual choruses performing today."[27] Cleveland's soaring, expansive moans on "The Love of God" anticipate his emotional vocal leads with the Angelic Choir. Gospel enthusiasts credit *The Love of God* as the initial entry of the church choir in the battle for religious radio dominance and record sales, a position held, at that time, by quartets, soloists, and piano-led groups.

While in Detroit, Cleveland rekindled his working relationship with the Meditation Singers, a group that now included future soul star Laura Lee Rundless and future gospel choir leader (and Cleveland collaborator) Charles Fold. Cleveland accompanied and sang with the Meditations on a handful of selections he produced for Specialty Records at Chicago's Universal Recording Studio on July 8, 1959.[28] But the timing was poor; at the same time that the Meditations recorded at Universal, Specialty owner Art Rupe was winding down the label's recording activities. As a result, only two Meditation Singers Specialty sides saw the light of day; the rest weren't heard until decades later, on a Specialty Records reissue CD.[29] Nevertheless, *Billboard* bestowed a four-star rating upon that one Specialty disk, "My Soul Looks Back and Wonders," released almost simultaneously with HOB's *The Love of God*.[30]

Despite his achievements as a songwriter, arranger, choir director, group leader, accompanist, and music minister, Cleveland sought a solo career. He had wanted that for a long time. He told an audience of gospel announcers in 1974 how, in the early 1950s, he sat for thirty-two straight working days in the waiting room of Chicago's Vee Jay Records, hoping for an audition—to no avail. He added that when Vee Jay came looking for him six years later, it was six years too late. "I'm glad I am with Savoy," he told the announcers.

"Vee Jay went out of business. Many a precious gem is thrown away because of lack of recognition. We must be able to recognize and polish the nugget."[31]

Savoy wasted no time polishing the nugget. The week after Cleveland's signing, Roberts and Mendelsohn hustled him into the studio for a recording session, backed by his erstwhile colleagues, the Gospel All Stars.[32] The six sides recorded that day were coupled into three singles and marketed throughout the remainder of 1960. A month later, the company advertised the first release, "Just Like He Said He Would" / He's Alright with Me" in *Billboard*. Sparing no superlatives, Savoy cited the disc as "the greatest spiritual ever made."[33] However, the most remarkable cut from the session, "Just to Behold His Face," is a beautifully passionate reading of Lucie Campbell's 1941 gospel composition. Letting loose in his tear-stained foghorn, Cleveland gives the song the same emotional reading he lent to "The Love of God."

It was evident that James Cleveland was on his way to becoming a gospel solo artist, but his choir directing days were not over, at least as far as Savoy was concerned. The company understandably hoped he would produce the same magic for Savoy that he had for HOB. He couldn't use the Voices of Tabernacle, because they were signed to HOB, but he *was* working with another choir. Annette May Thomas, daughter of gospel star Brother Joe May, had invited Cleveland to move to Los Angeles and replace her as music minister at the city's New Greater Harvest Baptist Church. It was a new congregation, established four years earlier by the Reverend T. M. Chambers Jr., son of the Reverend T. M. Chambers Sr. of Los Angeles's Zion Hill Baptist Church.[34] Cleveland accepted Annette's invitation, but transporting the entire New Greater Harvest church choir, an untested one at that, from Los Angeles to one of Savoy's preferred recording studios in New York would have been impracticable.[35] On the other hand, there was a local church choir with recording provenance that happened to be signed to Savoy. So, sometime in 1962, on the recommendation of Fred Mendelsohn, Cleveland approached Roberts about borrowing his Angelic Choir for a recording. Years later, Roberts recalled their conversation:

> James called me to ask if he could record with me. And I told him I would be happy to record with him, but I would appreciate it if he would do it differently. And he asked me how. And I said, "Let's record it live in church." And the reason I thought of doing that was because [he] had recorded with

a choir out of Detroit called the Voices of Tabernacle. But I knew my choir could not meet the standards of the Voices of Tabernacle in a studio session. They were all professional singers and I just had Mary, Jane, and John Doe from up the street, down the street, and around the corner. But I knew if you put them in the church atmosphere, we would do well.[36]

Cleveland expressed reservations. It would be more difficult to edit technical errors out of a live recording than out of a studio session. But Roberts was persistent. "I always felt that when you have to clean up a song too much," he said on a videotaped interview, "you lose some of the fervor that the original interpretation of the song may have had."[37] Still, Cleveland did not know of any gospel choirs that had recorded a live album in a church, in front of a congregation. He may not have known about them, but gospel choirs had indeed recorded live in-service albums, including one right there in Newark.

5

In Search of the Authentic:
The Live In-Service Recording

Attempts to capture on phonograph records the authenticity of the African American worship experience go back almost as far as the African American sacred recording industry itself. According to historian Lerone Martin, between 1925 and 1941, approximately one hundred African American preachers took advantage of the "new method [of recording for the phonograph] to preach an old gospel message."[1] Singles by the Reverends J. M. Gates, F. W. McGee, D. C. Rice, and other recording preachers attempted to simulate the live worship or revival experience by forming a studio "congregation" of two or more singers to participate aurally on the session. The small assembly assented to the minister's demonstrative sermonettes with the rhythmic fidelity characteristic of a church congregation. Their responses included improvisatory interjections of "Hallelujah," "Amen," "Yes," and occasional wordless moans. Before or after the recorded sermonette, a song leader or group from the simulated congregation would raise a familiar hymn, gospel song, or spiritual, and the rest would pick it up, sometimes clapping along to the rhythm. While sermonettes with singing were typically recorded in a studio, Martin notes that Gates's 1926 disks were recorded in his Atlanta church, with members of the congregation on hand to respond to the sermon and sing congregational hymns.[2] If so, they represented the first live recording audience in modern gospel music history.

Just like radio broadcasts of religious services, writes Martin, these sermon recordings carried religious messages to consumers who might not have heard them otherwise.[3] Ironically, religious leaders used the same media—radio and recordings—through which popular culture was disseminated to fight back against the spread of popular entertainment in the African American community, all the while shepherding their community back within the confines of traditional Protestant values.[4] Seeing the potential of radio and records to promote their ministries beyond their sanctuaries, African American pastors, and especially those from the Holiness and Pentecostal sects, pursued them aggressively to attract more members and money to their churches and also to build new levels of prestige for themselves.[5] Whether the disks were recorded in a studio or a church, the record company's marketing efforts hyped their authenticity. For example, a 1927 *Chicago Defender* ad for the Reverend F. W. McGee's famous sermon, "Jonah in the Belly of the Whale," boasted that the side would "make you feel that you're right in the church. You hear it all just as it actually happens."[6] It was a studio recording.

Although the Great Depression devastated the record industry and ended the recording careers of many preachers, a few continued to produce recorded sermons into the 1930s and the 1940s. Some even began their recording careers during the period. For example, beginning in 1933, the Victor Talking Machine Company pressed and sold disks by Elder Solomon Lightfoot Michaux. A preacher in Newport News, Virginia, Michaux (1885–1969) originated his popular broadcast from radio station WJSV. On sides waxed in 1934 for the Conqueror label, Bishop Oscar "Sin-Killing" Sanders simulated the in-service experience of his racially integrated Christ Temple Apostolic Church in Muncie, Indiana.[7] The preaching, the piano-accompanied congregational singing, and the spirited rhythm of Sanders's disks—he even covered Michaux's trademark song, "Happy Am I"—gave phonograph listeners a taste of a soul-stirring worship service in a rural southern church transplanted to 1930s northeastern Indiana. In 1935, Decca artist Reverend Nathan Smith and his Burning Bush Sunday School evoked the Sunday school experience, with adults leading children in singing and instruction.

The Reverend Benny C. Campbell, whose recording career began on Conqueror in 1938, offered feverish congregational singing and hand clapping on a string of singles for Apollo Records between 1947 and 1950. The Reverend Samuel Kelsey (1897–1993), pastor of a Church of God in Christ congregation in Washington, DC, patterned his 1940s-era releases after 1920s-era recording pastors like Gates, Rice, and McGee by inviting congregational singing, and even a trombonist, to accompany his spoken word messages. Interesting to note is that he bases the sermonette on his 1947 MGM recording of "The Storm Is Passing Over" on the verses of the fourth chapter of Mark that form the basis of "Peace Be Still." But with rare exceptions, such as some of Gates's twelve-inch 78-rpm releases, these studio simulations of church services were limited to three and four minutes.

On the other hand, folklorist and song collectors Alan Lomax, John Work, and Lewis Jones captured live recordings of African American congregational singing in authentic church settings for Fisk University and the Library of Congress Archive of American Folk Song. One example, taped in August 1941, features a lively service held at the Church of God in Christ on the Moorehead Plantation in Lula, Mississippi.[8] To an accompaniment of guitar, tambourine, and hand clapping, the congregation sings zesty renditions of "I Got a Hiding Place" and "I'm Gonna Lift Up a Standard for My King." Each selection features unison antiphonal singing between an impassioned lead vocalist and the congregation. Less than a year later, the song collectors captured a Sunday evening Holiness Service in Clarksdale, Mississippi, held at a Church of God in Christ church led by a Reverend McGhee, with guitar and trombone accompanying the lively singing and shouting.[9]

Professor Braxton Shelley posits that the live gospel music recording phenomenon derives from "early radio programs that featured actual worship services of churches like Chicago's First Church of Deliverance during the 1930s." Citing Dr. Tyron Cooper's 2013 dissertation, *Holding to My Faith: Performing Belief in Contemporary Black Gospel Music 'Live' Recording Productions*, Shelley asserts that weekly church radio broadcasts "allowed listeners to experience the character and spirit of Sunday morning worship services" and that they "led to these church choirs and subsequent artists recording live [so as to] capitalize off of their ability to appeal to an audience base with an affinity for the spontaneous, transcendent moments characteristic of African American worship."[10] Lerone Martin argues just the opposite: that, among other things, recordings of phonograph preachers "drafted the blueprint for trendy black religious broadcasting."[11] These arguments are not necessarily contradictory. Although 1920s phonograph preachers may have stimulated the rise of religious broadcasting among African American churches (though nonblack ministers and evangelists had been broadcasting on radio since the birth of the wireless), the electrically charged atmosphere of live radio broadcasts of church services no doubt played a role in the industry's adoption of live gospel recordings. For example, whether or not the Capitol Records singles by the Echoes of Eden Choir were recorded, as alleged, in St. Paul Baptist Church, their release was based on the Los Angeles church's popular radio broadcasts and attempted to immortalize those authentic "transcendent moments" on record. On several of the choir's recordings, individual members inject spontaneity by responding reflexively during particularly moving moments, just as they would have done in church, such as when contralto Sallie Martin digs deep into her solar plexus to excavate a series of seismic low notes on "Just a Closer Walk with Thee."[12]

Around the same time, in 1947, the Reverend G. W. Killens, the Louisiana-born pastor of Mount Calvary Missionary Baptist Church in Oakland, California, was immortalized on disk while preaching to an audience in the Oakland City Auditorium. Singles of Killens's thunderous oratory and the audience's enthusiastic response, issued initially on Ollie Hunt's independent Bay Area imprint Olliet Records, were sufficiently popular to be rereleased in 1951 by the Bihari Brothers on their Los Angeles RPM label.[13] The year 1949 witnessed live sermon recordings by the Reverend William M. Rimson, pastor of Detroit's Greater Love Tabernacle Church of God in Christ, issued initially on the Religious Recordings imprint, and by the Reverend Louis H. Narcisse. Like Killens a Bay Area pastor, Narcisse made a test pressing of "Get Back Jordan" for Jaxyson Records. Not released until the 2000s, on a Jaxyson Records compilation by Acrobat Records, the side captures the fervency of worship, complete with congregant hand clapping and spontaneous exhortations.[14]

The decade of the 1950s opened with sixteen sides by gospel singer Edna Gallmon Cooke leading the Young Peoples Choir from Springfield Baptist Church of Washington, DC. The record labels state that the sides were "recorded during church services" but with the exception of "God Be with You," a spoken benediction by Springfield Baptist's pastor, the Reverend J. J. Abney, none of the sides offers any aural impression of being made during a service—no congregants can be heard in the background.[15] On the other hand, a congregation is intensely engaged with Deacon Leroy Shinault on his long-meter rendition of "Lord I Come to Thee," captured on a 1957 release by Ping Records and presumably recorded in a Chicago church. Shinault raises the hymn and the congregation responds by singing a keening melody characteristic of long-meter hymnody.

In 1951, only three years after Columbia Records introduced the ten-inch long-playing 33^1/$_3$-rpm disk into the marketplace, Decca Records, by then a significant force in African American popular and religious music, and on its way to becoming a major player in original cast recordings of Broadway musicals, released what may well be the first commercial album to feature a live African American worship service with gospel singing. *The Wedding Ceremony of Sister Rosetta Tharpe and Russell Morrison* chronicled the very public July 3, 1951, nuptials of Tharpe, Decca's biggest spiritual star, and New York Savoy Ballroom executive Russell Morrison. The combined ceremony and gospel music program was recorded in front of fifteen to twenty thousand Tharpe fans at Griffith Stadium in Washington, DC. Decca's folk and R&B director Paul Cohen and R&B department assistant Joe Thomas culled nearly three hours of taped material to make the collection a souvenir of, according to the album notes, a "100% unrehearsed, live occasion."[16]

The final product was a ten-inch LP with four cuts per side and, for those without a phonograph capable of playing the new 33^1/$_3$-rpm records, a corresponding album of four double-sided 78-rpm disks. A portion of the album contained highlights from the formal wedding ceremony, presided over by the Church of God in Christ minister and aforementioned recording preacher, the Reverend Samuel Kelsey. The rest were selections from the music program that preceded and followed the formal vows, including selections by Tharpe and the Rosettes, her female background vocal group, and Decca labelmates the Harmonizing Four of Richmond, Virginia. Decca's rationale to capture Tharpe live, however, was inspired neither by records of St. Paul's Echoes of Eden nor by the many recorded sermons of the 1920s, nor even by the company's use of the long-playing album to release soundtracks of Broadway musicals, but by Norman Granz's *Jazz at the Philharmonic* releases. The jazz impresario's series of recorded jam sessions captured jazz performances in all their "on-the-spot spontaneity."[17]

But if Tharpe's wedding album opened the door to album-length live in-service recordings, few African American gospel artists walked through it in the 1950s. Recording sessions continued to occur in the controlled confines of professional music studios and radio stations. A prime example is a ten-inch album recorded on March 31, 1954, for Choir Records of Hollywood. The disk featured the Voices of Victory, the home choir of the Victory Baptist Church of Los Angeles, California, directed by Thurston Gilbert Frazier (1930–74).[18] Frazier, who arranged and sang on the album's selections and directed the choir, sought with this release to reproduce an authentic Baptist Church service, from invocation to doxology. Engineered by Francis Allan Enig, *A Service by the Pastor and the Choir of the Victory Baptist Church* opens with a spirited reading of "I'm So Glad Jesus Lifted Me," a song featured on the weekly radio broadcasts of Chicago's First Church of Deliverance and recorded by the Voices of Victory for Decca in 1953. After the introductory singing, Victory Baptist's pastor, the Reverend Doctor Arthur Atlas Peters, recites prayers and delivers a sermonette while the choir presents a program of spirituals, gospel songs, and hymns, such as "Great Change in Me" and "Blessed Assurance." Robbie Preston, the mother of organist and singer Billy Preston, handles piano responsibilities. As on the St. Paul Echoes of Eden singles, members of the Voices of Victory can be heard punctuating the recording atmosphere with spontaneous vocal interjections, exclamations, and hand clapping as they embrace the spirit of the service. The disk was pressed without track breaks, suggesting the presentation was to be enjoyed as one continuous listening experience.

The Voices of Victory release came closer to capturing an authentic church service than Tharpe's public nuptials, which sounded like a gospel musical at which a wedding ceremony broke out. But for all its attempts at authenticity, what's missing from the Voices of Victory disk, as from most of its predecessors, was the audible pleasure of a live recording audience or congregation. That's because it was not recorded in Victory Baptist Church at all but in the Capitol Records studio in Hollywood. The Voices gathered in the same studio, and around the same microphones, as Nat King Cole and Frank Sinatra. Nevertheless, a *Billboard* reviewer gushed, "Every so often a small or new LP diskery turns out an album of such merit that it deserves the widest exposure. Here is one."[19]

King Records of Cincinnati, another "small or new diskery," as *Billboard* terms it, added the missing audience component when it recorded the Spirit of Memphis quartet singing "Lord Jesus" in front of an audience at Memphis's Mason Temple on October 7, 1952. The unknown producer captured the quartet's unaccompanied singing but, more important, he preserved its interaction with an aurally enthusiastic audience. The sung performance, which consumes both sides of the single, focuses so heavily on the interplay between audience and quartet that the singing is almost secondary.[20] A year later, King would record Brother Claude Ely, the "Gospel Ranger," singing and playing guitar at a white Pentecostal service in a Letcher County,

Kentucky, courthouse. Among the products of that live session was a King single of "There Ain't No Grave Gonna Hold My Body Down," a song that would thenceforth become associated with Ely. Country music historian Kevin Fontenot suggests that this 1953 disk was the first time people unfamiliar with the Pentecostal church had a chance to experience the music.[21]

The Mason Temple in Memphis served as the venue for another live recording, Bessie Griffin's November 1953 presentation of "Too Close to Heaven." Supported by pianist Charlotte Nelson, the Caravans accompanist whom James Cleveland replaced in 1954, Griffin sang Alex Bradford's smash hit, and Memphis radio station WDIA was there to record it for its short-lived Starmaker imprint.[22] Like the Spirit of Memphis release, Griffin's performance filled both sides of the 78-rpm disk. Although these two Memphis recordings were made at gospel music programs and not in church, similarities exist between church worship and a gospel program. Both feature interactions by the audience or congregation and attempts to conjure spirit possession, or individuals "getting happy," during the performance.

Meanwhile, on the West Coast, Specialty Records owner Art Rupe heard about Killens's live record from Brother Joe May. May wrote Rupe in 1952 that Randy Wood, owner of one of the nation's most successful mail-order music companies, told him that the Killens disk was "the best seller of today."[23] Forever looking for the next best thing, Rupe began taping live performances of his gospel artists whenever he could, including a 1952 appearance in Los Angeles by the Sallie Martin Singers, then Specialty Records artists. The results were hit-and-miss, largely because of the limitations of mobile recording equipment.[24] A particularly forceful voice, for example, could cause significant distortion that, at that time, might ruin an otherwise pristine performance. Another risk was when a singer, caught in the spirit, "ran off mike" while singing, leaving a gaping hole in the audio. Too much authenticity was anathema to producers whose skills were honed in the controlled conditions of recording studios.

Serendipity was on Specialty's side, however, when Rupe's producer, Robert "Bumps" Blackwell, captured a July 22, 1955, program at Los Angeles's Shrine Auditorium, which included the aforementioned appearance by James Cleveland and the Caravans. Other artists recorded that night included the Pilgrim Travelers, the Swan Silvertones, Brother Joe May, Annette May Thomas, and Sam Cooke with the Soul Stirrers. It is one of the most significant aural illustrations of live gospel music during its golden age. The taped program was not released to the public until the 1970s, when portions appeared on a Specialty LP with wrongheadedly overdubbed instrumentation. In 1993, however, half the program, without overdubbing, was released on CD by Fantasy Records in association with Specialty. The CD version of the 1955 Shrine Concert better illustrates the emotional energy that an audience or congregation provides gospel artists—a mutually supportive exchange that simply cannot be replicated in the sterile studio environment. A similar example is a SAR Records limited release of an amateur tape recording of a July 1955 program on which the Soul Stirrers and Sam Cooke sing an extended and hypnotic version of their Specialty hit "Nearer to Thee" to screams from female fans.[25]

Also in 1955, record man Mike Adrian and album jacket designer Curt Witt inadvertently altered the paradigm of recording African American sacred music on the long-playing album format while wandering around 125th Street and Eighth Avenue in Harlem. In search of objects to photograph for an album cover assignment, the two happened on a worship service in progress. Intrigued by the music and hand clapping, the men ascended the steps to the church. There they encountered the congregation of the local United House of Prayer for All People, a denomination founded in 1919 by Marcelino Manuel da Graça, better known as Bishop Daddy Grace (1881–1960). Not only were the men welcomed warmly, but they came away captivated by the church's music and spirit. They returned again and again, finally visiting with a tape recorder in hand. The two sides of *A Night with Daddy Grace*, released in 1955 on the Harlequin label, is the product of that live in-service taping. It features prayers, testimonies, singing by a vocal troupe called the Grace Emanuel Singers, and selections by the Grace Heavenly Band. Directed by Willie Williams, the Grace Heavenly Band was a "shout band" of brass players performing in the lively harmony that remains the distinct domain of the United House of Prayer for All People and is rarely heard outside its denominational walls. The album notes heralded its "on-the-spot excitement" and reckoned that the music therein "makes much of today's rock and roll sound thin and commercial in comparison."[26] This 1955 release may well be the first instance of a live in-service worship experience preserved on a long-playing album.

Around the same time, an African American church congregation in Detroit could be heard audibly appreciating traditional or folk preaching and gospel singing on album-length sermons by its pastor, the Reverend

Clarence LaVaughn Franklin. Born near Indianola, Mississippi, on January 22, 1915, C. L. Franklin grew up listening to the Reverend Gates's recorded sermons. He was drawn to the religious life and in June 1946, after ministering to congregations in Mississippi and Tennessee, he was installed as pastor of New Bethel Baptist Church in Detroit. By harnessing the power of radio, records, and national preaching and singing tours, Franklin built New Bethel into an influential ministry not only in Detroit but throughout the nation. As early as 1949, Detroit record-store owner Joe Von Battle was recording Franklin's Sunday morning sermons. By 1953, Battle was pressing them, complete with singing and the spontaneous reactions from the church congregation, on his J-V-B label and selling them at his Hastings Avenue record store in Detroit. He also leased the recordings to Chess Records, which issued Franklin's sermons on its own imprint. Chess continued its relationship with Franklin after the J-V-B issues ceased, establishing a special Sermon Series devoted almost exclusively to Franklin's messages. One of the most stunning examples of congregants or audience members being swept into the music was a 1956 solo by Franklin's fourteen-year-old daughter, Aretha, of "Take My Hand, Precious Lord." Halfway through her church performance of Thomas Dorsey's beloved hymn, captured on tape by Battle, a female congregant shrieked uncontrollably and repeatedly, evidently slain in the spirit.

In 1954 the choir of the Reverend James Lofton's Church of Our Prayer, also from Detroit, released a two-part single, "Great Day," for the local Prosperity label. Recorded in the church, this cover of the Ward Singers' "Who Shall Be Able to Stand" features spontaneous exclamations of joy by the choristers.[27] But if there was any audience participation, it was tamped down so as not to interfere with the recording process.

In Brooklyn around 1958, the Washington Temple Church of God in Christ produced an album called *Gospel Singing in Washington Temple*. Led by Bishop Frederick D. Washington (1913–88) and his wife, the powerful vocalist Ernestine Washington (1914–83)—both having recorded as far back as the early to mid-1940s—the church boasted a music ministry led by music director Alfred Miller. Anthony Heilbut cites Miller as being the first pianist on records to play in the modern gospel style introduced in the mid-1930s by Roberta Martin. Not only did the church's music ministry (which included its own "Angelic Choir") record many projects in Washington Temple, but it also hosted HOB Records' star-studded fifth anniversary celebration musical, which was recorded live in the mid-1960s and released as an album.[28]

Toward the end of the 1950s, Dot Records released a gem of a live album by Clara Ward and the Ward Singers. Bestowed the unimaginative title of *Gospel Concert*, the album captured the group not in a church but at a June 18, 1958, live appearance at New York's celebrated Town Hall. Accompanied by Sam Windham, the same steel guitarist who worked with the Angelic Choir, gospel organist Herman Stevens, and a lineup of top jazz musicians, including Milt Hinton on bass and Osie Johnson on drums, the Wards present a variety of gospels, spirituals, and hymns. "Didn't It Rain" features Windham's stimulating steel-guitar work. It documents the Wardses' unfettered exuberance in front of a live audience or congregation.[29]

Folklorist Alan Lomax was busy again in October 1959 when he captured the Reverend Robert Crenshaw, one-time member of the Skylarks and Swan Silvertones quartets, during a worship service at New Brown's Chapel in Memphis. The highlight of the album was Crenshaw's lifting of the long-meter hymn, "I Love the Lord, He Heard My Cry," with sung congregational response. Meanwhile, that same year, but in the world of southern gospel, Starday Records of Nashville, Tennessee, recorded the eleventh anniversary of Wally Fowler's "Gospel and Spiritual All Nite Singing Concerts" at the city's Ryman Auditorium, then home of the Grand Ole Opry. In November 1948 Fowler, founder of the Oak Ridge Quartet, initiated the practice of bringing southern gospel's most popular quartets and soloists together at the Ryman for an all-night congregational sing-along.[30]

The first known live commercial recording of a Newark, New Jersey, gospel choir is by the Back Home Choir from Greater Harvest Baptist Church. Its appearance, alongside hometown heroes the Drinkard Singers, at the 1957 Newport Jazz Festival, was preserved on LP by Norman Granz, of the aforementioned *Jazz at the Philharmonic* series, for his one-year-old Verve label.[31] But the first known live *in-church* commercial recording of gospel music in Newark occurred at the Abyssinian Baptist Church on Kinney Street and under the pastoral leadership of the Reverend Raphus P. Means. Alex Bradford, Abyssinian's minister of music at the time, was a nationally known gospel music personality and recording artist with as much drive and ambition as James Cleveland. Known as the "Singing Rage of the Gospel Age,"[32] Bradford was born in Bessemer, Alabama, on January 23, 1927. As a youngster, he was fascinated by the musical and theatrical flamboyance of

Prophet Jones, founder of the Triumph the King of Christ Universal Do-
minion Kingdom of God and Temple of Christ.[33] Bradford was also drawn
to the sanctified church in general and attempted to join, but his staunch
Baptist mother kept him seated firmly in the pews of the Baptist Church.[34]

Bradford was as gifted a songwriter as he was a singer. In addition to
writing songs for his own groups, he wrote classics for the Roberta Martin
Singers, such as "Come On in the Room" and "Too Close to Heaven." Ap-
pearing as "I'm Too Close," Bradford's composition proved successful for
Martin, but it was his own recording for Specialty in 1953, with his Bradford
Singers, that put him on the national gospel circuit. He signed with Savoy
in 1959, recording his debut sides for the company's Gospel subsidiary in
September of that year.

In April 1960, as Dunstan Prial reports, John Hammond, discoverer of
major American talents from Billie Holiday and Aretha Franklin to Bob
Dylan and Bruce Springsteen, wanted "to replicate the sound and feel of
an actual Sunday morning service."[35] Because the recording, produced for
Columbia Records, label home of Mahalia Jackson, was to take place on a
weekday morning, Hammond and Bradford invited as many Abyssinian
members as were available to gather at the church for the recording session. This, writes Prial, "provided an incalculable dimension to an already
supercharged atmosphere. . . . This was no longer a recording session. This
was church."[36]

Indeed, it *was* church. The album's most riveting selection, Bradford's
rousing "Said I Wasn't Gonna Tell Nobody," demonstrates how a spirit-filled
congregation becomes, in Shelley's words, "affective laborers" in arranging
a song through its spontaneous responses. After rousing leads by Calvin
White and Margaret Simpson, the song wound to a close, but extempora-
neous shouts from the congregation encouraged the choir and soloists to
pick it back up and reprise the chorus on the spot.[37] It is one of the first
recorded examples of the false ending, a technique that would become standard for gospel choirs and especially for Dr. Mattie Moss Clark's Southwest
Michigan State Choir of the Church of God in Christ, which used the false
ending often on record. "Said I Wasn't Gonna Tell Nobody" wound up in
the repertories of church and community choirs for years to come.

The recording was marvelous, but there was one problem: Bradford was
signed to Savoy, not Columbia. Herman Lubinsky allegedly snuck into Abyssinian that morning to make certain Bradford did not utter one note on

the recording. To Lubinsky's satisfaction, Bradford can't be heard on the album.[38]

In its November 7, 1960, issue, *Billboard* deemed Abyssinian Baptist Gospel Choir one of its Spotlight Winners of the Week. "This is the McCoy," the reviewer wrote, "with the recording reproducing the fervent, ecstatic emotions of the group."[39] The Abyssinian Baptist Gospel Choir was invited to appear at the second annual Newport Folk Festival. The choir hit the stage Sunday evening, June 26, 1960, singing alongside Odetta, the New Lost City Ramblers, and Theodore Bikel.[40] Then, on May 28, 1961, Abyssinian pastor Means and some church members walked out of the West Kinney Street facility. The following day, Bradford hosted a meeting at his home to discuss plans for a brand new church. At that meeting, Means, Bradford, and other participants birthed the Greater Abyssinian Baptist Church.[41]

Six days before the November 7 *Billboard* review, King Records engineers John Roswick and Carl Averbeck set up microphones in the Bible Way Church of God in Cincinnati, Ohio, to record the pastor, choir, and congregation in an authentic worship service. The most all-inclusive of live in-service recordings to that point, *Let the Church Roll On* featured choral and congregational singing as well as an opening prayer and sermonette by Bible Way's charismatic pastor, the four-foot-ten Reverend "Little" Abraham Isaac Jacob Swanson XII. King packaged "Little Abraham Introduction," which opened side two, as a single. Retitled "Reverend Swanson's Prayer," the single became a radio favorite that gospel music fans of a certain age remember fondly to this day.[42]

Although recorded between December 14 and 16, 1962, and therefore after Cleveland and the Angelic Choir began their live in-service collaboration, Arhoolie Records founder Chris Strachwitz captured fervent Pentecostal worship services at St. Luke's Powerhouse Church of God in Christ in Phoenix, Arizona. The pastor, Reverend Louis Overstreet (1921–80), was a transplant from Louisiana who played electric guitar and bass drum simultaneously. One of the tracks Strachwitz captured that December is a remarkable instrumental called "Holiness Dance." Its rhythmic rawness and persistent ostinato evoke the ancient ring shout associated with praise houses established by enslaved Africans in America.[43]

Thus, by 1962, the stage had long been set for what James Cleveland, Lawrence Roberts, and the Angelic Choir were about to undertake.

6

This Sunday—In Person

Despite the number of live in-service recordings prior to 1962, James Cleveland's concern had merit. In an age when hit-making machines such as Motown recorded multiple takes to get a song just right, a live performance was typically a one-shot assignment. Also, there were the acoustics of the church and the reliability of remote recording equipment to consider. As anyone who has produced a live program knows from painful experience, the audio technology that works well at rehearsal can malfunction during the actual performance. Further, some pastors may not want to convert their holy sanctuary into a commercial recording studio.

But Savoy wasn't a complete live recording Luddite. It had begun planting the seeds of in-service recordings when it produced a full-length album of preaching and singing by the Reverend J. C. Crawford, pastor of Newark's Beulah Baptist Church on January 22, 1962. Entitled *A Nail in a Sure Place* and released on the Gospel subsidiary, the album was a follow-up to a single Crawford and his congregation recorded on Gospel in 1960.[1] Savoy released it about the same time as the Angelic Choir's debut album; they were both reviewed by *Billboard* in its May 19, 1962, issue.[2] Then, on June 24, about a week before the first James Cleveland–Angelic Choir session, Savoy recorded a full-length album by Elder Solomon Lightfoot Michaux. It was the first commercial disk Michaux made since his 1947 sides for Super Disc Records and featured his wife as a soloist and the Radio Church of

God Choir in a reproduction of their popular radio broadcast.[3] The album, engineered by Herb Fisher at Medallion Studios, was released in fall 1962. But Michaux's album was a recreation of his radio broadcast, the choir responding in lockstep to the pastor's declamations, and Crawford's album was cast in the mode of the recording preachers and singing congregations of the late 1920s. Still, Roberts knew what his choir was capable of doing. He heard it every fourth Sunday morning at First Baptist. "He always said church recording had more soul, more feeling, and you can get into the music better," Bootsy said. "And the people get more involved."[4] Cleveland ultimately consented, and the first live recording session for the Angelic Choir was scheduled for July 1, 1962.

The midday heat hung heavy over First Baptist Church that Sunday in early summer. By the time the recording session began, the temperature had climbed to a sweltering 86 degrees. Making things worse, the portable fans that would normally have kept congregants comfortable during the worship service were shut off to eliminate ambient noise. The choir and the congregation turned to cardboard hand fans to beat the heat. "You had to come prepared to stay there a few hours," said Gertrude Hicks.[5]

Savoy engineers Paul Cady and Herb Fisher served as the onsite recording team; the name of the mobile recording service they used is lost to time. Robert Logan remembered Cady in particular as "very easygoing, soft-spoken, a nice man. He ran the wires from the [mobile recording] truck right to the church and the mikes." As for the equipment, Logan recalled it as "antiquated" in comparison to today's technology. "They had just the regular mikes—the lead mike, the instruments. [Cady] tried to get [a] good sound but back then, the technology was new."[6] Supervising the production was Fred Mendelsohn.

"It was one of the most exciting afternoons I can remember," Mendelsohn told writer Viv Broughton, recalling that the album was made "under very tough circumstances. We were in the cellar of this very old church, before the Angelic Choir and Rev. Lawrence Roberts rebuilt their church. . . . We ran the equipment down there. It wasn't of the best kind. In fact, I think we recorded monaural." But despite the technological challenges, "we could hear the excitement when the choir was singing, and when James was singing, and especially when the choir was really getting the spirit."[7]

Pianist-organist Alfred White was joined by three Cleveland associates, Thurston Frazier (1930–74) of the Voices of Victory and Voices of Hope, organ wunderkind Billy Preston (1946–2006) from Los Angeles, and pianist Leslie Vernon Bush (1929–81), a Voices of Tabernacle alumnus. On the drums was Joseph Marshall Jr. (1913–92), an in-demand session musician who worked with the Duke Ellington and Jimmy Lunceford bands. Born in Pensacola, Florida, but raised in Chicago, Marshall learned his craft from two of the city's most influential bandleaders, Major N. Clark Smith (1877–1935) and Captain Walter Dyett (1901–69).[8]

Roberts opens *This Sunday in Person—James Cleveland with the Angelic Choir* (also referred to as *Christ Is the Answer*) by introducing "Professor Reverend James Cleveland."[9] He then relinquishes his pulpit to Cleveland, who for the remainder of the album proves a more than capable preacher, song leader, and emcee.

Like his idol, Eugene Smith of the Roberta Martin Singers, Cleveland introduces each selection with a brief religious message, a personal reminiscence, or a narrative related to the theme of the song. For the album's anchor selection, "Christ Is the Answer," Cleveland reminds the congregation that faith in God is the solution to life's problems. He reiterates this theme during the preface to "It's in My Heart": "Some folks wonder why we sing as hard as we do, or why even though sometimes when things aren't going so well, we keep hanging on to Christ." Cleveland answers his own parenthetical question by referring to his personal salvation experience and conviction that God will make everything right. A trio of sweetly harmonizing female choristers assist on the track. And on "Only Believe," recorded in 1960 with the Voices of Tabernacle, Cleveland declares God to be a source of daily respite, especially "when the bills are due and you don't know where the money is coming from." During "Jesus Will Bring Things Out," he offers more examples of liberation from daily challenges: "If you feel like you're all alone and don't have a friend," or "don't have but a dime in your pocket . . . Jesus will make it all right."

Cleveland leads seven of the nine issued selections. The choir supports him with sung responses to his calls. On "Trust Him," however, the Angelic Choir assumes the dominant role, singing with the youthful exuberance it demonstrated on "It's the Holy Ghost."[10] Two other songs recorded at the session, "He's Got Everything You Need" and "Let Jesus Lead You," have never been released.

The musicians' responsibility on this album is chiefly to support Cleveland and the Angelic Choir; there are no solo opportunities. And despite a few spontaneous hallelujahs and other declamatory shouts, the live recording audience remains relatively passive. Perhaps the novelty of an ever-present recording apparatus, the oppressive heat, or both, tamped down the First Baptist congregation's enthusiasm. Nevertheless, since there are no track breaks between the selections, like the 1954 Voices of Victory album, the first volume of the Cleveland–Angelic Choir collaboration was clearly intended for listening in one sitting. But unlike the Voices of Victory disk, *This Sunday in Person* does not endeavor to follow the traditional Baptist order of service; instead, it feels like an informally organized religious revival or song service.

Billboard lauded the Cleveland-Angelic Choir release on the front page of its November 3, 1962, issue, calling it an example of "a spiritual album moving well in the field."[11] Roberts was equally pleased with the results. "It was truly an exciting evening and one that I shall never forget," he wrote in his autobiography, *The Gospel Truth*. "Technically, there were some errors (as could be expected) and you could indeed find them if you wanted to sit down and pick them out like you would little fish bones out of the fish. More importantly, there was an interlocking spiritual connection between all persons in the church, and together we ultimately reached utopia."[12] Like the Voices of Tabernacle, this partnership with the Angelic Choir was an early example of Cleveland's ability to lift a choir to its maximum capabilities. "Within everybody, there's a certain well of creativity," Cleveland once said. "There are so many sitting there in the choir that don't even know their own potential. I draw them out and I get a whole lot of stuff out of them that they're not even aware they have."[13]

The positive response to the album not only alleviated the apprehensions Cleveland had about live in-church recordings, but he sounded as if he enjoyed the experience. Savoy was also pleased with the results and released one single from the proceedings, "Trust Him" / "He Will Bring Things Out" (Savoy 4182). Besides being standalone representations of the album, the 45-rpm single steered the listener to the larger body of work by stating on its label that the selections are an "excerpt from 'This Sunday In Person' Savoy LP #14059."

Savoy wasted no time approving a second live session for Cleveland and the Angelic Choir. It was scheduled to coincide with a New York appearance by Cleveland and the Voices of Tabernacle at gospel announcer and promoter Joe Bostic's three-day Gospel Music Festival, held at Randall's Island Stadium September 7 to 9.[14] But the follow-up session, held at First Baptist on Friday, September 14, 1962, produced only one commercial single: "Redeemed" / "Leave It There" (Savoy 4188). For reasons that no one could recall more than five decades later, nothing else from that program was issued.

Savoy scheduled the next live session for Sunday, December 9, 1962, since Cleveland and Preston were planning to be back in New York to record a solo album of traditional hymns later that week.[15] The goal for the December 9 recording was to rerecord all the material from the September date, including "Redeemed" and "Leave It There." The Nutley weather on December 9 could not have been more different from the July session. The temperature hovered near freezing and snow fell gently on the church roof, "like a Christmas card come to life," according to the album notes.[16] Thurston Frazier returned to direct, Preston was back on organ—presumably, the entire crew of musicians had returned. Paul Cady was the sole onsite engineer, and Savoy released this session.

Not having heard the results of the first try, one cannot know for certain, but it may have been a blessing that the album was rerecorded, as it captured an intense spirituality in First Baptist that far surpassed *Christ Is the Answer*. As anyone involved in managing gospel music programs or recordings knows, the overall spirituality, meaning the exuberant atmosphere triggered by the members' sensitivity to the presence of the Holy Ghost, cannot be planned. Besides, this time the Angelic Choir and the First Baptist congregation seemed more at ease in the presence of recording microphones. The less oppressive temperature couldn't have hurt things, either.

As on *Christ Is the Answer*, Roberts relinquishes his pulpit to Cleveland, who takes full advantage, delivering spoken introductions to the songs, peppering the session with spontaneous interjections, and aurally encouraging the Angelic Choir and the congregation to participate fully in the service. The sound of individuals "getting happy," or exulting in the spirit, can be heard in the background, motivating Cleveland to sing and preach with even more conviction. By "I'm Saved," the penultimate track in terms of album placement but in reality the ninth of eleven total cuts (two closing selections were not issued), Cleveland is so invigorated that he explains how he feels by paraphrasing Jeremiah 20:9: "Like the man with fire shut up in his bones," he shouts.

It is interesting that the album's apex is not Cleveland's or the choir's singing, but sixteen-year-old Billy Preston's inspired organ solo on the beloved nineteenth-century hymn, "How Great Thou Art." As Cleveland recites the lyrics, Preston runs up and down the Hammond B3 keyboard, the instrument emoting like an evangelist in the throes of spirit possession. He even simulates the song's reference to "roaring thunder" by leaning on the left side of the keyboard, much to the delight of the choir and congregation. It remains one of the most affecting organ solos in the gospel music lexicon.

On the album's concluding track, "He's All Right with Me," Cleveland introduces a motif that he and the Angelic Choir will reprise on *Peace Be Still*—shifting the tempo midway through from a staid 4/4 to a rousing 2/4, or what Cleveland describes here as "churching it up a little bit." Perhaps recognizing that not all record purchasers would be familiar with the sprightly music of Pentecostal and Holiness church services, Cleveland breaks the fourth wall to instruct record listeners to "go get your Bible and turn to the 150th Psalm." He then paraphrases: "Praise him upon the loud sounding cymbals, and then on down at the end, it says praise Him with the timbrel and dance." Pentecostal and Holiness churches often cite Psalm 150 to clarify their use of spontaneous and enthusiastic worship music. For the non-Pentecostal First Baptist membership, the rollicking music stimulates a nostalgia for the southern folk church tradition of their forebears. Once the musicians roll into the sanctified beat, the assembly claps hands, a chorus of tambourines clash, drums pound, organ and piano improvise on the spirited melody, and a group of singers vamp on "I feel all right." The album does not end as much as fade, leaving the listener with the impression that the service continued long after the tape machine was turned off. An interesting note is that, according to Savoy's matrix number sequence, "He's All Right with Me" wasn't the session's final selection but the seventh of eleven total cuts.[17]

Preston's vivacious organ solo so impressed the Savoy team that they subtitled volume 2 *How Great Thou Art*.[18] *Billboard* considered volume 2 to be as sellable as volume 1, pinning four stars on the album in its March 16, 1963, issue.[19]

Cleveland had become a live recording convert. He told *Billboard* columnist Robert Darden in 1989, "I prefer a live session because so much more heart and expression comes through. A well-arranged studio album is always good. But as a missionary, many times the people who hear a live album respond to it as if they were there. Secondly, when you put a gospel artist in a church with a supporting choir that he or she works with 52 Sundays each year, you get a much more relaxed sound. You get something when people sing with the support of their church members, friends, and families you could not get in the studio."[20]

The last live performance to be recorded commercially in First Baptist Church's wooden edifice was not by James Cleveland and the Angelic Choir but by the group near and dear to both Cleveland and Roberts: the Roberta Martin Singers.

Perhaps inspired by hearing *Christ Is the Answer*, Eugene Smith, the business manager of the Roberta Martin Singers, told Martin biographer Ronald Greer that he had approached Roberta earlier in 1962 with the idea of recording the ensemble live in church.[21] However the idea came about, the success of the first two Cleveland–Angelic Choir live albums would have been enough to convince Savoy to move forward with a live album on the Martin Singers, one of its best and most consistent sellers.

It is not surprising that First Baptist Church was bulging with attendees eager to be present for the Roberta Martin Singers' in-service recording on Wednesday, March 6, 1963. Entering the sanctuary to applause were some of the era's most respected gospel singers assembled in one group: Roberta Martin, Eugene Smith, DeLois Barrett Campbell, Gloria Griffin, Norsalus McKissick, Archie Dennis, and "Little" Lucy Smith on piano.[22] The Angelic Choir membership made up a large percentage of the live recording audience; Roberts encouraged them to attend as ambassadors of the church. Choir member Inez Reid said she would have attended anyway; for her, being in the presence of such famous singers in her own church "made us look more famous, too."[23] But Gertrude Hicks attended purely out of respect for her pastor. "The Roberta Martin Singers wasn't quite my cup of tea," she admitted. "They sang that slow stuff and I like to pick [the tempo] up!"[24]

It is fascinating that Eugene Smith cited Mark 4:37–39 in his narrative introduction to "The Storm Is Passing Over" that Wednesday: "Our lives are sometimes filled with storm clouds," he intoned, "and we can find no rest until we pray to our heavenly father and hear him say, 'Peace, Be Still.'

Then we can feel the storm is passing over because we have the peace, deep down, in our soul."[25]

Billboard gave four stars to both of the album's singles, the Gloria Griffin–led "I'm Grateful" (released in spring 1963) and "What Would You Do without Jesus" (released in fall 1963).[26] In hindsight, producing this recording was inspired. *From Out of Nowhere* remains the only commercially available example of the Martin Singers singing live during their glory years. Less than six years later, Martin died and the group disbanded shortly thereafter.

Not long after the Martin Singers' live recording, First Baptist Church was granted a fifteen-year construction loan, the little wooden church on Harrison was razed, its timbers carted off, and a hole dug on the footprint of the old church. As collateral for the loan, four First Baptist deacons—Ernest Nunnally, Fred Roundtree, Joseph Reed, and Roscoe Granthan—mortgaged their homes; Roundtree mortgaged two houses.[27] Roberts's grandparents George and Annabelle Holmes did likewise. Robert Logan remembered that at first it was very difficult for the church to get the construction loan. But one Saturday night, he said, the Angelic Choir "did a concert for Marvin Fish, president of National Newark and Essex Bank Company. It was a special concert for him and his friends. They wept; it turned their hearts and they provided the loan."[28]

Many members, including Gertrude Hicks, traveled to Nutley to watch the church building come down. "It kind of hurt a little bit," she remembered.[29] But the church wasted no time marketing its new capital project: the front cover of the Angelic Choir's next studio album, recorded on June 26, 1963, at Beltone Studios at 1650 Broadway in New York, boasted architect E. T. Bowser Jr.'s black-and-white rendering of the striking edifice that was planned.[30] The album notes stated that the Angelic Choir's "progressive patterns in music, songs, and arrangements are as modern as their new church."[31] Dennis Bines, a veteran Newark-area gospel musician, songwriter, and promotion man for Bishop Jeff Banks and the Revival Temple Mass Choir, said Roberts foresaw First Baptist not only as a place of worship but also as a recording studio for the Angelic Choir and other artists.[32]

"We had some hard times trying to build a church," Bootsy acknowledged. "The contractor walked out after a while, and half the church still had to be finished. My husband and Freeman [Johnson], they would go up every day before they started working on the church, [when] it was just a hole in the ground, and they would pray over the hole and ask the Lord to bring it up, bring it up."[33]

In a show of ecumenical goodwill, Trinity Temple Seventh-day Adventist Church in Newark invited the First Baptist congregation to use its edifice at 35 Hillside Avenue for worship services until construction was completed. "Being Seventh-day Adventists meant they worshipped on Saturday, so that made the church available for us on Sunday," Robert Logan explained. "So we rented that church for over a year, and we brought our instruments, our organ anyway, from First Baptist Church. They had their own piano."[34] It turned out to be a more convenient location for First Baptist members living in Newark or East Orange. It also meant that, at least for the foreseeable future, Trinity Temple would serve as the site for live recordings by James Cleveland and the Angelic Choir.

7

Peace Be Still

If you didn't know that the tall, rectangular, nondescript brick edifice on Hillside Avenue once housed Trinity Temple Seventh-day Adventist Church, you might think it is a gymnasium, a community center, or perhaps a banquet hall. Once inside, however, you realize it is a sacred space—unassuming, but sacred nevertheless. Dark wooden-paneled wainscoting adorns the walls and surrounds the slightly raised wooden altar. The altar is tiered in the back to accommodate a small choir. This is where the Angelic Choir stood to sing for Sunday worship and on Thursday evening, September 19, 1963, for their third Sunday Service recording session with James Cleveland.

A special schedule of preparatory rehearsals for the session was announced during First Baptist Sunday services in late August and early September. The Angelic Choir—now numbering between sixty and seventy-five members—began studying the songs they would record. "My husband would go over the songs with the choir before James would come," Bootsy said, "and then James would rehearse [with us] all week long. [James] would come and stay with us. He was like a brother. He put a bathroom in our house upstairs."[1]

Robert Logan remembered it like this: "James Cleveland would come to town and we'd have maybe one or two rehearsals, and they'd sometimes last hours and hours. He'd start at seven or eight at night and you'd be out until twelve o'clock, because he was a perfectionist. People who have a great gift in them want to do everything to a T. And we *should* do it to a T to please the Lord."[2] "We only had about, I'd say, four rehearsals," Inez Reid recalled. "We didn't have that many rehearsals because Reverend James Cleveland and Reverend Roberts were just that good with music. It didn't take us long to learn a song."[3] For Reid, who had never heard "Peace Be Still" before the September rehearsals, learning it was relatively simple because Cleveland and Roberts took time to teach each section of the choir—soprano, alto, and tenor—its part.[4] "Reverend James Cleveland said it was nice to work with us because it wasn't hard to teach us songs," Reid said. "We caught on so fast."[5]

Although the first two Sunday Service sessions were literally held on Sundays, *Peace Be Still* was scheduled for a Thursday evening. Recording on a Thursday at Trinity Temple was so odd that, decades later, Bootsy Roberts questioned whether the date in Savoy's session book may have been given in error. She distinctly recalled Sundays being the only day in the week Trinity Temple was available for their use.[6] Complicating the dating further, producer Fred Mendelsohn told Viv Broughton that the recording happened on a Sunday because Trinity Temple "was the only church not already in use on a Sunday."[7] This dating holds up logically, and Bob Porter, who helped compile the Savoy discography, believes that "If Fred said it was Sunday, it was Sunday."[8] On the other hand, Robert Logan, whose mind is sharp and his memory lucid, insists without the shadow of a doubt that not only did the *Peace Be Still* recording take place on a weekday—in his recollection, it was either a Thursday or Friday—but that it was held in the evening.[9] Musicians Union payment stubs for the instrumentalists would help break the tie, but none can be found. And because the album was not recorded in a commercial studio, there are no documents detailing the session—take numbers, personnel, dates, times, and so on.

The numerical order of matrices assigned to selections that Savoy recorded in September 1963 is not necessarily helpful, either. The matrix numbers immediately following *Peace Be Still* (63–287 to 63–298) were assigned to a Wednesday, September 25, Imperial Gospel Singers session date even though, chronologically, the Southwest Michigan State Choir of the Church of God in Christ recorded for Savoy four days earlier, on Saturday, September 21.[10] That the September 21 recording was made offsite in Detroit likely accounts for the fact that it was assigned higher matrices than the locally produced Imperial Gospel Singers session, which probably was entered into the log immediately after the session took place. The accuracy afforded these session dates, notwithstanding the matrix order, also argues for September 19 as the recording date of *Peace Be Still*.

Assuming, then, that the recording date was indeed Thursday, September 19, the shift from Sunday to Thursday might have been to accommodate Cleveland's schedule of singing appearances. Having accepted Annette May Thomas's invitation to serve as music minister and choir director at New Greater Harvest Baptist Church in Los Angeles, he would have needed to be back on the West Coast in time to lead the music for Sunday service.[11] Possible, but not convincing, in that his commitment to the New Greater Harvest music ministry didn't stop him from traveling later in the 1960s, and his frequent unavailability eventually cost him his church assignment. On the other hand, that the Cleveland Singers were present on *Peace Be Still* suggests the troupe was touring the area with their leader and may have been engaged to appear at a local church that Sunday. Whatever the reason, if Cleveland was in town, Savoy would have wanted to eke every ounce of utility out of him before he returned to the West Coast.

Notwithstanding the mystery surrounding the recording date, everyone interviewed for this book who participated in the Trinity Temple recording session that September evening recalled the church being full to capacity. Who was there? "Everybody" remembered Reid, "and not only church members [but] our friends that didn't belong to that church. It was just a fully packed church."[12] Deacon Raymond Murphy remembered the entire recording session taking "just a couple of hours, but it was like a service. You weren't there because it was a recording. We were there having service. It was just recorded as a service."[13] Fred Mendelsohn's recollection of the session aligned with those of the choir members. "We got the crowds and it was a piece of magic," he told Broughton. "There too, you could feel the excitement running high and that's what makes an album. The inspiration was there."[14]

The "excitement running high" at the session made it an oasis in a time of national tragedy. Four days before the recording session, on Sunday, September 15, 1963, the Sixteenth Street Baptist Church in Birmingham, Alabama, was the site of a racially motivated bombing that took the lives of four young members: Addie Mae Collins, Cynthia Wesley, Carole Robertson, and Denise McNair. Among the twenty others injured was ten-year-old Sarah Collins, who lost an eye in the blast. Tensions in the wake of the bombing spilled out into mass protests on the streets of Birmingham, leading to more deaths when protestors and police clashed. The incident—the latest in a string of bombings in Birmingham—stimulated international outrage and contributed to the passing of the Civil Rights Act of 1964.

But the Angelic Choir members interviewed for this book who were present for the *Peace Be Still* session did not recall that the Birmingham tragedy affected either the mood of the title track or the spirit of the session. As Bernadine Hankerson recalled, the atmosphere at Trinity Temple was "very spiritual. We wasn't [so] disturbed [by the news] that we couldn't serve the Lord. We knew the Lord and we were there to praise and lift up His name. That was the purpose. So anything that happened anywhere else, we were just there to praise the Lord and thank Him that we were able to make it." She added, "We knew [the bombing] had happened but it wasn't ruling life."[15] And although some African American churches took precautions after the Birmingham bombing to make sure a similar incident would not happen on their premises, none of the Angelic Choir members was concerned about personal safety at Trinity Temple. "If they had any concerns," Murphy noted, "they kept it to themselves."[16]

If producing the first two volumes of the Sunday Service collaboration went more or less according to plan, the third volume turned out to be a challenge. Engineer Paul Cady, now experienced in wiring First Baptist Church for sound, had to recalibrate his learning to accommodate the cavernous Trinity Temple. Running wires from the mobile recording truck parked on Hillside Avenue to the microphones in the church, he and Roberts positioned the featured soloists on one microphone, sopranos on a second microphone to intensify the treble sound, and a third microphone for altos and tenors. Roberts miked the organ, piano, and drums; placed a shield around the drums to stop its sound from bleeding into the other microphones; and draped a heavy cushion or blanket over the piano for the same reason.[17]

Another, and more significant, challenge was finding musicians for accompaniment, for Thurston Frazier and Billy Preston, critical contributors to the first two volumes, were unavailable. Frazier's absence may have been due to his hospitalization at the time. Since Savoy did not list the personnel on the back cover of *Peace Be Still*, as it had done on the prior two volumes, the identity of the three-piece band for the session has been a source of speculation. Members of the Angelic Choir interviewed for this book better remembered which musicians did *not* play on the session than those who did. The consensus was that neither James Cleveland nor any of the Angelic Choir's regular musicians were on piano, organ, and drums. Gertrude Hicks, the choir's chief piano accompanist, admitted she "wasn't good enough" at the time to play on a recording.[18] The drummer is assumed to be Joe Marshall, because he played on the other live albums and was a Savoy studio stalwart in the early 1960s. Herbert "Pee Wee" Pickard was offered as one possibility as organist, but Pickard told this author he "did not play one note on *Peace Be Still*."[19] When the question was posed to gospel music historians and enthusiasts familiar with the period, suggestions ranged from Charles Barnett of the Cleveland Singers to Charles Craig of the Voices of Tabernacle. But musicians pay attention to other musicians, and without missing a beat, the organist Robert Logan recalled who was on keyboards: John Hason on piano and Doctor Solomon Herriot on organ.

Born in 1942, John Wesley Hason Jr. had a storied through tragically short career with James Cleveland. He was skilled on both piano and organ and, according to Logan, was traveling with Cleveland at the time. Hason can be heard playing piano on the Cleveland Singers' May 1963 Savoy session, which produced the first recorded version of "I Had a Talk with God," a song also on the *Peace Be Still* playlist. His résumé would include multiple recording credits on albums produced under Savoy's *James Cleveland Presents* series and on albums on the Atlantic and Zanzee imprints by the Institutional Church of God in Christ Choir of Brooklyn, New York. Hason also formed his own small group, the John Hason Singers; they recorded a single for Savoy's Gospel subsidiary in 1965 and a full album in 1975.[20] He is known to a wider audience for his on-screen role as the accompanist for the choir in the church scene from the 1980 film *The Blues Brothers*. At the time of his death in 1987, Hason was a musician for the Victory Temple Church of God in Christ in San Francisco.

Born June 16, 1936, in New York,[21] Doctor Solomon Herriot Jr. may seem at first blush as a most unusual choice to play organ on this session, in that his musical training was honed in the classical world. According to a brief biography from a program of his music, Herriot began piano lessons in 1946 with Vereda Pearson and organ lessons three years later with Doctor Lawrence F. Pierre. He attended Mannes College of Music, the Juilliard School, and Guilmant Organ School. He continued his organ studies under the tutelage of Hugh Guiles, Edgar Hilliard, Bronson Ragan, and Virgil Fox.

He also studied choral conducting with Richard Weagley of Riverside Church and William Whitehead of Fifth Avenue Presbyterian Church. In October 1961 he was named head organist and choirmaster at New York's Mother African Methodist Episcopal Zion Church.[22]

Nevertheless, Herriot made a few forays into gospel. For example, he accompanied Lillian Hayman and the Messengers on their 1961 gospel album for Richard Simpson's eponymous label.[23] Simpson engaged Herriot as organ accompanist for sides by the Richburg Singers, also released on his own label, and on a 1964 album produced for Vee Jay Records. Herriot accompanied the Gospel All-Stars on a 1964 album called *Deep River* for the Gospel Recording Company (not the Savoy subsidiary) and directed the Mother AME Zion Choir on a 1968 Fantasy Records recording of Duke Ellington's *Second Sacred Concert*. In 1976 Herriot helped install Mother AME Zion's new pipe organ.[24] Despite Herriot's robust classical training, the Reverend Dr. Malcolm Byrd, current pastor of Mother AME Zion, who knew and worked with the organist, called him "a gospel musician who turned classical."[25] Byrd remembered Herriot as somewhat of a loner but someone who also garnered considerable respect throughout the community and was often referred to as the dean of black church music. What with Herriot's musical bona fides, it's no surprise he was engaged for the session when Preston was unable to participate. "Everyone in Harlem knew he played on *Peace Be Still*," Byrd said.[26]

With everyone ready—the choir behind the altar, the musicians miked, and Cady satisfied with the audio arrangement, the session commenced. To capture the atmosphere of the evening effectively, the following song-by-song description reports the order of the program as recorded, not as configured on the final album. I am indebted to Doctor Braxton D. Shelley of Harvard University for his inestimable assistance in explaining the music theory behind each selection.[27]

"Jesus Saves"

"Jesus Saves," an original James Cleveland song sung in D-flat at a moderate tempo, was the first selection committed to tape on the evening of September 19.[28] Hebrews 7:25[29] informs the lyrics: "Wherefore

He is able also to save them to the uttermost that come unto God by Him." The lyrics also borrow from Psalm 40:2: "He brought me up also out of an horrible pit, out of the miry clay, and set my feet upon a rock, and established my goings." An indirect influence is the refrain to "He Brought Me Out," a hymn written in 1898 by Henry J. Zelley (1859–1942). It begins with "He brought me out of the miry clay / He set my feet on the Rock to stay." Popular gospel songs of the era, such as Sam Cooke and the Soul Stirrers' 1954 single, "Jesus I'll Never Forget," employed the "miry clay" analogy to depict deliverance from difficulties.

As he did on the previous Sunday Service volumes, Cleveland assumes the role of chief minstrel. He introduces nearly all the songs with a brief narrative delivered authoritatively in his trademark rasp. For "Jesus Saves," Cleveland introduces what would become the album's salvation motif: "I know tonight for myself that Jesus saves, yes he does. I'd heard about it for a long time, but one Tuesday evening fourteen years ago, I learned it for myself. And I can tell you tonight he'll be to you just what you let him be."

After the introduction, Cleveland and an uncredited male vocalist (possibly Roberts) sing a duet in two-part harmony while the choir answers with the melodic response "Jesus saves, Jesus saves." Later, the tables turn and the choir assumes principal responsibility as Cleveland and the male vocalist trade interjections. Then, out of nowhere, a female singer enters the fray, shouting "to the utmost" and "he'll turn you around," following each with gut-wrenching "yeahs." The compound triple 9/8 beat, known colloquially as the "rocking chair" rhythm because it simulates the fluid motion of a rocking chair, is accentuated by Marshall's percussive drumming as the choir and musicians juggle alternating crescendos and diminuendos. For Shelley, Cleveland's juxtaposition of piano and forte, or quiet and loud choral sounds, likens the use of the choir "as an almost orchestral instrument."[30] Cleveland would employ this juxtaposition, or use of the choir as instrument, again on "Peace Be Still."

After the Angelic Choir sings multiple lines of "To the utmost / Jesus saves," the musicians drop off temporarily. Cleveland breaks the silence by announcing: "This is how the old church did it." Reprising the technique he used on *How Great Thou Art*'s "He's All Right with Me," Cleveland alters the tempo from 9/8 to duple meter and leads the Angelic Choir on a feverish, hand-clapping, sanctified-church-style rendering of the chorus, centered on a sung "Hallelujah"—a kind of vamp, notes Shelley, with harmonies in

E-flat and B-flat.[31] Although to the listener the shift appears spontaneous, Gertrude Hicks recalled that any such techniques were rehearsed beforehand: "We had a sense of direction of where we were going."[32] A keen ear can hear a split-second tape edit immediately after Cleveland's comment, possibly to eliminate unwanted silence or errors made by choir members or musicians during the tempo change.

As this special section pulses along, with the choir clapping on the backbeat and singing at a thunderous volume, Cleveland begins rapping tunefully on a variation of his opening remarks on salvation: "Ain't but one thing I've done wrong / Stayed in sin just too long / God in my hands / God in my feet / Made my joy so complete." The energy dissipates around the eight-minute mark, giving the choir a moment to cool down and Cleveland a chance to tee up the finale, which he does by using the chorus as lyric fodder. "One day I was so filthy and unclean / I was in the gutter of life. What did he do for you, Brother Cleveland? He picked me up, yes he did, yes he did, yes he did." He finishes by shifting the musical time to rubato, declaring, "And if they let me in the White House tonight, and they wanted somebody to be a witness for him, I could lift my hands and say, 'Hallelujah! Jesus saves!'" With this, Cleveland and the Angelic Choir conclude. Shelley points to Cleveland's thrice changing of musical time as among the song's most interesting characteristics.[33]

With a running length of nearly ten and a half minutes, "Jesus Saves" was among the longest gospel song presentations committed to vinyl by that point. The length gave listeners unfamiliar with the rhythm and spirit of African American gospel music a chance to hear the dramatic ebbs and flows, the dynamic peaks and valleys, play out over a period longer than radio play permitted. It also demonstrated a technique, now ubiquitous in gospel music, of starting a selection by singing in a subdued manner, then building the song's intensity to an emotional climax, and liberating the tension through a gradual cooling down to the conclusion. Indeed, what made this and all the Cleveland-Angelic Choir Sunday Service collaborations distinctive was that listeners from every walk of life, including those who might never set foot in an African American church, experience how hymns and gospel songs were performed in front of a congregation, in an authentically reconstructed African American prayer or revival service.

Since its introduction on *Peace Be Still*, "Jesus Saves" has been covered in whole or in part by a number of gospel artists, such as Cleveland protégés Jessy Dixon and the Gospel Chimes (1965); Doctor Charles G. Hayes and the

Cosmopolitan Church of Prayer (1982); the Voices of Victory of the Salem Baptist Church of Omaha, Nebraska, with the Reverend Bruce Parham on lead (2001); and Luther Barnes and the Sunset Jubilaires' 2003 gospel quartet interpretation. Douglas Miller's 1985 solo version of "Jesus Saves" was fully Pentecostal-flavored. Moreover, artists from Daryl Coley to the Edwin Hawkins Music and Arts Love Fellowship Conference Mass Choir have incorporated lyric snippets such as "To the utmost, Jesus saves," and "He will pick you up and turn you around" into their arrangements. Likewise, the miry clay imagery in gospel song persists through such selections as the Newsboys' 1991 "Kingdom Man" and 2004's "For All You've Done," by the internationally popular Australian Christian worship band Hillsong.

Perhaps the most popular cover came in 1984, when Little Cedric and the Hailey Singers recorded "Jesus Saves" for GosPearl Records. The song catapulted the album of the same title to number four on the *Billboard* Top Gospel Albums chart and helped make the teen gospel quartet GosPearl's top-selling artist of the mid-1980s.[34]

"Peace Be Still"

"Peace Be Still" is based on Mark 4:37–39: "And there arose a great storm of wind, and the waves beat into the ship, so that it was now full. And [Jesus] was in the hinder part of the ship, asleep on a pillow: and [the disciples] awake him, and say unto him, 'Master, carest thou not that we perish?' And he arose, and rebuked the wind, and said unto the sea, 'Peace, be still.' And the wind ceased, and there was a great calm."

The hymn's melody comes from "Master, the Tempest Is Raging," composed in 1874 by Doctor Horatio Richmond Palmer (1834–1907), who also composed the popular gospel hymn "Yield Not to Temptation," and its lyrics come from a song text written by Mary Ann Baker (1831–1921), a Baptist and temperance-movement supporter who lived in Chicago. The composition came about when Palmer, music director of Second Baptist Church, then located at Monroe and Morgan Streets on Chicago's Near West Side, asked Baker, a Sunday school teacher at Second Baptist, to set some biblical stories to song texts that could be used in a series of Sunday school services. According to historian and author Karen Lynn Davidson,

> Mary Ann Baker was left an orphan when her parents died of tuberculosis. She and her sister and brother lived together in Chicago. When her brother

was stricken with the same disease that had killed their parents, the two sisters gathered together the little money they had and sent him to Florida to recover. But within a few weeks, he died, and the sisters did not have sufficient money to travel to Florida for his funeral nor to bring his body back to Chicago.

Of this trial Baker said, "I became wickedly rebellious at this dispensation of divine providence. I said in my heart that God did not care for me or mine. But the Master's own voice stilled the tempest in my unsanctified heart, and brought it to the calm of a deeper faith and a more perfect trust."[35]

Palmer published their composition in 1874 in his *Songs of Love for the Bible School* hymnbook.[36] By 1881 the hymn was sufficiently popular that it was sung at several funeral services held for assassinated US President James Garfield.[37] The first known commercial recording of the hymn was made by the Edison Phonograph Company in December 1912. Released in March 1913 on a Blue Amberol cylinder, the recording opens with a solemn reading of Mark 4:35–41 by the Reverend Doctor William H. Morgan.

Born in Whiton Park, England, in 1861, William Morgan emigrated to the United States with his parents in 1870. The family settled in Ironton, Ohio, and, at age eleven, Morgan took employment with the Iron and Steel Works. In 1883 he entered Ohio University but left after two years and enrolled at the Hamline College of Minnesota, where he graduated in 1889. He continued his studies in New Jersey, at the Drew Theological Seminary in Madison, and, as a student, pastored a church in Port Morris. In 1897 Morgan accepted the pastorate of the Central Methodist Episcopal Church in, of all places, Newark, New Jersey. It was during his tenure in Newark that he recorded the four-minute Edison cylinder. After a windy organ introduction, the Edison Mixed Quartet, a mixed-voice group probably composed of Elizabeth Spencer, Cornelia Marvin, Harry Anthony, and Donald Chalmers, follows Morgan's recitation with a faithful a cappella rendition of Palmer's "Master," titled for the cylinder release as "Peace! Be Still."[38] Morgan went on to record several more religious cylinders for Edison from 1913 to 1921, all of them featuring his recitation of scriptural passages with choral or quartet singing afterward.

The arrangement of "Peace Be Still" that Cleveland taught the Angelic Choir in New Jersey in 1963 originated on the other side of the nation, in Los Angeles, California, a few years prior. One day, leafing through his copy of the *Broadman Hymnal*, as he liked to do from time to time, the Reverend

James Ewell stopped at number 471, "Peace Be Still." He thought it might make a great arrangement for a gospel choir.

An amateur hymnologist, Ewell was born to a sharecropper family in Dermott, Arkansas, on February 25, 1924, and raised in nearby Augusta, Arkansas.[39] In 1944 he migrated from Arkansas to Los Angeles, where he joined Reverend John Branham's St. Paul Baptist Church, the same church whose Echoes of Eden choir recorded for Capitol Records. Participating in the church's music ministry, Ewell sang "Standing in the Safety Zone" to open the church's Sunday radio broadcast.

At some point in the 1950s, the Reverend William H. Wofford, assistant pastor of St. Paul and a fellow transplant from Arkansas, moved to Bethany Baptist Church. Ewell went with him. Gwendolyn Cooper Lightner became Bethany Baptist's music minister. Born in rural Brookville, Illinois, on June 28, 1925, Lightner took piano lessons while in elementary school and continued her music studies at Southern Illinois University at Carbondale and at Chicago's Lyon and Healy Academy of Music.[40] Although skilled in the western European classical music repertory, Lightner became fascinated with gospel music. She sought out Kenneth Morris, a composer and publisher who had served as minister of music and organist at Chicago's First Church of Deliverance in the late 1930s. Morris, who introduced the Hammond organ to First Church of Deliverance and, via its Sunday evening radio broadcast, to churches throughout the country, helped Lightner incorporate the bounce of gospel music into her keyboard technique.[41]

At Reverend Branham's invitation, Lightner moved from Chicago to Los Angeles in the early 1940s to accompany the Echoes of Eden.[42] With National Baptist Convention wunderkind J. Earle Hines (1916–60) directing the choir and soloing, Sallie Martin and her adopted daughter Cora assisting, and Lightner on piano, the Echoes of Eden became popular through its broadcasts over radio station KFWB. Soon, celebrities like actress Jackie Beavers were showing up at St. Paul to enjoy Branham's sermons and the spirited singing of the Echoes of Eden.

In 1957 Lightner and Thurston Frazier organized a community choir called the Voices of Hope to perform for a March of Dimes charity event. The choir was so well received by the public that its members, one of whom was Reverend Ewell, wanted to keep it going. It was for Bethany Baptist Church as well as for the Voices of Hope that Lightner arranged "Peace Be Still." The Voices of Victory, which released the 1954 in-service disk under the direction of Thurston Frazier, learned it from them. "My father was always looking for new hymns to learn and sing," Melodi Ewell Lovely, Ewell's daughter, a musician in her own right, recalled. "He took ['Peace Be Still'] to Gwen and asked her to play it for him. From there, they basically arranged it as a gospel song."[43]

"Peace Be Still" began to spread beyond Bethany Baptist and the Voices of Hope. Singer-songwriter Joe Peay, founder of the Triumphs gospel group, remembered hearing the arrangement sung by the Voices of Victory on Sunday radio broadcasts from Los Angeles's Victory Baptist Church, pastored by the Reverend Arthur Atlas Peters. Peay described his first encountering of the arrangement:

> I arrived in L.A. in 1962. A local church radio choir [Voices of Victory] was singing "Peace be Still" on their [radio] broadcast. They did a marvelous job. Firstly, a gentleman would come on and narrate the encounter of Jesus Christ on that ship. That's what got my attention. The guy did such a phenomenal job on it. He would do this every Sunday for the radio broadcast. When I became friends with Thurston Frazier, I asked him who wrote the song. He showed me the hymn book it was in.
>
> Soon thereafter, Thurston invited [the Triumphs] to appear on a television program with his community choir. He taught the choir "Peace be Still." I always recognized James Cleveland as an opportunist, so after the first rehearsal, I said [to Frazier], "I'll bet your friend James Cleveland will take that song and record it and make a hit out of it." Those are the very words that came out of my mouth. A few months later, the record was released by Savoy. James changed the arrangement somewhat, and the rest was gold.[44]

Cleveland had moved to Los Angeles by 1962, when the Voices of Victory's "Peace Be Still" could be heard on radio. As a friend and associate of Frazier—the two would form a gospel music publishing partnership called Frazier-Cleveland and Company[45]—he would have been aware of Lightner's arrangement, if he hadn't heard it from Lightner herself. Still, by September 1963, neither the Voices of Victory nor the Voices of Hope had recorded her arrangement.[46] That left the door wide open for Cleveland, who never saw an open door of opportunity he didn't stride confidently through.

"At one time, Thurston Frazier and the Voices of Hope would sing 'Peace Be Still,'" Annette May Thomas said. "[Reverend Cleveland] liked it so much that he went on and recorded it. We always liked Gwendolyn Cooper Lightner's intro to it, the little piano run she always did. When Reverend

[Cleveland] recorded it, he used that same run. That was her arrangement. I think they were a little upset, but James liked it and he recorded it. But he was *able* to record it. It wouldn't have gotten the publicity it got if Reverend Cleveland hadn't recorded it. What he did was similar, but different."[47] Melodi Lovely said her father "was never bothered by the fact that he wasn't acknowledged as being an arranger of the hymn," Lovely said. "If it did, he never expressed it, not to me. I never heard him express it."[48]

In Hason's hands, Lightner's piano introduction to the Angelic Choir's "Peace Be Still," coming as it does after the alternately relaxed and rollicking "Jesus Saves," signals that the mood is about to change. The opening is sweetly somber—no James Cleveland spoken introduction (if he did one, it wasn't recorded), rapt silence from the congregation, just Hason and organist Herriot introducing the song with intense harmonic flourishes, echoes of the subdued instrumental introduction of the Gospel Clefs' "Open Our Eyes." Marshall's light brushing of the toms and cymbals are meant to evoke the sound of churning waves and distant thunder.

With an unhurried 9/8 gospel waltz tempo firmly established,[49] Cleveland's first sung word, *master*, is a calm but firm attempt to rouse the sleeping Jesus. Its veiled power is said to have thrilled author James Baldwin, who told Anthony Heilbut that Cleveland "could kill him with the simple reading of 'Master.'"[50] Cleveland rests for two beats, then a keen awareness of the advancing waves drives him to an anguished plea of unnerving sonority: "The TEMPEST is raging!" When Cleveland stretches out the word *tempest* to give it sufficient gravitas, he does so on his top note, which in his sandpaper-rough voice adds a frightened urgency to his cry, as if he were literally staring down the naked power of a quickly approaching storm and wondering whether it might already be too late. Spiritually aroused by Cleveland's ferocious reading, several congregants and choristers, Ernest Nunnally most audibly, respond with interjections of admiration and encouragement.[51]

By opening with a vocal solo instead of choral singing, as the Voices of Hope had done, Cleveland transforms the disciples' communal plea for salvation into a personal entreaty. He concludes the section with a direct plea, "Get up, Jesus!" a now almost compulsory exclamation for covers of "Peace Be Still." "James did a tremendous job of transforming ["Peace Be Still"] from the exclusive choir format by placing in it a solo," Peay observed. "I don't know if somebody told him to do that, or Thurston [Frazier] advised him, or James did it himself, but James created that solo part, which really set the ball off in another direction."[52]

Meanwhile, Marshall's insistent 9/8 tempo, now sounding like war drums galvanizing a military regiment for battle, portrays in percussion the impending clash between the Savior and the storm. The Angelic Choir enters as anxious witnesses, as if standing on the shore near the ensuing action. The choir raises the sonic tension incrementally, its staccato cadence itself a form of military tattoo: "Whether the wrath of the storm-tossed sea / Or demons or men or whatever it be / No water can swallow the ship where lies / The Master of ocean and earth and skies." At the words "They all," the tautness created by their voices in cacophonous communion reaches its apogee in a thunderous chord and then abruptly drops into silence, the crashing waves halted by the command of Jesus. The force calmed, the choir whispers the line "sweetly obey Thy will."

The choir's sudden plunge from fortissimo to pianissimo elicits a cacophony of gleeful endorsements from the choir and, presumably, some in the live audience.[53] It marks out a dramatic arc, Shelley notes, which parallels the escalation of an approaching storm—heightening the tension to a breaking point and then releasing it as Jesus speaks "Peace! Be still!"[54] But Cleveland is just getting started. He directs the choir to reprise the segment, but this time, he interjects the lyrics like a preacher in full rapture, raising the intensity alongside the group and joining them on their second free fall, prompting another round of spontaneous exhortations of admiration. Where the Palmer-Baker original climaxes once, the Cleveland–Angelic Choir arrangement climaxes twice, in keeping with Lightner's arrangement.[55] To historian Will Boone, repeating the climactic moment of the song is more than just a musical technique; it's a "musical declaration of the phrase so common among black Sanctified and Pentecostal believers—'if He did it once, He can do it again.'"[56]

"I thought it was fantastic the way we modulated up high and then came down low," Bootsy recalled of this section of the song.[57] Pearl Minatee's daughter, the Reverend Doctor Stefanie Minatee, thought so, too. "I think the choir climbing to [the word] *peace* really has something to do with [the song's popularity]. They don't stay on the same plane; the choir climbs."[58] Veteran gospel announcer Linwood Heath also points to this technique as one of the reasons the song became popular. "To bring you up and then come down, there was something about it that was just—we hadn't heard that in Philadelphia. And then when they came down sweetly [on] 'Sweetly obey thy will,' it just really touched your heart. I believe it was God's doing. It just ministered to people and it was something unique about it, something that just hit us when we heard it."[59]

To Marshall's persistent pulse and punctuations from Hason's piano and Herriot's organ—at one point, Herriot simulates thunder with a rapid arpeggio—the ensemble finishes the six-minute scene by reversing the antiphonal effect, as they did during "Jesus Saves." The choir now leads and Cleveland, whose pleas opened the piece, is the respondent. For every sung utterance of *peace* by the choir, Cleveland shouts "Yes!" as if answering the voice of God during a moment of religious ecstasy. The song fades to an end peacefully, calmly, the wind and the waves having subsided and the disciples now safe.

"Peace Be Still" is spectacular sacred theater. It raises gospel music to new heights of artistic accomplishment and, as Professor Johari Jabir notes, serves as "a bridge between the early folk/blues style of gospel and the soulful sound of gospel inspired by modern jazz, pop, and soul."[60] Like the Gospel Clefs, James Cleveland and the Angelic Choir foretell the coming of the contemporary gospel music movement six years before Edwin Hawkins's "Oh Happy Day" made the transition official. Skillful editing-room technique by Roberts ensures that the 9/8 tempo of "Peace Be Still" and snippets of its motive, played reflectively on piano and organ, bleed seamlessly into Cleveland's oratorical introduction to "Jesus Saves."

Whether planned or not, reversing the order of "Jesus Saves" and "Peace Be Still" on the album makes narrative sense. "Jesus Saves" is a celebration of Jesus's redemptive power. It exemplifies the awe expressed by the disciples, who exclaim, "What manner of man is this?" in the passage in Mark immediately after Jesus's actions. On the other hand, "Peace Be Still" describes Jesus's act of intervention that prompted such praise and gratitude. Reversing the two places the miracle and the gratitude in the proper order. But in actuality, it was probably a commercial decision. The track to highlight was made manifest by the enthusiastic response from the choir and live audience. Shelley's 2017 article on how a lead single was selected from a live album by gospel artist Richard Smallwood is instructive: "In the live recording, audience members become affective laborers whose praise serves to sell and—one might add—sanctify new sonic materials. . . . The performance of previously unheard compositions must be met with a certain response if it is to be accepted as commercially viable."[61] Employing this argument, one can infer that the audible appreciation for "Peace Be Still" by the choir and live recording audience was sufficient for Cleveland, Roberts, and Mendelsohn to make it the album's lead single. Since Gwendolyn Lightner's arrangement of "Peace Be Still" was unknown to Angelic Choir members until they rehearsed it, and completely unknown to most members of the live audience—the "affective laborers"—until they experienced it that September evening, the interjections during the live recording could be likened to the reaction of an informal and uncompensated focus group. Even though the choir rehearsed the song, those anticipated but nevertheless spontaneous improvisatory elements that give every gospel song performance its own DNA kept things fresh and somewhat unexpected. The reactions gave Savoy the feedback it needed to select "Peace Be Still" as the radio single.

Since radio preferred programming songs around three minutes in length, the six-minute "Peace Be Still" had to be divided into two parts for the 45-rpm disk. Savoy was already familiar with this practice, having divided the Ward Singers' lengthy 1953 single, "I Know It Was the Lord," into two parts. But it is likely that a preference for hearing and, in some instances, programming the song on radio in its entirety, without the distracting interruption of flipping over a 45-rpm disk, contributed to the overwhelming sales of the *Peace Be Still* album, where the performance could be heard without interruption.

"I Had a Talk with God"

Gerri Griffin sat patiently with her parents in the basement of Trinity Temple, waiting to be summoned to the main sanctuary. She had just celebrated her eleventh birthday two days earlier, but Gerri was no newcomer to musical performance. She had sung in front of church congregations since the age of two. But being selected personally by James Cleveland to solo on "I Had a Talk with God" could be the budding talent's chance for national exposure.

Born in New York on September 17, 1952, Geraldine Griffin was the second of four children of Herbert "Chuck" Griffin and Anna Quick Griffin.[62] The family resided at 2224 Second Avenue in East Harlem's Thomas Jefferson Homes.[63] Anna had been a member of the Daniels Singers, a New York gospel group that sounded like a sanctified version of the Roberta Martin

Singers. Chuck was a community organizer who formed a nonprofit to offer economically disadvantaged East Harlem youth a variety of positive out-of-school activities—from sports to singing. A student at East Harlem's PS 57, Gerri channeled her irrepressible energy into singing folk songs, writing poetry, and playing piano. A fan of South African singer Miriam Makeba, Gerri knew from an early age that she wanted to pursue music profession-ally. Though the family was raised Methodist, they attended Grace Temple Church of God in Christ because Gerri's uncle, the Reverend Norman Nelson Quick, was its pastor. Gerri sang at Grace Temple and became the unofficial mascot of the church's basketball team.[64]

Gerri couldn't have asked for two better career advocates than her mother and Bernice Cole (ca. 1921–2006). Like Anna, Bernice was a na-tional gospel recording artist. Around 1951, she joined the Angelic Gospel Singers, a female gospel group from Philadelphia that had scored a national hit with their debut single, "Touch Me Lord Jesus." Bernice sang with the Angelics until 1957 and returned to the group sometime in the mid-1970s. Both Bernice and Anna had deep tentacles in the East Coast gospel music community, both were resourceful, and neither was shy, especially when it came to promoting Gerri's talent. "My mother never ceased to amaze me how industrious and resourceful she was when it came to making and creat-ing opportunities for me," Gerri recalled. "Bernice was as big an advocate for me as my mother was."

In 1963 Cole learned through the church grapevine that James Cleveland was scheduled to appear at Mount Moriah Baptist Church in Harlem. She and Anna decided to attend the Mount Moriah program, Gerri in tow, and to see whether they could persuade Cleveland to give Gerri an informal audition. "They wrangled a solo for me at that [Mount Moriah] service," Gerri said. "They had to find a box or something for me to stand upon, to reach the microphone at the podium, because I was so young and small."

Gerri sang "Somebody Bigger Than You and I" for Cleveland and the Mount Moriah congregation that day. "I never got emotional when I sang before," she said, "but I guess I kind of got that it was important, or whatever it was, and . . . I remember hitting the last notes of that song and starting to cry. It was very emotional, and my mother came and got me and *she* was crying. In the next couple of days, James Cleveland was at my house."

Cleveland visited the Griffins' East Harlem apartment about a week prior to the *Peace Be Still* recording. He brought three background singers with him; Gerri recalled the group being composed of two men and one woman, Gloria Griffin (no relation) of the Roberta Martin Singers, who was part of the Cleveland Singers at that time. "My mother cooked dinner for them," Gerri said. "James Cleveland sat at the piano and taught me the song."

Earlier that year, in May, the Cleveland Singers made the first recording of James's new composition, "I Had a Talk with God," with Billy Preston on organ and John Hason on piano.[65] The track was added to the Cleveland Singers' Savoy LP, *The Sun Will Shine after Awhile* but, as of mid-September 1963, that album—the last Cleveland worked on prior to *Peace Be Still*—had yet to be released. Cleveland wanted to try the song again and decided to do so with the Angelic Choir and the Cleveland Singers at the September 19 session.

After Cleveland announces the title of the song and Hason offers a brief introduction on piano, Griffin sings the first line, "I had a talk with God last night," in B-flat. The youthful energy in her voice, tinged with stomach butterflies, sparks words of tender encouragement from several members of the choir and from Cleveland, who gently whispers, "Sing, Gerri." Although Griffin builds vocal confidence incrementally, her performance nevertheless possesses a vulnerability absent from the May 1963 Cleveland Singers version. They captured the song in one take that evening. "I just went up to the mike and started singing," Gerri said.

Shelley finds this song "probably the most harmonically rich of all those on the album." He notes that the song's construction—complete with secondary dominants, diminished triads, and other rarely used harmonies—appear in several iterations of one large musical idea that culminates with the choir's statement of the title lyric.[66] "I Had a Talk with God" is the only track on *Peace Be Still* that prominently features the Cleveland Singers and the choir together. Aside from Cleveland's, Gerri delivers the album's longest vocal solo.

The juxtaposition of an eleven-year-old girl singing about having a heart-to-heart chat with God just four days after the Sixteenth Street Baptist Church bombing was not lost on historian Will Boone: "While the news reports and headlines were speaking of a world in which it was terrifying to be a young black girl . . . the sound of Griffin's voice declares a counter-narrative. . . . She sounds empowered by the assurance that 'He said he'd all my battles fight.'"[67]

Griffin remembered remaining at the recording session for a little while after her solo, but then she and her parents went home. She does not recall being paid for her solo, nor was compensation on her mind at the time. "It was not like they brought me in at the last minute and I was some big star," she said. "Nobody knew who I was, and I was only eleven. So I doubt if they paid me anything, because what [Cleveland] did was, he did me a favor. . . . That's what it amounted to. He was as big as they came back then, and to have this kind of a break, my mother probably would have paid *him*!"[68]

"I Had a Talk with God" became one of the better known tracks on *Peace Be Still* but not because of radio play. In fact, Gerri doesn't remember the song ever appearing on local radio, though she adds, "My mother knew [New York radio announcer and promoter] Joe Bostic. She knew all of those people. Knowing her, she probably called into the radio station and told them my daughter is on that album and got them to play it!" Instead, Cleveland's song became famous when repurposed as "I Had a Talk with My Man," a soulful love ballad recorded in 1964 by songstress Mitty Collier. Years later, Collier told music historian Robert Pruter that while she was under contract to Chess Records, she and Billy Davis, her manager and producer at the time, were at the Chess studio in Chicago when Davis came upon session musician Leonard Caston listening to *Peace Be Still*. He was searching for songs to teach his church choir. Hearing "I Had a Talk with God" gave Davis the idea that with a few word changes, the most important of which was replacing *God* with *man*, the song could be a great soul ballad for Collier.[69]

Davis's intuition was correct. "I Had a Talk with My Man" entered the *Cash Box* Top 50 R&B singles chart at number thirty-eight in October 1964 and the Top 100 singles chart at number eighty-three. It made the top ten of the R&B singles chart by November of that year.[70] Pleased with the response, Davis and Collier followed the single with another secularization of a Cleveland composition. "No Cross, No Crown," from volume 4 of the James Cleveland and the Angelic Choir's Sunday Service partnership, became "No Faith, No Love."[71] In 1967 Collier recorded yet another repurposed Cleveland composition, "That'll Be Good Enough for Me."

Collier recalls that Cleveland was not pleased to learn that his gospel songs were being rearranged into R&B hits. Moreover, "I Had a Talk with My Man" and "No Faith, No Love" were credited not to Cleveland but to

Davis and Caston, with arrangements contributed by Riley Hampton. Collier reminded this writer, however, that Cleveland did the same thing in 1975 to songwriter Jim Weatherly when he transformed his love ballad, "You're the Best Thing," an early 1970s hit for both Ray Price and Gladys Knight and the Pips, into a gospel radio favorite with the Charles Fold Singers as "Jesus Is the Best Thing That Ever Happened to Me."

In retrospect, "I Had a Talk with God" was a gospel song pleading for pop conversion. Its melody and construction were drawn from early 1960s pop balladry, and Gerri's plaintive solo gave it a girl group sensibility in synch with Chess sides as well as with early Motown ballads. It would be naive to think that Cleveland, as a songwriter, was not inspired, at least in part, by black popular music while writing "I Had a Talk with God." Ray Charles's 1956 hit "Hallelujah I Love Her So" inspired Cleveland to write and record "That's Why I Love Him So" with the Gospel All Stars the following year. Plus, he was becoming an astute businessman whose new publishing partnership with Thurston Frazier undoubtedly benefited from lessons learned the hard way peddling tunes on the cheap to Roberta Martin. If his religious faith and unwillingness to raise the ire of the church community kept him from becoming a full-fledged R&B singer, Cleveland in later years did not shy away from working with popular music icons such as Quincy Jones, Aretha Franklin, Natalie Cole, and Elton John. So if Thomas A. Dorsey gave gospel music its initial bounce and Roberta Martin its light classical ornamentation, James Cleveland injected religious songs with elements of pop balladry. Not that he was the only one: Savoy labelmates Leon Lumpkins and Bishop Charles Watkins knew their way around a pop melody, too, as evidenced by their gospel hits, "Open Our Eyes" and "Heartaches," respectively. So did Reverend Lawrence Roberts, with his appropriation of Charles's "Hit the Road Jack" for "It's the Holy Ghost" on the Angelic Choir's first album.

And as for Gerri Griffin, her wish for a career in musical performance ultimately came true, but not from "I Had a Talk with God"—with the exception of a complimentary article in the *New York Amsterdam News*, she wasn't cited as the soloist anywhere. She did share the stage with the Roberta Martin Singers, but more important, she leveraged her mother and Bernice Cole's advocacy, as well as her own talent and gumption, to secure a spot in the cast of the musical *Hair* and, more visibly, as lead singer for the Voices of East Harlem, a youth choir her parents organized out of her father's East Harlem Youth Federation. With the passion of a gospel choir, the unfettered choreography of street dancing, and declarations of universal brotherhood, the Voices of East Harlem recorded three critically acclaimed albums. They shared the stage with some of the era's most influential soul, folk, and rock acts, from Ike and Tina Turner to the Who. They toured Europe and appeared at the Isle of Wight Festival. They even traveled to Accra, Ghana, to be part of the *Soul to Soul* music festival (a documentary film and album of the event are available).

Looking back, Gerri Griffin Watlington, who now dedicates her work to the church, remembers her participation on *Peace Be Still* as "almost a fluke. Had Bernice not found out [Cleveland] was going to be in New York, had she not arranged that, I would never have been on it."[72]

"Where He Leads Me"

At this point, Cleveland and the Angelic Choir shift from a newly composed song to a standard hymn, "Where He Leads Me." In 1890 a Salvation Army officer named Ernest William Blandy wrote the lyrics to "Where He Leads Me" to express how the Lord led him to forgo a comfortable position at an established church for a more challenging ministry in New York City's infamous Hell's Kitchen neighborhood. The opening line, "Where He leads me, I must follow," is Blandy's Christian pledge of fidelity to Jesus and his teachings. Supplying the melody was John Samuel Norris, a Methodist born on the Isle of Wight who became a Congregationalist minister and served churches in Wisconsin, Michigan, and Iowa before he passed away in Chicago in 1907.[73]

By 1963 "Where He Leads Me" was a popular selection in African American Protestant hymnbooks. It appeared as number forty-six in the National Baptist Convention's *Gospel Pearls*, a staple for gospel singers since its publication by the Convention's Publishing Board in 1921. An arrangement by Philip P. Bliss, who with Ira Sankey in 1874 coauthored the first hymnbook to use the phrase "gospel song" in its title, was included in *Gospel Quintet Songs*, a 1920s folio associated with the Christian and Missionary Alliance Colored Gospel Quintet (also known as the Cleveland [Ohio] Colored Quartet). The song was recorded around February 1929 by country blues guitarist Blind Willie Harris, who cut a version in New Orleans for Vocalion. In April of that year, the Southern Sanctified Singers recorded the hymn in Chicago for Brunswick Records.[74] In the early 1950s, tenor Thomas Johnson led the

Harmonizing Four of Richmond, Virginia, on a smooth and imperceptibly rhythmic reading of the hymn for Gotham Records. Around the same time, Ray Crume led Chicago's Highway QCs gospel quartet on a more soulful version for Vee Jay Records. In 1961 Mahalia Jackson rendered the song with great solemnity on one of the eighty-four five-minute television segments packaged and distributed nationally as *Mahalia Jackson Sings*.[75]

The song also became popular among southern gospel groups, with recordings that included a 1941 release by the influential Rangers Quartet on Conqueror, appearance on a 1966 Starday album by the Lewis Family, and a version by the Blue Ridge Quartet in 1970.[76] Country music icon Hank Williams performed it on a 1951 WSM radio broadcast, with his Drifting Cowboys band members providing vocal harmony like a southern gospel quartet. A sixty-year-old Jimmy Davis, two-term governor of Louisiana and composer of "You Are My Sunshine," included the hymn on his 1959 Decca album, *Suppertime*.[77]

For *Peace Be Still*, Cleveland sets "Where He Leads Me" in D-flat and, structurally, as a call and response between him, the choir, and the live recording audience and congregation. He opens with the declaration "I told God one day these words," and then launches into a meter-less falsetto reading of the hymn's refrain as Herriot improvises on the organ in support. While the following verse, "I'll go with Him through the valley," is not one of Blandy's originals, it does fit with Blandy's second and third verses, "I'll go with Him thro' the garden" and "I'll go with Him thro' the judgement," respectively. Then, placing Blandy's intentions in his own words, Cleveland retorts, "If it means I'll have to cry sometimes / If it means I'll have to fold my arms sometimes / "I'll be with Him all the way." The choir echoes Cleveland's "with Him all the way" in a whispered harmony as the first side of the album draws to a close as solemnly as it opened.

"This song stands apart from all the rest [on the album]," notes Shelley, "because of the light, falsetto-like phonation that Cleveland employs throughout the song."[78] And it is the first time, though not the last, on *Peace Be Still* that Cleveland will raise a traditional church hymn for the purpose of leading congregational singing, another effort to recreate the authentic African American worship experience for the phonograph-record-listening public, and perhaps encourage listeners to sing along.

But although "Where He Leads Me" restates the themes of discipleship and faith as articulated on "Peace Be Still" and "Jesus Saves," it also reminds listeners that the call might be unclear initially and provoke personal resistance. Like Blandy's reaction to the call to minister in an undesirable location and, like Cleveland's initial resistance to live recording, walking in faith produces rewards.

"God Is Enough"

After "Where He Leads Me," the choir recorded "God Is Enough," but for some reason it was neither included on *Peace Be Still* nor released commercially until Cleveland and the Angelic Choir attempted it again for the next Sunday Service volume, 1964's *I Stood on the Banks of Jordan*. The 1964 version is a duet between Cleveland and an effervescent soprano from the Angelic Choir, possibly Marjorie Raines (at one point during the soprano's final solo turn, a fellow chorister shouts "Sing, Margie!"), with the choir punctuating the duet with bursts of dense harmony.

Sustaining the slow, even tempo of "Where He Leads Me," Cleveland introduces a theme he would expound on again in "Heaven, That Will Be Good Enough for Me," his 1965 hit with the Cleveland Singers. In stark contrast to prosperity theology, which assures financial blessings to faithful Christians, James sings in "God Is Enough" that material possessions pale in comparison to the grace of God and the reward of eternal life. On "Heaven," Cleveland sings, "I've never been to Paris in the spring or the fall / I've never been to India to see the Taj Mahal / But if I can make it to Heaven, that will be good enough for me / Because Heaven is a place I want to be." Similarly, on "God Is Enough," he offers "Rubies and diamonds I don't possess / But I've got Jesus and, with Him, I'm blessed." The line also conjures the hook of "That's Enough," a 1956 hit for the Gospel Harmonettes, led by its composer, Dorothy Love Coates ("I've got Jesus, and that's enough"). In any event, this testimony to the limitless power of God is articulated through a sung conversation between Cleveland, Raines, and the Angelic Choir. It calls to mind an opera or Broadway musical recitative.

Unissued on *Peace Be Still*, "God Is Enough" must have pleased Cleveland, Roberts, and the Savoy team the second time around, as it became the flip side of "No Cross, No Crown" (Savoy 4318), one of *I Stood on the Banks of Jordan*'s two single releases. Oddly, as far as is known, the song was never recorded again after 1964—by Cleveland, by the Angelic Choir, or by any other African American gospel artist.

"My All and All"

The other unissued selection from the September 19, 1963, session is "My All and All." Cleveland and the choir attempted it again during the 1964 *I Stood on the Banks of Jordan* session, but it did not make the final cut on this volume either. In fact, James Cleveland and the Angelic Choir never recorded "My All and All" together. It does not show up on an Angelic Choir record until 1967, when the troupe featured it on their own album, *The Soul and Faith of the Angelic Choir*. It's there we discover that the song is a gospelization of Marvin Gaye's April 1963 single, "Pride and Joy."[79] Instead of "You are my pride and joy," the choir sings "You are my all and all."

With Freeman Johnson handling the lead vocal, the song's gospel-meets-Motown vibe was augmented by the accompaniment of electric guitar, tambourine, bass, and drums. Like 1961's "It's the Holy Ghost," "My All and All" was an example of Roberts converting popular R&B songs into church arrangements. Notwithstanding its radio potential, "My All and All" was never released as a single and, as of this writing, the two unissued *Peace Be Still* matrices remain undiscovered.[80]

"I'll Wear a Crown"

Although attributed to James Cleveland, only the arrangement of "I'll Wear a Crown" belongs to him. The song, also known as "I Shall Wear a Crown," is a spiritual and therefore precedes modern gospel music. It was recorded in Chicago on July 3, 1928, by Church of God in Christ pianist Arizona Dranes.[81] It was her final recording session for OKeh Records and, as it turned out, in her lifetime. In 1950 Dave Dexter, artists and repertoire director of Capitol Records' R&B line, paired the Reverend R. A. Daniels, a blind preacher from Portland, Oregon, with the Mount Zion Church Gospel Choir of Santa Monica, California. Their energetic, tambourine-soaked version, cut as a Capitol single, was likely an intentional decision on Dexter's part to capitalize on the popularity of St. Paul Baptist's Echoes of Eden, also on Capitol.[82] Eight years later, the Stars of Faith, with Henrietta Waddy on lead vocal, recorded an equally energetic version of the song for Savoy.[83]

Notwithstanding Cleveland's arrangement credit, "I'll Wear a Crown" on *Peace Be Still* sounds like another example of Lawrence Roberts's playful blend of religious lyrics with elements of R&B and rock 'n' roll. Set in B-flat, the arrangement employs the stimulating "twist" dance rhythm that had been popular since the 1959 release of "The Twist" by Hank Ballard and the Midnighters and Chubby Checker's mainstream 1960 cover.[84] The rhythm section of organ, piano, and drums is helped by the choir's hand clapping. Perhaps more than any other song on the album, "I'll Wear a Crown" benefits from Joe Marshall's rock 'n' roll experience, the thudding of his toms ricocheting off the walls and ceiling of Trinity Temple. Shelley also hears the song's heavy syncopation, its lyrics cutting against the grain of the 4/4 meter.[85]

The lively twist beat is an effective complement to lyrics about facing down death with optimism instead of despair. Cleveland opens with a spoken evocation of the hereafter: "Those of us that have sent up our timber, we have laid up a crown of life, and we shall wear a golden crown." Every line he utters receives assent from a sole female voice (possibly Gertrude Hicks). To reinforce the image of entering heaven, Cleveland and the Angelic Choir pull lines liberally from spirituals and from the Reverend W. Herbert Brewster's "Move On Up a Little Higher," Mahalia Jackson's breakout hit of 1948. The Angelic Choir quotes "Move On Up a Little Higher" in the chorus: "Soon as my feet strike Zion / Lay down my heavy burden / Put on my robe in glory / Shout and tell my story." Cleveland then improvises on Brewster's composition, adding "see my mother / shake hands with my brother," then transitions into the folk spiritual "All God's Children Got Shoes." He disappears off mike, momentarily overcome by the spirit, though he can be heard shouting phrases imperceptibly in the distance. His return to the microphone signals the song's conclusion.

Shelley hears "a kind of narrative teleology that drives the song forward" in how the two main sections of the song treat the title lyric in opposite ways. "The A section opens with 'Watch ye therefore' and ends with 'We shall wear a golden crown,' while B opens with 'I shall wear a crown' and ends with 'I shall wear a crown.'" He also notes the song's "bluesy emphasis on the subdominant IV, which stands in contrast to 'The Lord Brought Us Out' [the selection that follows "Crown"]. Halfway through the chorus, you can hear/feel the move to IV, in this case an E-flat chord, at 'oh, I shall wear a crown.'"[86]

The song remains a popular selection in the gospel music repertory. Soloist Gene Martin recorded it during an A. A. Allen revival service at New York's Rockland Palace. Like Savoy's Sunday Service series, Allen's disks were live in-service recordings of revival-like events that featured spirited interaction with the recording audience and congregation.[87] Whether or not he was invoking the Cleveland–Angelic Choir version, Martin also interpolates the spiritual "All God's Children Got Shoes" several times during his version of "Crown" as David Davis and Tommy Downing accompany him on organ and piano, respectively. Detroit choir director, songwriter, and arranger Thomas Whitfield presented "I Shall Wear a Crown" under the title "Soon as I Get Home" in a 1983 live recording with his Thomas Whitfield Company. Although the aforementioned versions of the song were performed to a vigorous beat, Whitfield characteristically offers a slow and sumptuous reading with jazz and classical flourishes.[88] Whitfield's arrangement was the version sung by a choir at the August 31, 2018, funeral of Aretha Franklin—an appropriate choice, since Detroiters Franklin and Whitfield were both profoundly influenced by Cleveland. "Crown" was also among the traditional gospel classics rendered by a chorus of renowned gospel singers at the appropriately titled *Gospel Pioneers Reunion*, recorded in 1994 by southern gospel maven Bill Gaither and released commercially as a DVD and CD in 2016.

Like "Peace Be Still," "I'll Wear a Crown" exemplifies what religious music scholar Jon Michael Spencer calls a distinguishing factor of Cleveland's lyric content and, ultimately, his personal theology. Citing Louis-Charles Harvey's mid-1980s article "Black Gospel and Black Theology," Spencer writes that, for Cleveland, "Jesus is the answer to the problems in black life." But there is a price to pay. Although Jesus serves as "friend, protector, and liberator," there is a certain "cross-bearing" that Christians must experience to gain entrance to eternal happiness.[89] The metaphor for "weather[ing] the storms and rains of life" is cross-bearing; that is, there is no gain without pain. No cross, no crown. As a common church aphorism goes, one must go *through* to get *to*. Cleveland's personal theology is sprinkled liberally throughout *Peace Be Still*.

"The Lord Brought Us Out"

The fastest-paced selection on *Peace Be Still* is "The Lord Brought Us Out," a song in 4/4 time written by Cleveland and not recorded commercially prior to its inclusion on this session. After Cleveland's spoken introduction—"We can brag tonight because the God we serve is able"—the musicians lurch into a steadily rolling march tempo. The song's sole musical motive is repeated antiphonally between Cleveland and the choir. Behind them, the piano and organ play a simple, repetitive bass ostinato of B-flat-F-G-A as the choir augments the rhythm with fervent handclapping and percussive tambourine shaking.

Shelley adds, "Tonally speaking, 'The Lord Brought Us Out' is in B-flat major with some modal mixture, especially on the 'Oh yes,' which culminates on a D-flat major chord, a borrowed chord from the parallel minor. The relative stasis of its harmonic character, the fact that the first three statements of the title lyric occur on an uninterrupted tonic (I) chord, really stands out in comparison to songs like 'I'll Wear a Crown,' where the movement to the subdominant (IV) has expressive weight."[90]

Lyrically, Cleveland turns once again to the subject of divine rescue introduced on "Peace Be Still." Here, he cites three biblical stories instead of one: Daniel in the lion's den (Daniel 6:1–28); the rescue of Shadrach, Meshach, and Abednego from the fiery furnace (Daniel 3:16–28), and Jesus meeting the Samarian woman at the well (John 4:1–26). The assumption is that if God saved these individuals—Daniel from carnal destruction, the Hebrew boys from incineration, and the Samarian woman from spiritual corruption, He will save everyone. Cleveland reiterates the cross-bearing theme of "I'll Wear a Crown." Weathering the storms of life is the way to gain entrance to heaven. In jubilant antiphony, Cleveland declares, "The Lord God almighty done" and the Angelic Choir responds with "brought us out." They repeat this phrase together three times and conclude with a soaring, confident, and extended "Oh yes," the B-flat-F-G-A ostinato fueling the motive power of the choir's sustained notes.

Perhaps because it is more of a spontaneous congregational chant than a through-composed song, "The Lord Brought Us Out" was not reprised on future albums by Cleveland or the Angelic Choir.

"Shine on Me"

Cleveland and the Angelic Choir return to classic hymnody with a B-flat rendition of "Shine on Me." The melody comes from "Maitland," a nineteenth-century composition by George N. Allen (1812–77). The hymn's chorus, based loosely on Psalm 31:16 ("Make thy face to shine upon thy servant: save me for thy mercies' sake") has its origins in a folk spiritual. It was recorded by African American artists as early as 1923, when the Wiseman Sextette sang it for Billy Sunday music director Homer Rodeheaver's Rainbow Records; in 1927 by the professional jubilee choir Sandhill's Sixteen (Victor); and in 1929 by Blind Willie Johnson as "Let Your Light Shine on Me" (Columbia).[91] Country gospel singers Ernest Phipps and His Holiness Singers also recorded the hymn for Victor in 1928. In the introduction to his recorded version, blues guitarist Huddie William "Leadbelly" Ledbetter (1888–1949) explained that "Shine on Me" was sung on plantations by African Americans prior to emancipation.

Cleveland opens "Shine on Me" with his now almost obligatory spoken introduction. "Sometimes our ways get mighty dark," he intones in his sandpaper-rough baritone, "and we need the Lord to come into our heart." Unconsciously echoing Leadbelly, Cleveland informs the choir and live audience that "Shine on Me" was sung in the "little wooden church on the hill" as a long-meter hymn. To render a long-meter, or lining-out, hymn in the African American church, a church deacon lifts, or raises, a lyric line and invites the congregation to sing it back to him in a heavily ornamented melody. While this recorded version maintains the drawn-out tempo, it is not sung as a long-meter hymn; there is no antiphonal interplay with the Angelic Choir or congregation. Rather, it is sung as a congregational hymn and in harmony. As a result, "Shine on Me" is a showcase for the vocal power of the Angelic Choir (fortified, undoubtedly, by singing from the congregation) and for Cleveland's improvisational skills, which portend his calling to religious ministry. Hason and Herriot follow Cleveland and the choir with Roberta Martin-esque ornamentation from the middle section of the keyboard.

Shelley finds Hason's keyboard work particularly interesting: "The rumbling chords in the left hand of the piano fill the space while the choir and soloists are breathing. It's like a performance of freedom, and a performance of pregnant pauses."[92]

It is interesting that, when Cleveland declares, "Sometimes our ways get mighty dark," not only does he restate the cross-bearing current that runs throughout the album, but it is possible he is making a veiled reference to discrimination and racially motivated violence. The metaphor of a lighthouse lighting the way toward salvation certainly fits on an album brimming with imagery of raging storms and wind-tossed seas. And by invoking pastoral "little wooden church" imagery, Cleveland is reminding the congregation and choir not only of their shared southern religious roots but of the transformational power of traditional worship. The singers, the live recording audience, and, in turn, the record-buying public can leave their troubles on the altar and breathe in a deep, satisfying gulp of old-time religion—the type that sustained their forebears. Cleveland is also unconsciously channeling early-twentieth-century US immigrant entertainers who sang songs that evoked nostalgia for a simpler time in the pastoral Old World—more paradigmatic than realistic—as a way to cope with the often-alienating New World.[93] For Cleveland, the "wooden church" down south represents an oasis of safety and predictability in a world that is anything but, even if that southern experience was sufficiently demeaning, debilitating, and dangerous to effect mass migration. This juxtaposition of old hymns sung in a modern setting is yet another thematic element running through the entirety of *Peace Be Still*.

"I'll Be Caught Up to Meet Him"

References to the Reverend W. Herbert Brewster's "Move On Up a Little Higher," having already adorned "I'll Wear a Crown," remain firmly fixed in Cleveland's consciousness as he opens the equally apocalyptic "I'll Be Caught Up to Meet Him." In a half-spoken, half-sung one-minute opening narrative, Cleveland describes heaven, in Brewster's words, as a joyous place "where there will be no more crying, no more sorrow" and "always howdy, howdy, and never goodbye." In other words, the storms of life have been calmed and the Christian, if faithful, can anticipate eternal happiness.

"I'll Be Caught Up to Meet Him" is based loosely on the concept of the Rapture as referenced in 1 Thessalonians 4:16–18, and particularly this line: "Then we which are alive and remain shall be caught up together with them in the clouds, to meet the Lord in the air: and so shall we ever be with the Lord." The words and music were composed around 1944 by Clarence E. Hatcher under the full title "I'll Be Caught Up to Meet Him in the Air." Around the time he composed "Caught Up to Meet Him," Hatcher, born in Brooklyn, New York, was a member of Brown's Inspirational Singers, organized by Beatrice Brown. Members of the Indianapolis, Indiana, gospel troupe, which sang in the measured elegance of the Roberta Martin Singers, included gospel pianist-arranger Kenneth Woods Jr. and Meditation Singers and television star Della Reese.[94] Heralded as "America's greatest gospel pianist" in the mid-1940s, Hatcher founded a publishing company in Brooklyn and wrote other gospel music favorites. Handling the arrangement was Virginia Davis, a Chicago-based musician who wrote and arranged hundreds of gospel songs during gospel's golden era.[95] Davis's "Wonderful," a dreamy pop-gospel ballad recorded in 1956 by the Soul Stirrers, was restyled by the Stirrers' erstwhile lead vocalist, Sam Cooke, as "Lovable." It was Cooke's first secular single.

Probably because of its Brooklyn provenance, "I'll Be Caught Up to Meet Him" bounced around the East Coast gospel music scene before Cleveland and the Angelic Choir picked it up. Sometime in the 1940s, the influential Mary Johnson Davis Singers of Philadelphia were captured on acetate singing the song, and the Banks Brothers' Back Home Choir of Newark included it on their 1958 RCA Victor album, *I Do Believe*.[96] The Back Home Choir's version was zestier than the heavy-handed waltz employed by Cleveland and the Angelic Choir. Also, the Back Home Choir recorded "I'll Be Caught Up to Meet Him" as an ensemble, whereas Cleveland assumes lead vocal duties for the *Peace Be Still* album. He also reverses the placing of the chorus and verse as rendered by the Back Home Choir.[97] Around the same time as *Peace Be Still*, the Metropolitan Baptist Church of New York City's Prayer Meeting Chorus recorded the Back Home Choir's version for its own in-service album.[98]

The only song on *Peace Be Still* set in A-flat and with a moderate 6/8 tempo, "Caught" features what Shelley calls a fascinating "double call-and-response,"[99] as Cleveland personalizes a moving couplet popular in 1950s and 1960s gospel: "One of these mornings / It won't be long / You'll look for James / And he'll be gone." During the vamp, Cleveland embarks on a metaphorical search for his sister and his brother who have passed through the pearly gates (in reality, his siblings were very much alive at the time).

Like other selections on *Peace Be Still*, "Caught Up to Meet Him" has remained a church choir staple. It has been recorded live by the Combined Choirs of the Fourth Missionary Baptist Church of Houston, Texas (1969), by Dr. Jonathan Greer and the Showers of Blessings Choir of the Cathedral of Faith Church of God in Christ (1980), by the West Angeles Church of God in Christ Mass Choir (1990), and Professor Ronnie Felder and the Voices of Inspiration of Brooklyn, New York (2002). To this writer, the Angelic Choir's enthusiastic evocation of Heaven, and Cleveland's vocal runs from deep growl to falsetto, are compelling, but the Back Home Choir's recorded version, with its bouncy tempo, is far more engaging.

"Praise God"

Of all the live recordings of African American worship services prior to
Peace Be Still, none contained the best-known and most beloved hymn of
doxology in African American Protestant worship: "Praise God from Whom
All Blessings Flow:"

> Praise God, from whom all blessings flow;
> Praise Him, all creatures here below;
> Praise Him above, ye heavenly host;
> Praise Father, Son, and Holy Ghost. Amen.

With lyrics written in 1674 by Anglican Bishop Thomas Ken (1637–1711), one
of the fathers of modern hymnology, "Praise God" has the oldest provenance
of any selection on the album. Ken wrote the four lines for two separate
hymns, "Awake, My Soul, and with the Sun" and "Glory to Thee, My God,
This Night," to be sung at morning and evening worship at Winchester
College in Hampshire, England, where he served at the time he composed
these two hymns.[100]

Though "Praise God" was a product of the seventeenth and eighteenth
centuries—it was published in 1709—its melody is attributed to sixteenth-
century French composer Louis Bourgeois (ca. 1510–59). Bourgeois was
supervising composer for the 1551 edition of the *Genevan Psalter*, a book
of metrical hymns commissioned by John Calvin, the French theologian
whose beliefs helped form the Calvinist tradition. The tune was commonly
known as "Old Hundredth" because of its initial use as the melodic setting
of Psalm 100, the "Song of Thanksgiving." As a unified composition, "Praise
God" made its way into the hymnbooks of African American Protestant
churches as they expanded in number after Reconstruction. It is often
used for a service's doxology, meaning an expression of praise to God that
concludes the formal service. Perhaps the close association of "Praise God"
with the formal order of worship service and not commercial gospel singing explains why it was not recorded by any gospel artist prior to *Peace Be
Still*, though a few choirs did incorporate it into their live recordings after
1963.[101]

With all the austerity of a senior choir, the Angelic Choir chants the
"Old Hundredth" in D-flat major as Reverend Roberts, as presiding pastor,
recites the lines. But his recitation is about as close as "Praise God" comes

to gospel music. Its inclusion on the album as a text made the program feel like a traditional worship service, not a gospel music album, with the congregation invited to join in the singing prior to dismissal.

Although the choir sounds fatigued from a long evening, it reenergizes during the rococo "Amen." To Shelley, the sevenfold amen makes the selection "a kind of double doxology."[102] Then, after singing the first syllable of the final "Amen," the choir pauses for nearly four seconds, waiting for Roberts to direct them to sing the final syllable on the tonic chord. As they conclude, Roberts's softly spoken "Amen" overlays the choir's singing of the second syllable (-men) as the cymbals hiss and the recording ends. In addition to being the oldest song on *Peace Be Still*, "Praise God" is also the shortest of the album's nine selections, clocking in at just two minutes and eleven seconds.

The air was heavy with solemnity at the conclusion of the September 19 recording session, the time nearing, or perhaps past, the midnight hour. The storm had been quieted, the choir had rendered profuse praises to God for not only rescuing them from certain destruction but for also offering them eternal life in exchange for their Christian fidelity. The peaceful stillness in Trinity Temple was palpable as Paul Cady switched off the recording mechanism. As he boxed the tapes and marked the boxes, as Marshall disassembled his drums, and as Herriot shut down the organ, the choir and congregants broke the silence with pleasant chatter and bursts of discreet laughter. They relived the night's highlights and lowlights with one another as they gathered their belongings and headed toward the church exits to meet the serene night sky and face another Friday workday, just a few hours away.

The Reverend Lawrence Curtis Roberts. Reverend Lawrence Roberts collection.

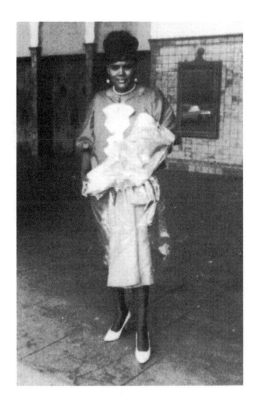

Dolores "Bootsy" Roberts.
Reverend Lawrence Roberts
collection.

Gospel Chordettes/Lawrence Roberts Singers, late 1950s. The Reverend
Lawrence Roberts, front left. Rev. Lawrence Roberts collection.

Zion Hill Baptist Church Young People's Choir, 1953. Reverend Lawrence Roberts
collection.

First Baptist Church, 1950s. Razed in 1963. Reverend Lawrence Roberts collection.

The Reverend James Cleveland, mid-1960s. Courtesy of Malaco Music Group.

The Angelic Choir of the First Baptist Church of Nutley, New Jersey, ca. 1964. Photo by Al Henderson. Courtesy of Newark Public Library.

Edison Blue Amberol cylinder cap of first known commercial recording of "Peace Be Still," recorded in December 1912. Courtesy Grey Roots Museum and Archives Collection, Owen Sound, Ontario, Canada.

The Reverend James Ewell.
Courtesy of Melodi Ewell
Lovely and Edward Ewell.

Interior of Trinity Temple Seventh-day Adventist Church, Newark, where *Peace Be Still* was recorded on September 19, 1963. The church has a new sanctuary and now uses this space for prayer meetings and special events. Photograph by author.

Album cover of *Peace Be Still*, Harvey Williams, artist. Courtesy of Malaco Music Group.

Harvey Williams, artist of the *Peace Be Still* album cover and many other Savoy album covers of the 1960s. Courtesy of Keith Van Williams with special thanks to Robert Rogers.

... .CORC...... , INC.
)5-53 FERR. STREET
NEWARK 5, N J   September 25, 1963

SAVOY LABEL COPY
33 1/3 RPM

SAVOY 14076   SAVOY 14076-A

"PEACE BE STILL"

JAMES CLEVELAND

and the

ANGELIC CHOIR

(directed by Rev. Lawrence Roberts)

VOL. III

1. PEACE BE STILL
2. JESUS SAVES
3. I HAD A TALK WITH GOD
4. WHERE HE LEADS ME

SAVOY 14076   SAVOY 14076-B

"PEACE BE STILL"

JAMES CLEVELAND

and the

ANGELIC CHOIR

(directed by Rev. Lawrence Roberts)

VOL. III

1. SHINE ON ME
2. THE LORD BROUGHT US OUT
3. I'LL WEAR A CROWN
4. I'LL BE CAUGHT UP TO MEET HIM
5. PRAISE GOD

Savoy label copy for *Peace Be Still.* Courtesy of Malaco Music Group.

New edifice for First Baptist Church. The first Sunday service in the new building was held on February 14, 1965. Photograph by author.

Gertrude Hicks at piano, First Baptist Church, September 1971. Courtesy of Robert Logan.

The Reverend Lawrence Roberts (seated) with Doris Duke (standing), First Baptist Church, early 1970s. Courtesy of Robert Logan.

The First Baptist Church music ministry in action, September 1971. Gertrude Hicks leads a song. The Reverend Lawrence Roberts accompanies on piano and Connie Pitts (far right) claps along. Courtesy of Robert Logan.

8

The Performativity of
"Peace Be Still"

As has been mentioned several times thus far, "Peace Be Still" was recorded during the 1963 Birmingham campaign, arguably the most important operation of the classical southern period of the civil-rights movement. Nevertheless, 1960s-era Angelic Choir members interviewed for this book said that neither the song nor the album nor their performance was directly inspired or influenced by the Birmingham church bombing or any other current events from the front lines of the movement. This is not to suggest that no choir members or listeners interpreted "Peace Be Still" or other album selections as a commentary on the troubles or as a therapeutic response to the trying times. Indeed, Professor Robert Darden, who leads Baylor University's Black Gospel Music Restoration Project, considers "Peace Be Still" the "second gospel song most associated with the healing that eventually followed the terrible events of Sunday, September 16" (the first, in his estimation, was Dorothy Love Coates and the Gospel Harmonettes' album cut, "The Hymn," recorded for Vee Jay in 1964).[1]

So, if not in explicit response to civil-rights gains or losses, what were James Cleveland and the Angelic Choir trying to communicate through "Peace Be Still" and other album selections? What fueled the indelible impression "Peace Be Still" left, and continues to leave, on its listeners? Since black sacred music is clothed in multiple layers of meaning, let's first consider a *coded messages* theory. In his master's thesis, "Sit In, Stand Up and Sing Out! Black Gospel Music and the Civil Rights Movement," Michael Castellini contends that gospel songs, like their folk spiritual forebears, contain coded messages that speak to an African American worldview. Song lyrics employing biblical texts embed socially relevant messages in religious metaphor. If folk spirituals, "draped in scriptural imagery and sung by people well versed in their seditious meaning . . . referred to earthly as well as heavenly release from hellish oppression," so too, do gospel songs.[2] Scriptural imagery of this kind, Castellini writes, is what anthropologist and political scientist James Scott refers to as the "hidden transcript," or the "folk cultural discourse that diverts direct aggression into folktales, humor, fantasy, play, ritual, music, and other forms."[3] Singing a gospel song or a spiritual with a hidden transcript falls within what Scott calls the realm of "infrapolitics," or daily acts of resistance that appear opaque to the external world but, to the black community, the message is crystal clear.[4]

"Gospel music has always operated primarily in the realm of infrapolitics," Castellini argues, "by strategically masking its oppositional expressions in biblical allegory and religious symbolism to deflect the repressive reaction of hostile whites."[5] In other words, gospel songs and singing are a sacred shorthand decipherable by those in the African American religious community but not easily decipherable by individuals outside it. "Black people's singing was in a specific context of social circumstance," explains civil-rights leader, minister, and religious music scholar Wyatt Tee Walker. "Simply put, what Black people are singing religiously will provide a clue as to what is happening to them sociologically."[6]

The life-preserving necessity of communicating in code was not easy for southern migrants to simply switch off upon settling in the North. During a 2005 interview that was posted in 2018 on the website JerryJazzMusician, Nick Salvatore, author of *Singing in a Strange Land: C. L. Franklin, the Black Church, and the Transformation of America*, posited, "When a group of people is living in an oppressive and dangerous culture, how do they speak out against it? If you are African American, how do you speak out against an oppressive culture like that found in the Mississippi Delta of 1947? It was very dangerous, and plenty of people were killed trying to do so. So, when black people came to a city like Detroit from a state like Mississippi or Arkansas, while they discovered a freedom that didn't exist for them in the Delta, they weren't sure how to express themselves after being raised in a culture that threatened them for speaking out. In the process of finding one's voice, church hymns and sermons became critically important."[7] As the children of migrants or as newcomers themselves, the members of the Angelic Choir could certainly bear witness. Having to earn a living outside their church and choir activities and, as we shall see, living in a region with racial tensions simmering beneath the surface, they were careful to not draw the wrong kind of attention.

One cathartic and confidential way to communicate the anger and frustration of living as a black person in America, then, was to sing it out. Whether advancing the collective cause of freedom or expressing private sorrows and joys, singing is a vehicle for African Americans to, in the words of Bernice Johnson Reagon, "evidence their reality."[8] Regardless of whether that reality is at the community level, at the personal level, or both, "gospel music, at bottom," concludes Walker, "is religious folk music that is clearly identifiable with the social circumstance of the Black community in America."[9]

Professor Johari Jabir of the University of Illinois at Chicago goes one step further. He asserts that coded messages in "Peace Be Still" are not just embedded in the lyrics but also in its dramatic music arrangement. "'Peace Be Still' is a song about peace but it is not a peaceful song," he writes. "It does not use the bourgeois style of peaceful music to obscure the violent truth of Black life in America. Cleveland's arrangement of vocals, instrumentation, and lyrics is the 'manner that reflects the matter,' to borrow a phrase from Richard Wright's discussion on depicting the violence of Black life in writing. . . . [Its] language, logic, and sound . . . expose the violent contradictions of race, rights, protest, and citizenship indicative of the Black experience in America."[10] In sum, the performativity of "Peace Be Still," or its ability to effect change in the world, adroitly articulates the African American worldview in words and music, and in plain sight, but without fear of reprisal. James Cleveland and the Angelic Choir did not need to spell out their message for it to be heard and understood.

On the other hand, historian Will Boone believes the lyric content of "Peace Be Still" may be more transparent than opaque. At the 2014 conference of the Society for Ethnomusicology, Boone offered a second potential translation of "Peace Be Still" by citing African American studies professor Ashton Crawley's concept of the "aesthetics of possibility," or a preference for expressing joy over pain as itself a "radical act of resistance." Boone explained that the album's periodic outbreaks of palpable joy, despite life's trials, outweigh the need to garner strength from one specific tragic incident, such as the Sixteenth Street Baptist Church bombing in Birmingham. In assembling the *Peace Be Still* album, Boone argued, "Cleveland and the Angelics told a story of salvation, deliverance, joy, and celebration. It was not a new story, but a very old one; applicable to current events but ultimately concerned with things that are timeless. . . . It is through this so-called otherworldly practice that people and communities are empowered, that they come to see the world otherwise; that they come to believe in the possibility of political freedom because they have glimpsed existential freedom."[11]

In other words, existential freedom, or the transformative power of joy expressed by "Peace Be Still" and other tracks on the album, inspires believers to not just stand the storm of racial prejudice but to overcome it and emerge victorious. It's a philosophy not inconsistent with the passive resistance strategy employed by the Reverend Doctor Martin Luther King Jr. and the Southern Christian Leadership Conference at the exact moment in time the album was recorded. Indeed, Freedom Rider and King associate Reverend C. T. Vivian could just as easily have been talking about "Peace Be Still" when he said that "Anytime you can get something that lifts your spirits and also speaks to the reality of your life, even the reality of oppression, and at the same time is talking about how you can really overcome; that's terribly important stuff."[12] This aligns with Emily J. Lordi's definition of *soul logic*, or "the special resilience black people had earned by surviving the historical and daily trials of white supremacy." Linking soul logic to its gospel roots, Lordi asserts that "soul musicians, through a series of practices drawn from the black church, modeled virtuosic black resilience on a national stage."[13] Lordi's definition of soul logic, which includes both vocalists and musicians, gives further credence to Jabir's suggestion that "Peace Be Still" makes its point both lyrically and musically.

The act of overcoming or, in gospel song parlance, "shouting troubles over," through the allegorical use of biblical stories in song is, like coded messaging, a mainstay of gospel music. It's what the Angelic Choir members meant when they expressed their commitment to "praising the Lord" during the *Peace Be Still* session. To them, thanking the Lord for helping them overcome life's trials was just as important as beseeching the Lord for continual assistance. Theirs is the gratitude of survivors, not the pleas of victims. They are not "poor pilgrims of sorrow" but victorious warriors and standard bearers for Christ. Endurance is itself a form of protest; survival informs the antagonist that the protester cannot be kept down or, in the words of Isaiah 54:17, "No weapon that is formed against thee shall prosper." Incorporating into this argument the Angelic Choir's status, as summarized by Gertrude Hicks, as "everyday people, no stars," one is reminded of a comment made by country-girl-turned-stage-actor Nina in Anton Chekhov's *The Sea Gull*: "What's important is not fame, not glory, not the things I used to dream of, but the ability to endure. To be able to bear one's cross and have faith."[14] Again, Lordi's soul logic proves instructive: "People who had soul believed in—had to believe in—the value of pain, and they showed how it could be alchemized into artistic expressions of deep feeling. Both the belief and its creative expression secured one's place in a community of other black people who understood that suffering had meaning and who lived that understanding through a life-affirming style."[15] "All classes of a people under social pressure are permeated with a common experience; they are emotionally welded as others cannot be," Alain Locke wrote. "With them, even ordinary living has epic depth and lyric intensity, and this, their material handicap, is their spiritual advantage."[16]

So whether as a coded message, an expression of joy to supersede pain, or a declaration of endurance, "Peace Be Still" struggles to make sense of the madness of man's inhumanity to man. "All great music teeters on the edge of madness," writes British commentator Norman Lebrecht in a May 2019 review of Stephen Johnson's book, *How Shostakovich Changed My Mind*. "In life's crises," Johnson suggests that "each of us comes up against an internal siege . . . and music comes to our relief."[17] Jabir concurs: "Gospel songs like 'Peace Be Still' are a distinctly religious example of how Black people 'make sense' of a social order that does not—even on its own terms—make sense."[18] For Locke, African American art converts "the brands and wounds of social persecution" into "the proud stigmata of spiritual immunity and moral victory."[19]

And for African Americans, making sense of the madness through the medium of music in 1963 meant cloaking it, like the folk spirituals, in biblical metaphor, letting the music be their voice and tell their story. This is consistent with Nick Salvatore's comments. Prior to the passage of the

1964 Civil Rights Act, gospel artists on major record labels were, with rare exception, hesitant to express—and, in some cases, prohibited from expressing—explicit social statements on phonograph records. Radio stations, fearing backlash from sponsors, were reticent to program records deemed controversial. For example, when researching material for his book, *Roosevelt's Blues*, historian Guido van Rijn discovered that of the approximately 25,000 blues and gospel records released between 1902 and 1945, only 349, or about 1.4 percent, contained direct political references.[20]

In the same book, van Rijn raises another excellent point about the hidden transcript. He tells the story of Lawrence Gellert, a white Hungarian immigrant who lived with a black woman in 1920s North Carolina. Inspired by the music produced by his friend's church, Gellert set about recording African American protest music in Georgia and the Carolinas. Of the five hundred recordings Gellert captured between 1924 and 1937, van Rijn reports that "half the songs he collected contained outspoken political protest, a surprising number compared to the mere 5 percent of protest songs in the Library of Congress recordings collected by John and Alan Lomax and the even smaller percentage on commercial recordings."[21] The musicians Gellert recorded evidently trusted him, likely because the music collector was of the community. But one wonders whether the musicians would have felt as comfortable expressing their opinions had Gellert been recording for commercial purposes. In this case, Matthew 10:27 is better rendered as "What I tell you in darkness, that speak ye *not* in light." At least not explicitly.

This wasn't just an African American music phenomenon. Consider the radio ban of "The Pill," Loretta Lynn's 1975 single about birth control. The line "Makin' love in the green grass" in Van Morrison's 1967 hit "Brown Eyed Girl" was edited out for radio play. Even the Beach Boys' now-iconic "God Only Knows" from 1966 was deemed blasphemous by some radio stations because the rock song used the word *God*. But songs by black artists explicitly protesting discrimination would likely have had difficulty being released in the first place. Bosses of major imprints with gospel catalogs like Savoy, Vee Jay, Peacock, and Nashboro would not have authorized the release of a single that did not stand a chance of garnering radio play and potentially prejudice programmers against their less radical offerings. That "Peace Be Still" received wide radio play suggests that no radio station found its message so explicitly subversive as to endanger its relationship with its advertisers or more conservative listeners. Indeed, Dorothy Love Coates and the Gospel Harmonettes' 1964 version of "The Hymn," which explicitly refers to "the little children" who "lost their lives in the church bombing," was not released as a single by the black-owned record company Vee Jay.

Instances of explicit social messaging on African American religious records prior to 1964 were almost unilaterally released by small, independent labels with regional distribution and aimed specifically at the African American market.[22] As Darden highlights in the second volume of *Nothing but Love in God's Water*, his sweeping survey of black sacred music and the freedom movement, recordings such as "Where Is Freedom" by the Friendly Four, which encouraged "freedom fighters everywhere," was released around July 1963, on a South Carolina label called Movement Records, an imprint likely established for that one release.[23] Brother Will Hairston of Detroit (1919–88), who made a career out of writing and recording movement songs like "Alabama Bus" (1956) and "Shout School Children" (1957), released his material on indie Detroit labels J-V-B, Knowles, and Natural. But whereas Hairston felt comfortable recording a tribute to Emmett Till, the teenager from Chicago whose horrific 1955 murder catalyzed the modern civil-rights movement, Dootone Records, a black-owned independent label that experienced national success with the Penguins' "Earth Angel" in 1954, released actor and musician Benjamin Sherman "Scatman" Crothers's "The Story of Emmett Till" in 1956 under the nom de plume of the Ramparts.[24]

In the early years of King's civil-rights efforts, northern black churches, with notable exceptions, supported their southern brethren prayerfully but passively, holding fund-raising events for the local chapter of the NAACP but steering clear of explicit protest activities. More direct involvement happened around 1960, when reports of bloody sit-ins and the harassment and brutality directed at the Freedom Riders began troubling the waters of the nation's social conscience. Moreover, as Andrew Billingsley affirms in *Mighty like a River*, blanket criticisms of the response of African American churches to racism and discrimination do not take into account the various ways churches and their flocks are equipped to respond to social and political crises. It depends on whether they are conservative, semiactivist, or activist congregations.[25]

The conservative church, Billingsley writes, is concerned primarily with the spiritual and religious needs of its members. Semiactivist churches not only care for their members' spiritual and religious needs, they also tackle relevant social issues by hosting guest speakers, community meetings, and discussions. These two types align with C. Eric Lincoln's description of spiritual, or privatistic, churches, which focus energy and resources on their members.[26] On the other hand, activist churches (*communal* in Lincoln's terminology) confront social crises head on.[27] They are involved in every aspect of their members' lives, including the political. Activist or communal churches were numerous in the South during the early 1960s. Sixteenth Street Baptist Church in Birmingham and Brown Chapel AME church in Selma, Alabama, are two examples of activist churches that provided succor to marchers, protesters, and civil-rights organizations such as the Southern Christian Leadership Conference.

Using Billingsley's nomenclature, First Baptist Church of Nutley would fall into the semiactivist category. Although the Reverend Lawrence Roberts and his staff did not march on the front line with Doctor King or protest in the streets of Nutley or Newark, the church did host ecumenical gatherings to promote fellowship, understanding, and collaborative worship among various religions well into the 1970s. On more than one occasion, Anthony Heilbut told this author during informal telephone conversations how Roberts shared with him his concerns about the larger issue of human rights.

That "Peace Be Still" was sung by a church choir adds yet another interpretive layer. In their seminal book *The Black Church in the African American Experience*, C. Eric Lincoln and Lawrence H. Mamiya introduce a concept called "convoking the culture"—to bring about "genuine corporate worship" by "assembling the faithful to a common place and a common experience of worship" so as to "transcend or to reduce to insignificance those social, cultural, or economic barriers which separate individuals in their secular interest."[28] Within the church, choral singing, an act of communal expression, offers a "sense of community" and a "temporary reduction of social alienation" through the "reaffirmation of a common bond."[29]

Because "Peace Be Still" was sung by a choir that, as a subset of a believing community, represents it (in this instance, First Baptist Church of Nutley), the song's infrapolitical message was affirmed by the community at large. A choir speaks for its congregation and with its congregation in the collective interpretation of a song. Allison Schnable of Princeton University might concur with this point. In her ethnographic study of a youth gospel choir, she writes that the "collective emotional experience of making music, the shared understandings of religious narratives in songs' lyrics, the ritual of performance in church services, and repeated co-presence in the sacred space of the church building create strong bonds among church members."[30] In this regard, the two most musically climactic moments of "Peace Be Still"—the twice calming of the waves represented by dramatic crescendos and decrescendos of the voices and musicians—characterize what Castellini calls the communal "elevated spiritual moment" that "*is* the message of gospel music."[31]

Looking at it from this perspective, "Peace Be Still" convoked cultural unity within the church walls of Trinity Temple and, via radio and phonograph record, within African American households throughout the United States. Like a radio broadcast of a church service, *Peace Be Still* as a long-playing album available for mass consumption was a way to gather the African American Christian body together for collective reaffirmation of a common bond and experience through music. The album, and its title track in particular, were intended to heal wounds inflicted by a myriad of daily indignities while also offering hope and encouragement for more than just the flock gathered at Trinity Temple on a mid-September evening in 1963. It was a reminder that no matter how tough life might be, no one anywhere had to battle the wind and the waves alone.

Although the Angelic Choir was not explicitly responding to the violence in Birmingham or the civil-rights movement generally, it did not mean that its members weren't personally angered and saddened over what was happening in the South. Many had family and friends living there but, as one member noted, the situation "didn't govern life." And, as the preceding arguments suggest, it would be naive to conclude that the sobering but ultimately uplifting message of "Peace Be Still" was bereft of any reaction or response to race prejudice or socioeconomic injustice, especially when racial injustice was alive and well in Newark long before the city's cataclysmic 1967 riot.

When in 1945 sociologists St. Clair Drake and Horace Cayton wrote, "Understand Chicago's Black Belt and you will understand the Black Belts of a dozen large American cities," Newark could easily have been among the dozen.[32] Southern migrants who arrived in Newark between the 1920s and the 1950s, including members of the Angelic Choir and their families and neighbors, confronted many of the same injustices their brethren experienced in northern cities like Chicago, Detroit, and New York.

Between 1940 and 1950, Newark's black population increased by nearly two-thirds, from 45,760 to 75,637, or a little less than one-fifth of the city population. In response, whites fled to the surrounding suburbs, dividing the area into what historian Kevin Mumford calls the "white suburb and the black city."[33] But while African Americans were swiftly becoming a majority in Newark, the city's power structure was still dominated by white males. Discrimination in public accommodations was forbidden by New Jersey state law, but that didn't necessarily prevent it from happening.[34] In 1949 singer and actor Lena Horne brought a racially mixed party to Caruso's Restaurant in Newark and was refused service. Citing the state laws forbidding segregation, Horne sued the restaurant and won.[35]

Horne's suit reflected a shift, begun prior to World War II, from passive acceptance by African American Newarkers of the status quo to active dissent. Emboldened by international outrage over the rise of fascism in Europe, blacks evoked anti-Hitler sentiments to call for antiracism in America.[36] Among the many reasons for their protest was the "invisible but assiduously observed color line" that dictated where in Newark African Americans could and could not live. Real-estate agents intentionally steered African Americans away from the suburbs, where the housing stock was better, to areas such as the Central Ward, where many dwellings were outdated and had outlived their usefulness. Of the more than forty thousand blacks living in Newark at the start of World War II, 90 percent were crammed into the Central Ward.[37] It was an enormous disappointment to the migrants; adding insult to injury, it seemed as if the worst domiciles were reserved for African American soldiers returning from the war.[38]

Notwithstanding the kind treatment Roberts reported receiving from Sebastian S. Kresge, Mumford notes that in postwar Newark, the flagship Kresge department store was one of the downtown establishments where segregation existed. Mumford also cites the restaurant in the S. S. Kresge 5 and 10 Cent Store on Broad Street for "randomly observed Jim Crow segregation." African Americans were usually seated in its main dining area, but when white-collar white workers crowded the café, the African Americans were relegated to counter service.[39] In response, African Americans pursued self-sufficiency by establishing their own businesses and service organizations.[40] The Coleman brothers' hotel and recording studio, discussed in chapter 2, are examples of entrepreneurship in response to exclusionism. Nevertheless, the "energetic center of civil rights" that Newark had become during World War II gradually faded as postwar communist hysteria turned what could have been a progressive mobilizing effort into "liberalism [that] was polite and passive."[41]

The 1950s witnessed the black population of Newark surge to 142,600, and the area's African American middle class successfully broke color barriers by settling in surrounding suburbs such as Orange and East Orange. Nevertheless, in 1960, when Roberts assumed the pastorate of First Baptist Church of Nutley, most of the African American population of Newark, where many First Baptist Church members and Angelic Choir members resided, were still consigned to the cramped and crumbling confines of the Central Ward.[42] When the local housing authority proposed to ease overcrowding by constructing the Columbus Homes, an integrated housing project, in the Italian American section of town, white ethnics pitched a fit.[43] Meanwhile, southern migrants still arriving in Newark in search of work joined the ranks of the unemployed, which for the city's African American working population hovered around 12 percent.[44]

If the Freedom Riders' arrival in Newark in 1961 redirected attention from the city's housing and employment discrimination to the struggles of southern African Americans, the Congress of Racial Equality (CORE) was intent on eradicating local injustices.[45] CORE established its first Newark branch office in 1963 and by July was organizing successful protests over unfair treatment of African Americans in employment and housing. Sit-ins at White Castle hamburger restaurants in Newark and Orange forced management to agree to new hiring practices that ensured jobs for African Americans. A "phone-in" to jam the switchboard at Newark Bell Telephone Company ended with a commitment on the part of company management to hire more black employees. Education was also an issue. By the 1960s, when the First Baptist Sunday Service recordings commenced, more than half of all African American adults in Newark had less than an eighth-grade education. Nearly half of African American youth between the ages of thirteen and sixteen were not in school at all, pushing the local high school dropout rate to an all-time high.[46] Thanks to CORE's organizing efforts, African Americans in Newark were once again speaking out about poor housing, high rents, absentee landlordism, income and education inequality, and police brutality.[47]

Sometimes the violence was just as blatantly racial in New Jersey as it was in the Deep South. For example, in August 1963, a month prior to the *Peace Be Still* recording session, the *New Jersey Afro American* reported on a row in Jersey City, just east of Newark, involving twenty-one-year-old Essie Marie Harvey. After Harvey, an African American, had been insulted and chased by a group of white boys, a group of her friends that included fourteen-year-old Serina Taylor came to her rescue. Members of the white group, held temporarily at bay, threatened to return. On Saturday morning, August 17, Taylor was sitting on the porch of her home at 118 Woodward Street in Jersey City when she was shot, "sniper style," by two young white men in a passing automobile. Vincent Lanza and James A'Polito were arrested for the shooting.[48]

If Nutley's white community was generally friendly to, or at least tolerant of, its African American neighbors and to those arriving from out of town to attend First Baptist Church, the town was not bereft of its own racially motivated incidents. Bootsy Roberts remembered instances of racial profiling by local police that required her husband's intervention:

> At nighttime, the young [men] would come in on the bus to go to a party in town, or they had a girlfriend in town, they would visit the girlfriend and walk to the bus stop. The police would pick them up. Little black boys, they would pick them up and then they would call my husband and say, "Do you know this boy or this guy?" My husband told them, "Every black boy you see, you call me. I don't know them all. You don't stop the little white boys when they're walking to the bus, so stop stopping these black boys walking to the bus stop after visiting their girlfriends!" He said, "What's good for the white boys is good for the black boys. Now you just stop it!"[49]

Notwithstanding racial tensions on the outside, the self-contained African American communities in and around Newark are remembered fondly by those who grew up there in the 1950s and 1960s as peaceful, orderly, and self-reliant. Still, Lorraine Stancil admitted that "there were some places we couldn't go. There were some tense moments, and as I began to question my mother about certain things, depending on where we were, if we were in the street, she would try to quell my questions and say 'not now.' When we were at home, it was a better time to openly discuss whatever was going on."[50] By 1967, a flammable mixture of economic and housing inequality, political disenfranchisement, and a frustration that things would never get better in Newark exploded into one of the worst urban riots in American history.

All this is to say that the Cleveland–Angelic Choir recording of "Peace Be Still" reflected the time in which it was produced, its response to those times embedded in biblical allegory and musical drama. But as societal norms changed, so too did the performativity of "Peace Be Still." According to Hayes and Laughton's *Gospel Discography*, nearly fifty versions of "Peace Be Still" were recorded between 1951 and the early 1990s. Only three predate the 1963 Cleveland–Angelic Choir recording. Of the three, only one—a 1951 version for Specialty Records by Dorothy Love Coates and the Gospel Harmonettes not released until the 1990s—used the Palmer-Baker hymn as its reference point. The other two, by the Mary Johnson Davis Singers (Atlantic, 1953) and Clara Ward (Dot, 1960), were written by Memphis preacher-songwriter Reverend W. Herbert Brewster. He set the same Bible verses to a wholly original melody. This suggests that the 1963 Cleveland–Angelic Choir "Peace Be Still" was the first time that African American artists released a recording of the Palmer-Baker version, thereby setting the standard for others to emulate.

Most gospel artists who covered "Peace Be Still" after September 1963 did so with fidelity to the Cleveland–Angelic Choir variant, but some employed the hundred-year-old hymn to express more explicit aspirations for personal healing and racial concord. That's because, by the mid-1960s, major record labels were not only becoming more tolerant of lyrics of social significance, they welcomed them. Veteran record man Ralph Bass (1911–97) was among those proactively promoting gospel songs with social messages. He had joined Chicago's Chess Records in 1959 after a successful seven-year run heading up Federal Records, a subsidiary of King Records.[51] Bass, as artists and repertoire man for the Chess subsidiary Checker, was eager to inject a youthful groove into gospel. Perhaps he took his cue from the Staple Singers, who supported Doctor King's commitment to justice, desegregation, and national amity that spoke explicitly to the African American worldview. Gospel songs that replaced the theme of man's relationship to God with man's relationship to his brethren came to be called "gos-pop." No doubt Bass's intentions were not wholly philanthropic; he recognized the potential of gos-pop to stimulate retail sales for the company. He explained in late 1968 that "The message of gos-pop is that there is more to gospel than just finding solace in the church. This follows the same message of Martin King, who was fighting for a new way of life. Kids are tired of hearing 'Jesus Give Us Help.' They want a positive message. Gos-pop teaches a way of life."[52]

An example of gos-pop as endorsed by Bass in the mid- to late 1960s is the Salem Travelers' Checker single "Give Me Liberty or Death." The song was written by group member Arthur Davis and recorded in February 1968, two months before the assassination of Doctor Martin Luther King Jr. To a fulsome musical foundation, the song contains statements such as "They learned that the word freedom / They've learned it is not just a word / They've been run over by horses and bit by dogs."[53] Other socially relevant Salem Travelers songs included their first hit, "The Children Goin' Astray," released in 1965 for One-Derful Records' Halo subsidiary, as well as Checker releases "These Are Trying Times" (1968), "Tell It Like It Is" (1968), "Keep On Holding On" (1969), "What You Gonna Do" (1970), and "Troubles of This World" (1970). On "Tell It Like It Is," Salem Travelers lead singer Robert Dixon laments that people who are criticized and scorned are "sick and tired of waiting for something to be done." To stinging psychedelic guitar riffs, Dixon declares, "The black and white should take a stand and rid this hate that's within man."[54]

Similarly, the Meditation Singers' Checker single, "Stand Up and Be Counted," a multiracial call to direct action released in February 1968 with writer credits to producer Gene Barge, declares, "Don't turn your back on bias and hate / You've got to look ol' Jim Crow in the eye / We can win if we cooperate."[55] The Violinaires of Detroit, also Checker artists during the 1960s, contributed "I Don't Know," a Gene Barge composition produced by Bass. After verses containing litanies of social dysfunction, the group sings the chorus, "I don't know what this world is coming to."[56] After King's death in April 1968, the record stores and airwaves were flooded with tributes to the fallen leader and pleas for unity to continue King's dream for social justice and racial unity.

One of the first uses of "Peace Be Still" for explicit social commentary came from poet and activist Nikki Giovanni. Born in 1943, Giovanni became associated with the Black Arts Movement, which conveyed messages of black pride through such vehicles as literary works and theatrical performances. "The Great Pax Whitie / Peace Be Still" opens Giovanni's 1971 Right On Records release, *Truth Is on Its Way*. It features a faithful interpretation of the Gwendolyn Cooper Lightner arrangement by Isaac Douglas and the New York Community Choir, under the direction of Benny Diggs, with Douglas handling the lead vocal. After the choir sings "Peace Be Still" all the way through, Giovanni recites her poem, "The Great Pax Whitie" with an evangelist's conviction and a proto-rapper's incisive and rapid-fire rhyming. It is significant that Giovanni replaces the exclamation point of "Peace! Be Still" with a colon, transforming peace from a command to an entity. Speaking directly to Peace, she describes the insidious indignities her people have suffered at the hands of a shameless white majority. As the New York Community Choir hand-claps to the 9/8 rhythm and vamps on the "Peace Be Still" motif, Giovanni implores African Americans everywhere to speak out against racism and intolerance.[57]

Giovanni's invocation of Cleveland and the Angelic Choir on *Truth Is on Its Way* doesn't end with "Peace Be Still." Side two of the album opens with a cover of Sunday Service volume 4's title track, "I Stood on the Banks of Jordan." Once again, Douglas and the New York Community Choir accompany Giovanni as she recites her poem, "All I Gotta Do." Drawing on the song's focus on watching and waiting, Giovanni expresses the frustration of a black woman waiting patiently for the coming of justice and human rights, knowing full well that the power structure will never fulfill its promises.

The following year, in a documentary film on the historic Wattstax benefit concert at the Los Angeles Coliseum, the Emotions, a sister group from Chicago (and former gospel singers the Hutchinson Sunbeams) are captured performing a nine-minute live version of "Peace Be Still" in a small church not unlike Trinity Temple or the razed First Baptist Church.[58] Exclamations of "Yes, Lord!" from congregants punctuate the air as the Emotions transition from a spoken introduction invoking the Crucifixion scene to a passionately sung version of the hymn, during which the sisters shift between close harmony and contrapuntal singing and shouting. "I believe I hear this voice crying out now," sings Sheila Hutchinson, transforming "Peace Be Still" and the biblical story on which it is based into a contemporary protest against racial oppression. Eventually, the trio invites the congregation to sing along. While the Emotions' fervent performance produces solemn nods from some congregants, it causes one young woman to seize up and faint.[59]

"All I Want Is Peace," recorded by the Heaven Dee-Etts of Trenton, New Jersey, and included in the group's 1976 album *The Good Times of the Heaven Dee-Etts*, turns "Peace Be Still" into an intensely personal plea for emotional healing. Accompanied by electric and bass guitar and drums, the group, led by Mary Glanton, opens the song in tempo rubato until the line "the wind and the waves," when it shifts into a plodding rhythm. "All that I want from my God is just a little peace of mind," Glanton shouts. "Sometimes, sometimes, sometimes, Lord, my pillow gets wet with tears, Lord, yes it does." Several times during the session, the urgency in the voices of the Heaven Dee-Etts overwhelms the recording apparatus.[60] But the transition of performativity from external to internal healing is made manifest in the song.

With an arrangement dramatically different from its forebears but consistent with the message of emotional healing, Vanessa Bell Armstrong's 1983 version of "Peace Be Still" is the best-known and arguably best-loved recorded version of the song next to the Cleveland–Angelic Choir version of twenty years prior. The genius behind Armstrong's version, from her second solo album for Onyx International Records, is fellow Detroiter Minister Thomas Whitfield. Born April 30, 1954, Whitfield was among a new generation of gospel choir directors influenced by James Cleveland, who helped commercialize the contemporary gospel sound even as he remained a steadfast proponent of the traditional style. Before his untimely passing on June 20, 1992, Whitfield had, in turn, influenced an even younger generation of choir directors, musicians, and gospel songwriters with his complex jazz- and classical-infused melodies and harmonies.[61] His influence is evident today in the music of gospel choir directors worldwide.

Accompanied by background vocalists that included Gwen Morton and musicians that included Whitfield on synthesizer and future gospel star Fred Hammond on bass guitar, Armstrong renders Whitfield's arrangement of "Peace Be Still" with intricately woven melisma, well-timed shouts, and over-the-stave soprano flights. By the end, she has translated the biblical story of Jesus calming the waters into a daily devotional, calling for peace "in your home, on your job, late in the midnight hour" and "when you don't know which way to turn." As with Giovanni, *peace* is not an entreaty but a proper noun. It's not a declaration to halt but a desired state of emotional solace. Not only did Whitfield earn his first Grammy nomination in 1984 for the arrangement, he also received a supreme compliment from the King of Gospel himself, James Cleveland. Detroit radio announcer and professor Deborah Smith-Pollard told *Billboard* gospel editor Lisa Collins that when Cleveland heard Armstrong's version of the song, he adopted the Whitfield arrangement for his own use. Cleveland said that "Thomas and Vanessa Bell Armstrong had understood what he had been trying to say 20 years earlier."[62]

The song remains an Armstrong staple. For example, at the conclusion of her 1998 Verity Records live album *Desire of My Heart*, Armstrong explains that "some people would be very upset" with her if she didn't "go back to some old, old stuff." She added, "I'll never forget where the Lord brought me from and where I got my beginning." She ends her medley of "old stuff" with "Peace Be Still," interjecting, "Even a cold gets worse at midnight, but whenever the Lord says 'peace,' He guarantees peace. I know that it will be." Toward the song's conclusion, she takes the coded message of "Peace Be Still" a step further. Flashing the two-finger peace sign popular in the 1960s and 1970s, Armstrong declares, "If you don't say nothing, the devil don't know what you are talking about." She, the choir, and members of the congregation and live audience flash the peace sign instead of singing the word *peace*. In so doing, Armstrong articulates peace as more than a state of individual calm—it's a state of collective calm with the power to overcome the most diabolical of forces, even if the believer has to achieve it by encoding it in sign language.

A tribute to the popularity of the Armstrong-Whitfield version came from none other than the Reverend Lawrence Roberts when, in 2005, he sang this arrangement with Paul Porter of the Christianaires, traditional gospel soloist Carolyn Traylor, and an all-star chorus. The context of its presentation was the Malaco Music Group's *Gospel Legends* video program. *Gospel Legends* was the brainchild of musician Darrell Luster, who gathered together legendary African American gospel singers, *Gaither Homecoming* style, to sing some of the most memorable songs in the Malaco gospel catalog. Adding "Peace Be Still" to the set list made sense because Malaco had purchased the Savoy gospel masters in late 1986 as well as the rights to the Vanessa Bell Armstrong album on Onyx that contained her version of the song.

Roberts opens with a narrative that erroneously places the site of the 1963 recording at First Baptist in Nutley but then transitions to a recap of the Bible verses on which the song is based. He then turns the song over to Porter, who mimics Cleveland's lead vocal techniques with impressive fidelity. Traylor enters during "the wind and the waves" section and from there she and Porter trade leads, singing, shouting, and squalling. Roberts, beaming like a proud father, leads the makeshift chorus. As with Armstrong, peace in the hands of Roberts, Porter, and Traylor is not an exclamation to stop but pleas to attain a desired state of inner peace.

Another telling modification in the performativity of "Peace Be Still," and next to Giovanni's the most explicit, occurs during a 1984 recording of the song by James Cleveland and the New Jersey Mass Choir, captured live at a program at Symphony Hall in Newark. It's a fitting selection to render in the city where, twenty-one years earlier, he and the Angelic Choir transformed a forgotten hymnbook selection into one of gospel music's biggest hits. This version employs the Whitfield arrangement, with its contemporary choral harmonies and chord changes. But where the 1963 recording was opaque in its response to the civil-rights movement, the 1984 release unveils Cleveland's personal hopes for amity. This comes at a point in the song when he addresses the spirit of the late Reverend Doctor Martin Luther King Jr.: "Martin, I know you're not here today in flesh, but don't worry about us. We're gonna have peace. The black and the white are coming together. We're loving one another. We're living next door to one another. We're going to school with one another. Don't worry!"[63]

"Peace Be Still" has also crossed cultural boundaries, as evidenced by the singing of the Cleveland–Angelic Choir version, albeit with Armstrong's vamp and coda, by Cleveland protégé Jessy Dixon. Surrounded by white Christian artists during a *Gaither Homecoming* video, Dixon sings with such emotion that the assembly gives him a standing ovation.

Besides thematic intention, whether for internal or communal peace, or as a spirited statement of survivorship, singing "Peace Be Still" in the twenty-first century triggers nostalgia among its listeners. Whether listening to a recording by a national artist or a live rendition by a local church choir, the song, almost without fail, stimulates instantaneous recognition, proceeded by exclamations of joy and gratitude and, in some cases, even tears. Ultimately, nostalgia for the idyllic old-time ways, even if not so idyllic in reality, is an effective coping mechanism, another means of emotional healing.

In the end, there are just as many interpretations of "Peace Be Still" as there are fans of the song. What is certain is that "Peace Be Still" remains a medium of healing and a proclamation of resistance. "I think ['Peace Be Still'] has lasted all these years and people still sing it," the Reverend Doctor Stefanie Minatee said, "because people are living in turbulent times and they are looking for something to hold to. When you say 'the winds and waves shall obey thy will,' whether [it's] the wrath of the storm-tossed sea, demons, or men, the lyrics just grab the listener."[64] Like the many musical techniques that make gospel *gospel*, it has a sensibility that comes from Africa. Because, says South African pianist Nduduzo Makhathini, "Historically, Africans always have explored healing that resides within sound."[65]

9

The Release of *Peace Be Still*

Since the October 12, 1963, issue of *Cash Box* contains a Savoy ad that lists volume 3 as among the company's "new and best-selling albums," it's clear that the record company didn't waste any time rushing the new Sunday Service album out to distributors and retailers.[1] Still, there's a nagging sense that Savoy Records didn't have as much faith in this volume as in the other two, at least initially, as company records show that it placed an order for only three thousand copies to be pressed. Savoy typed up the label copy on September 23, 1963, and at least on the first draft, did not include "Peace Be Still" as the album's subtitle. The song title was subsequently added to the copy in ink pen, suggesting the omission was an honest mistake, or perhaps the office was awaiting confirmation from Mendelsohn or Roberts on the target single.

Notwithstanding a presumed lack of enthusiasm from its record company, *Peace Be Still* began turning heads even before its release. "I can remember visiting the home of my friend Rev. Lawrence Roberts," gospel program producer George Hudson wrote, "to hear an unreleased, new album about which he seemed to be quite excited. As I walked in the house, Rev. Roberts and several members of the Angelic Choir were listening to a recording of a song called 'Peace Be Still.' And that was my introduction to what was to become the greatest team in Gospel record history."[2]

Using Michel Ruppli and Bob Porter's Savoy Records discography as their source,[3] one that mined the original Savoy files for its data, Cedric Hayes and Robert Laughton identified each selection on *Peace Be Still* by matrix number so one can differentiate between the session sequence and the final album sequence.

Side A:
SJC63–277[4]   Peace Be Still
SJC63–276   Jesus Saves
SJC63–278   I Had a Talk with God (identified erroneously on the album
    as "I Had to Talk with God;" the original label copy had the correct title)
SJC63–279   Where He Leads Me

Side B:
SJC63–284   Shine on Me
SJC63–283   The Lord Brought Us Out
SJC63–282   I'll Wear a Crown
SJC63–285   I'll Be Caught Up to Meet Him
SJC63–286   Praise God

The two unissued tracks discussed earlier were assigned these matrix numbers:

SJC63–280:   God Is Enough
SJC63–281:   My All and All

By breaking up the selections on the album, Roberts, Cleveland, and Mendelsohn had an inkling that each song on *Peace Be Still* could stand on its own, but only "Peace Be Still" was released as a single. It is possible that the length of the single's stay on the charts, as well as the fact that the following Sunday Service album, *I Stood on the Banks of Jordan* (volume 4), was recorded less than twelve months later, persuaded Savoy to not release additional singles from *Peace Be Still*.

"Sunday School Surrealism": The Album Cover

Herman Lubinsky was smitten the first time he laid eyes on the colorful and vibrant Dali-seque oil paintings that the artist, known simply as Harvey, was selling at a local street art festival. He decked the walls of his office at

Savoy Records with Harvey's oils—"every visible inch," according to record man Arnold Shaw.[5]

For decades, Harvey was something of an enigma among enthusiasts of his cover art, largely because he signed each work simply as "Harvey," with no surname, and the album credits cited him likewise. When I spoke to Reverend Lawrence Roberts in August 2006 about the mysterious Harvey, all he could remember is that the artist was a young man who did contract work for Savoy Records.[6] Thanks to research by John Glassburner and Robert Rogers, and interviews with Harvey's half-sister Margo Lee Williams and his son Keith, the shroud of mystery surrounding Harvey has been lifted. His name was Harvey Scott Williams.

Like Roberts, Harvey Williams was African American and a product of an arts-focused high school education. Born in Jersey City, New Jersey, on September 12, 1927, Harvey was the second child of Emma (Scott) Williams and Herbert Randell Williams. Emma was one of the first African American members of the Women's Air Corps (WAC) in World War II; Herbert became one of the top deputy collectors for the Port of New York and received the Gallatin Award, the US Treasury Department's highest civilian service honor.[7]

Demonstrating artistic proclivities at an early age, Harvey was accepted to the High School of Music and Art on West 135th Street in New York City—the same school that would inspire the hit musical *Fame*. By the time Harvey graduated, the United States was involved in World War II. Rather than begin a commercial art career, he entered the army to fight the Axis.

While in the army, Harvey married Elizabeth Butler, the daughter of a funeral home director. They had one child, Keith Van Williams. Upon his discharge, Harvey went to work at his father-in-law's funeral home, but in 1951, he resumed his art studies on Saturdays at New York's Art Students' League. He focused on painting the human form because portraiture was a lucrative way for an artist to make a living. The number of Harvey album covers for Savoy Records that feature well-defined hands clasped in prayer, or the "Hand of God" reaching down through billowy clouds, comes from Harvey's almost scientific fascination on perfecting the human figure on canvas.

Margo Lee Williams, former editor of the *Journal of the Afro-American Historical and Genealogical Society*, believes that it was Ernest Feine (1894–1965), Harvey's art teacher at the Art Students' League, who influenced her brother to emulate surrealism in his commercial paintings, which he exhibited in a few places around Manhattan. A photo in a July 1959 issue of the *Pittsburgh Courier* depicts Harvey and his father viewing one of his works, *Gift of the Magi*, which was exhibited at the Ceceile Gallery on West Fifty-Sixth Street and earned its Ceceile Award. Harvey also exhibited his work at the Greenwich Village Art Festival. It was there that Herman Lubinsky allegedly discovered the young man's work and began purchasing his canvases for his Newark office.[8]

Whether to save on the expense of cover portraiture or to emulate record labels such as Verve, Columbia, and Clef that employed talented cover illustrators such as David Stone Martin, Alex Steinweiss, and Jim Flora, Lubinsky employed Harvey around 1961 to design record album covers for Savoy Records and its subsidiaries. In 2006 Roberts explained that "Mr. Lubinsky would give [Harvey] a song, or myself or Mr. Mendelsohn would give him a title song of the album, and he would go off somewhere, back home, draw a picture, bring it back, and we would produce that cover."[9] A single parent, Harvey took his son Keith with him on his trips to Savoy, where he would receive $25 in cash for each cover he delivered. Although the majority of Harvey's approximately 175 album covers were for Savoy's gospel roster, he also painted fascinating covers for early 1960s Savoy jazz albums by the New York Jazz Quartet and Sun Ra.[10] "I thought they were cool because they were different," Margo said. "In many ways, it was my first real introduction into modern art on a personal level."[11]

Nevertheless, it was the outsized crosses, the Hand of God reaching down from the heavens, the roman numerals of the Ten Commandments buzzing around their stone tablets, staircases and railroad tracks leading into the ether, and Bibles floating weightlessly above landscapes reaching into infinity that marked Harvey's work. "Savoy's albums looked like no others," noted David Peterkofsky in the introduction of his *For Keeps* podcast in early 2019, on which Harvey was the subject. "Landscapes that seemed like equal parts Norman Rockwell and Salvador Dali, of all people. In retrospect, Savoy's 1960s artwork might best be described as 'Sunday School Surrealism'."[12]

For the front covers of the first two volumes of the James Cleveland and Angelic Choir Sunday Service collaborations, Harvey painted variations of the quintessential country church, complete with picturesque steeple, nestled among acres of green grass. In the foreground, the church's welcome sign contained the album title and artist details. If First Baptist of Nutley resembled the simple edifice in Harvey's painting, the pastoral setting looked nothing like the neighborhood surrounding First Baptist Church, which was residential. It didn't matter. The cover art enabled listeners who had never been to Nutley to imagine the music emanating from a little wooden church atop a grassy knoll. In many ways, the image graphically depicted what the music attempted to evoke—nostalgia for the traditional (i.e., southern) religious experience. This use of artistic paradigms to evoke authenticity and nostalgia is not unlike the practice by African American jubilee groups and gospel quartets of incorporating the words *southern*, *south*, or *Dixie* in their names, even if they were headquartered in Chicago or New York City. Zion Hill's L&N Gospel Singers, as we have seen, took their name from a railroad line that brought southern migrants to the urban North. And, as has been noted, evoking southern religion and its association with a principled folk culture helped people ripped from their roots to regain some sense of groundedness in an unfamiliar land.

With his experience painting the human form, Harvey probably found the *Peace Be Still* assignment as uncomplicated as the first two Sunday Service volumes. It was certainly one of the most explicit representations of an album title in Harvey's Savoy portfolio. Taking the biblical premise of the title track for his inspiration, Williams portrayed a white-robed Jesus standing alone at the bow of a one-mast wooden boat, arms outstretched to calm the dark clouds and churning waters. The disciples sit huddled in the stern, their faces and bodies nothing more than impressionistic smudges of pigment. Although Harvey's *Peace Be Still* oil on canvas is not nearly as eye-popping as other examples of his work, it is probably the best known and most viewed simply by virtue of the album's substantial ongoing sales.

Despite the remarkable number of gospel album covers Harvey painted for Savoy, he himself was not particularly religious. He believed in God but was not a churchgoer and preferred listening to classical music and Frank Sinatra. He knew he could not support his family from his artwork. A literal starving artist who survived several failed marriages, he taught at the Art Students' League while holding onto his full-time job as a riveter. Through the struggle, the activity of creating art was liberating. "Looking back on it," Margo recalled, "the years he was involved with his art, those were really positive times for him."[13]

Photographer Robert Rogers, an album art aficionado, dedicated his master's thesis to an examination of the work of Harvey Williams. He told David Peterkofsky during the January 2019 *For Keeps* podcast that the money Harvey made from selling his artwork barely covered weekly household expenses. "His art was being recognized," Rogers said. "He was an up-and-coming artist. He had the credentials. The family always felt like he should have charged more and pressed him to value his art more. I think it was just part of the struggles of being an artist that he had to realize that this couldn't sustain his life, and this couldn't sustain his family that he had. He had a young child at the time and had to care for him. . . . He only worked [on his art] for a short period of time."[14]

Williams precipitated his own mystery by signing *Peace Be Still* and his other album artwork as simply "Harvey," leaving off his surname. "Harvey had a huge ego," Margo said. "He wanted to be known by one name, like Picasso, Matisse, or Twiggy. He may have been amused now at the idea he was a mystery, but at the time, NO WAY! He loved whatever celebrity he achieved."[15]

Naturally, then, Harvey was proud of his album covers. "We always saw everything once it had become a cover," Margo recalled. "As soon as a cover would be created, he would bring that and show that to us. He was absolutely thrilled with the idea that he was on these gospel album covers. He was immensely proud of having that distinction."[16] Margo added that "after he divorced Keith's mother, Harvey was a riveter. For a while, he tried to survive on art, including doing paintings for rich patrons, signing their names so they could impress friends with their 'hidden' talents. His problem wasn't that he never made money, it's that he spent it faster than he could make it. Eventually, he went back to the funeral business."[17]

Rogers told Peterkofsky that later in Harvey's life, "his son and daughter-in-law presented him with some brushes and a canvas so he could paint again, but he'd contracted rheumatoid arthritis so bad that he couldn't even hold a brush. So when they gave it to him, he just wept and knew that he could never paint again."[18]

Harvey Scott Williams died on January 24, 1987, and is buried at Calverton National Cemetery on Long Island, New York. Williams's work has since garnered an avid following among album-art enthusiasts. Today, Savoy gospel albums with Harvey covers fetch prices on Internet auction sites that far outweigh those of contemporaneous releases. Nearly thirty years later, the family discovered gospel music enthusiast's John Glassburner's website dedicated to Harvey's album cover art and learned, to their delight, that their relative was a cult figure. "I'm thrilled to know," Margo wrote, "that his work will not end in oblivion."[19]

"The world that Harvey lived in didn't have gravity," Rogers said. "Everything floated around and it just sort of came to be. . . . Gospel at this time kept people together, and the fact that he pushed these boundaries that led into arguably more and more abstract art, and letting the cover be a nice place as a soapbox to present something that was different, to present something that was a little edgier, to present something to sort of push you into that third effect, where it was music and art but collectively it was a feeling, it was an emotion. He was like a shooting star. He came out with these brilliant images and this vibrant color, but flared out so soon and never to be seen again."[20]

Although its ads did appear in issues of *Cash Box* in late 1963, Savoy had dramatically reduced its budget for advertising in the trade magazines. Radio play and word of mouth were the two principal ways *Peace Be Still*, in album and single format, was marketed. Veteran gospel radio announcer Linwood Heath remembers vividly when the song first hit Philadelphia. In early 1964, Heath was apprenticing at radio station WDAS, answering phones and previewing records for announcer Reverend Louise Williams, the "Gospel Queen of Philadelphia." "There was no [promotional agent] calling radio stations at that time saying, 'Did you get so and so, did you give it a listen?'" Heath said. "Savoy and Peacock would mail us a box of albums or 45s and you just had to go through them." He continued that "Peace Be Still"

> by the Angelic Choir was sent to the station, along with some other recordings, by Savoy. When we played [it on the radio], there was something about it that just struck us. There was something about the atmosphere and the words, and yet it's a song in the hymnbook, but I never paid attention to it. The phones just lit up, they just lit up. People wanted to hear more and more, but at that time [Williams] didn't repeat any songs. It was just captivating to us in Philadelphia. It did something to us, the whole album; people were just buying that album. They just loved "Peace Be Still."[21]

Record retailers played *Peace Be Still* in their stores. That's how gospel songwriter and musician A. Jeffrey LaValley first heard it. He was twelve years old and traveling home from a visit to Madisonville, Kentucky: "We stopped at a record store on the South Side of Chicago and it was playing in the store. The piano got my attention first, then I heard the choir and was blown away. I had to have it. It was the first LP I ever bought."[22]

Meanwhile, in Washington, DC, "Peace Be Still" inspired a teenaged Richard Smallwood. "I heard it on the radio and immediately fell in love with it," recalled the award-winning gospel composer of "Total Praise," a song that has gone on to become as popular, if not more so, than "Peace Be Still." "'Peace Be Still' had to be played four or five times a day, and it was probably one of the most requested songs, if not the most requested song, during that period. Any time of day you turned on the radio, you'd wait just five or ten minutes, [and] you'd hear it. 'Peace Be Still' was like [Walter Hawkins's] 'Changed' or 'Going Up Yonder' during that day. It was like the biggest song in the country."[23]

Although Smallwood was familiar with the hymn—"I had to learn all the hymns in the hymnbook when I was growing up," he said—he was entranced by the arrangement and especially by John Hason's piano accompaniment. "That was my first time even hearing about the Angelic Choir. Of course, I went out to the record store and bought it, and played the grooves smooth. It eventually became my favorite James Cleveland record ever. That particular record caused me to go back and find the other volumes and then every volume after that until they didn't do any more."[24]

At the time, Smallwood was a member of Pleasant Green Baptist Church, where the pastor was the Reverend Cleavant Derricks, composer of the popular gospel song, "Just a Little Talk with Jesus." The Pleasant Green choir learned "Peace Be Still." "'Peace Be Still' was not 'Peace Be Still' unless you did that signature [piano] intro," Smallwood said. "As soon as you played the first three notes, the church would go up because they knew what you were getting ready to play. They knew that's what it was."[25] In his autobiography, *Total Praise*, Smallwood wrote that he became "a great admirer" of pianist Hason, "and for a while [he] influenced my approach to gospel piano playing."[26]

The song attracted international interest after Savoy authorized a 45-rpm version of "Peace Be Still" to be released in France on BYG Records; the title track was backed with "The Lord Brought Us Out" on the flip side. Meanwhile, a British Savoy release of *Peace Be Still* contained the aural components of the US release but used a photograph of a singing James Cleveland for its album cover instead of the Harvey artwork.

As far as the Reverend Lawrence Roberts was concerned, one of the best sales outlets for Angelic Choir singles and albums was First Baptist Church. Members would purchase records for themselves and for friends, he told Birdie Wilson Johnson. "When I had James's first album [volume 1], . . . [w]e could sell 2,000 in a given period of time right quick."[27]

But not every listener was won over initially. Joe Peay was somewhat disappointed with Cleveland and the Angelic Choir's recorded rendition of "Peace Be Still." "The sound wasn't right," he said, years later. "The choir, the voices, the microphones were not positioned right. You didn't get the full choir sound, especially the way that I heard it with Victory Baptist Church, as well as our [Southern California Mass Choir]. Oh my God, we'd make the walls shake! No one, in my opinion, could replace Thurston with that song. He was a performer as well as a singer. He was a formidable person."[28]

Nevertheless, on August 22, 1964, *Billboard* published the "Top Ten R&B Gospel Singles and LPs" as selected by the Reverend Louise Williams of WDAS, and *Peace Be Still* sat atop of it. Had Roberts seen the chart, he would most certainly have smiled knowing that his choir of "Mary, Jane, and John Doe from up the street, down the street, and around the corner" had bettered in sales the formidable Voices of Tabernacle, whose latest HOB release, *He's So Divine*, sat one position below, at number two.[29]

Radio station WLOK of Memphis, Tennessee, ranked "Peace Be Still" number four on its "Top Spiritual Selections" chart for September 7, 1964 (Mitty Collier's cover of "I Had a Talk with God," as "I Had a Talk with My Man," was number two on the survey's pop list that same week). Also in September, Miami, Florida, religious announcer Reverend Ira McCall listed "Peace Be Still" among the top three gospel songs making noise on WMBM-AM.[30] Nearly a year later, "Peace Be Still" was still number one in *Billboard*, but the album had dropped to number two on the Top Selling Spiritual LPs list, behind Cleveland and the Angelic Choir's follow-up Sunday Service album, *I Stood on the Banks of Jordan*.[31] In fact, Sunday Service volumes 3 and 4 flip-flopped between the number one and two positions during the brief period in 1964–65 when *Billboard* sporadically charted sales of gospel singles and LPs. Among the artists joining them on the list were the Staple Singers ("Hammer and Nails"), the Caravans ("Walk around Heaven All Day"), and the Consolers, a husband-and-wife duo from Miami, Florida ("Waiting for My Child").

Meanwhile, Savoy Records had live recording fever. On Saturday, September 21, two days after the *Peace Be Still* session, Savoy engaged audio engineers to hook up their equipment at Bailey Temple Church of God in Christ in Detroit, Michigan, to record the Southwest Michigan State Choir. Composed of singers from the Southwest Michigan Jurisdiction of the Church of God in Christ, the Southwest Michigan State Choir, led by Mattie Moss Clark, generated more volts of electricity when singing to an appreciative congregation in Bailey Temple than they did on their 1961 debut LP for Kapp, *Lord Do Something for Me*, recorded in a Detroit studio.

Indeed, the result of the Southwest Michigan State Choir's September 21 session, the Savoy album *Wonderful Wonderful* and its up-tempo single, "I Thank You Lord," cemented the reputations of Clark and the 250-voice mass choir.[32] It launched the Moss and Clark family gospel music dynasties—Bill Moss and the Celestials, the Clark Sisters individually and collectively, and soloists J Moss, Bill Moss Jr., and J. Drew and Kierra Sheard among them—as well as additional successful live in-service recordings from the choir spanning the 1960s that introduced such leading vocalists as Ora Watkins-Jones, Rose Marie Rimson-Brown, LaBarbara Whitehead, Donald Vails, and Vanessa Bell Armstrong.

Fred Mendelsohn became a believer. He told *Billboard* in February 1965, "You get something extra in a live recording—as in a church. The result may not be as perfect as a record made in a studio, but it has what is perhaps more important—sincerity and soul. . . . The buyers know exactly what they want, and they want authenticity." The same article indicated that Savoy was increasing its output of 'live' recordings as against studio recordings."[33]

To increase its output of live recordings, Savoy commenced a church-choir-signing spree. In addition to the Angelic Choir and the Southwest Michigan Mass Choir, Savoy added to its roster the Banks Brothers' Back Home Choir of Newark's Greater Harvest Baptist Church; evangelist Rosie Wallace and her Church of Love, Prayer, and Deliverance Choir; and the choir from the Church of God in Christ of Toledo, Ohio, which featured a young Rance Allen on bass guitar. If Peacock Records was the premier label for gospel quartets, Savoy Records was becoming the premier label for African American community and church choirs.

By this point, Savoy wasn't the only record company specializing in live in-service albums of African American church choirs. One woman made it her label's business model. Arkansas-born Idessa Malone (1913–87) became the first black woman to own a record company when she launched her Staff label in Detroit in 1947. Malone built her industry reputation recording the sounds of the Motor City's postwar jazz and blues scene; in late 1948, her recording of "Bewildered" by the Red Miller Trio hit the top spot on *Billboard*'s Best Selling Retail Race Records and Most-Played Jukebox Race Records chart. By 1960, after tussles with her business partners, Malone did a 180-degree turn. She transformed Staff Records into a religious label, recording sermons, talented organists, and the singing of amateur church choirs and groups. Among the first choirs she recorded was the one at Chicago's Fellowship Missionary Baptist Church, founded in 1950 by civil-rights leader Reverend Doctor Clay Evans. Malone took the choir into the city's Universal Recording Studio in 1962 and 1963 to cut their first two albums, which were released on the Fellowship imprint. But for the remainder of the 1960s and into the 1980s, Malone focused on live services recorded at churches. The congregations sold the albums to raise money for their general fund, building fund, or a special project—much as the Angelic Choir was using proceeds from the sale of its own releases to build a new church.

Ultimately, Malone's albums came closer to capturing authentic in-service worship experiences than did the Angelic Choir's recordings, those of Thurston Frazier and the Voices of Victory, or any other contemporaneous releases. That's because her albums tended to follow the order of service with fidelity: the choral singing, the prayers, the sermon, and the altar call. But because the choirs were not professional, or even semiprofessional, and some edifices lacked the optimal acoustics for recording, Malone's reproductions of Sunday-morning worship resulted in little commercially viable or radio-friendly material. Rare exceptions were "It Is No Secret," a Reverend Doctor Clay Evans solo from one of the Fellowship Missionary Baptist Church Choir albums; and "Great Consolation" / "A Prayer" by the Reverend C. T. Nelson of Greater Friendship Baptist Church of Cleveland, Ohio, which affected gospel radio in 1966. Nevertheless, Malone inspired a do-it-yourself recording industry among African American churches that recognized the economic potential in cutting a "vanity" record and selling it to support their ministry. Studios and record companies like Mark Recording, Custom Recording, Designer Records, Sound-O-Rama, and other whosoever-will-let-him-come shops were happy to accommodate the increased influx of traffic.

The vanity press phenomenon in gospel music received an enormous boost when a young Edwin Hawkins of Oakland, California, produced an album by his newly formed Northern California State Youth Choir of the

Church of God in Christ. Their custom-made *Let Us Go into the House of the Lord*, recorded in June 1968 at the Ephesian Church of God in Christ in Berkeley, California, opened with a softly rocking remake of a hymnbook staple, Philip Doddridge's 1755 "O Happy Day That Fixed My Choice," as "Oh Happy Day," with lead vocals by Dorothy Morrison. The choir's objective was to sell enough albums to pay its way to the 1968 Church of God in Christ Annual Youth Congress, but Hawkins got more than he bargained for when a San Francisco disk jockey began playing "Oh Happy Day" on the radio. Soon stations nationwide added the song to their playlists and "Oh Happy Day" became a national hit, the first officially recognized salvo of the contemporary gospel music era.[34] Record companies battled over the rights to sign Hawkins and his group (Buddah Records won). Like "Peace Be Still," "Oh Happy Day" demonstrated how an old hymn could be revived and rearranged to represent the musical tastes of a new generation of worshippers.

Although "Peace Be Still" engendered no controversy when released, the same couldn't be said about "Oh Happy Day." "Black deejays are divided on when and if to play the record, calling it irreverent to play among r&b disks or to dance to because of its sacred message," wrote Ed Ochs in the May 10, 1969, issue of *Billboard*. "Del Shields, WLIB deejay and jazz columnist, cautions the industry to 'go slow and take into serious consideration the deep sensitive feelings of the black people and their reaction to the manner in which this record would be programmed,' but adds that the record 'clearly shows that there is a swing back to the spiritual reclamation.'"[35]

Though not citing "Oh Happy Day" specifically, the reference is obvious in Reverend Lawrence Roberts's opening statement for a 1969 two-sided Savoy single, "Oh What a Day." "I heard one of our old songs being played on a rock and roll [radio] show," he declares. But as indignant as Roberts is on hearing a "Zion song" on a rock-and-roll radio program, he proceeds to rework the Hawkins arrangement of "Oh Happy Day" into "Oh What a Day" and passes the lead microphone to the Reverend Charles Banks and Dorothy Norwood, who are supported by none other than the Angelic Choir of First Baptist Church. It's a peculiar statement by an artist whose "I Can't Believe It" was played on nonreligious radio a decade earlier, but it does demonstrate the pushback that Hawkins and his contemporary gospel song received from the church community.

Notwithstanding the critical and commercial acclaim for their Sunday Service albums and other releases, Roberts and the Angelic Choir never lost sight of the fact that, in the end, their portion of the sales was to cover the construction of their new church. But after Cleveland took his royalties and Savoy recouped its expenses, what remained was insufficient to meet construction costs. To finish the job, the Angelic Choir had to tour the country as often as possible. The members spent long hours traveling from coast to coast, stringing together a series of one-nighters from Nutley to Los Angeles. "We traveled all over," Bootsy remembered. "We did nightly concerts with James Cleveland all the way to California. It took us a week to get there, but we were doing a concert every night and all the money we raised we sent it home. [One time] Freeman [Johnson] had to come back early, and my husband gave Freeman a bag of money, and he took that money back home, gave it to our trustees."[36]

"We would fly sometimes, other times we would just drive," Robert Logan said. "The choir usually traveled by bus, a reliable bus company out of Hackensack, New Jersey. I remember one of the longest drives we had, we went from Nutley to Erie, Pennsylvania, which is way up on Lake Erie. One particular tour in the early sixties, we left Nutley on Friday night and we reached Washington, DC, went to Kingsbury, Virginia, and to Chicago, Illinois. That's a lot for a weekend!"[37]

"We would go sometimes on an engagement far away, get off the bus, go home, shower, and go to work," recalled Bernadine Hankerson. "Sometimes you took your [traveling] bags to work or you'd get fired!" added Raymond Murphy.[38] First Baptist covered all traveling costs, but it did not compensate the singers and accompanists. All profits earned from performance fees went directly to pay down the First Baptist Church construction loan.

To relieve the long, tiring hours spent on the road, the Angelic Choir liked to play practical jokes on their leader. Remembered Vivian Carroll, "When the Angelics would go out to sing, and [Roberts] would preach, he would tell the congregation, 'I would like to introduce my wife, Dolores "Bootsy" Roberts.' Dolores and about ten of us would stand! We never knew who it was going to be. He would look around and say, 'Would the *real* Dolores Roberts stand up?' We would play that joke with him a lot, but he never knew when we were going to do it. That's what made it funny!"[39]

Roberts wasn't without turning the tables on his choir. He told Birdie Wilson Johnson,

> I never will forget the last time we were at the Apollo Theater, when I got the money that had to go to First Baptist. As a joke, I gave each choir member an envelope, those little brown envelopes that you used to get for anniversaries, and told them, "Here is something for you for this week's service." There was a note in there that said, "I love you, thanks so much for helping us to build First Baptist." They were throwing brown envelopes at me the whole night![40]

But like other African American artists of the era, the Angelic Choir was not immune to the insidious indignities of Jim Crow laws while touring the South. Roberts related one such incident to Johnson:

> We were on the way home from South Carolina doing a concert and one of our members got sick on the bus. We called for help and a white patrol car came up to aid us. And when he saw a bus full of black folks, he must have thought we were on a civil rights campaign. We explained to him we were gospel singers en route back to our church in New Jersey and he said, "Well, I will call you an ambulance." And he sped off and left her lying on the ground with all our choir members around. About ten minutes later we saw this light coming up the highway. It was a hearse from a local funeral home that they had sent to cart her to the hospital.[41]

The singer survived the ordeal, but sending a hearse instead of an ambulance to aid an African American experiencing a health emergency was a stark reminder of the long road ahead for achieving equality in America. The good news was that "ninety percent of [the mortgage payoff] was from the singing and traveling of the Angelic Choir," Roberts reported. "And this was done through the Civil Rights Movement and the torturous things that were going on in the South."[42] In the end, a combination of record sales, touring, and church contributions paid off the fifteen-year mortgage in five years.[43]

Everywhere they went, the choir sang "Peace Be Still." And whenever the Angelic Choir had the opportunity to sing on a program with James Cleveland, they followed a two-selection formula: "Peace Be Still" and "Jesus Saves." "They always tied those two together wherever we sang with [Cleveland]," Logan said. "Everywhere, those songs went together like a horse and carriage."[44] Brenda O'Neal remembered one engagement where a choir appearing on the program before the Angelic Choir had the audacity to sing "Peace Be Still" first. "I'll never forget it," O'Neal said. "Reverend Roberts said, 'Didn't they look around and see we were sitting there?' We went to laughing. We said, 'We're going to sing it right behind them!'"[45]

The Angelic Choir even sang an abbreviated version of "Peace Be Still" on television. In 1964, the group appeared on *TV Gospel Time*, the first nationally syndicated gospel music telecast. Because James Cleveland was unavailable to join the troupe for the taping, Freeman Johnson, the Angelic Choir member whose voice and comportment most evoked James Cleveland, took the solo. "He sounded like James Cleveland—looked like a young James Cleveland!" Roberts told Birdie Wilson Johnson. "And even had a voice in talking like James Cleveland."[46] From then on, whenever Cleveland was unavailable to join the choir on a gospel program, Johnson substituted as lead singer on "Peace Be Still."[47]

In addition to appearances "on all the TV networks in New York City at the time," according to Logan,[48] the Angelic Choir sang in Philadelphia, Detroit, Virginia, Georgia, and the Carolinas and even provided the music for a week's revival at a church in Bermuda.[49]

Perhaps the Angelic Choir's most visually striking performance of "Peace Be Still" took place in 1964 at the New York World's Fair in Flushing Meadow Park. The appearance was part of an outdoor gospel program organized by Joe Bostic, gospel announcer at New York radio station WLIB. Robert Logan remembered this:

> We were on the stage singing "Peace Be Still." Freeman Johnson was singing James Cleveland's part, and I was on the organ. For some reason, Lew Alcindor [basketball star Kareem Abdul-Jabbar] was standing on the stage with us. As we sang the song, suddenly it became dark and cloudy. A lightning storm came up out of nowhere. It was surreal. Everybody in the choir stand was like, "Wow—can you believe this? It was like God was speaking from Heaven, telling us that this is what it was like [in the Bible story]!"[50]

Linwood Heath witnessed the Angelic Choir at an early 1970s multiartist gospel musical program held at a stadium near Newark. James Cleveland, Albertina Walker, the Mighty Clouds of Joy, and the Hawkins Family were among the headliners. The Triboro Mass Choir opened and the Angelic Choir followed. "For me, and it's just my opinion," Heath said, the Angelic Choir "were a regular church choir. There was nothing exceptional about them. Gertrude [Hicks] got her voice out there and she could sing, and they might have other singers that were good, but at that time it was just God's doing of putting James [Cleveland] and them together."[51]

If Freeman Johnson was Cleveland's stand-in for the Angelic Choir, various groups served as stand-ins for the Angelic Choir when Cleveland was on tour. Anthony Heilbut remembers Cleveland fronting his pals the Caravans on "Peace Be Still" at an Apollo Theater appearance. In his memoir, Gene Viale recalled singing half of side one of *Peace Be Still* as a Cleveland Singer: "Finally, we moved on to the one everyone was waiting for, 'Peace Be Still.' . . . The audience was completely wrecked by the time [Cleveland] got through. I believe we then went into 'To the Utmost, Jesus Saves' and left the stage."[52]

Notwithstanding a growing national fan base, the Angelic Choir remained unfazed by their celebrity. "Everyday people. No stars," Gertrude Hicks stated matter-of-factly. "And we were not star-struck," Raymond Murphy added. "We were just a choir, and we enjoyed doing what we were doing—we didn't care who it was with. We weren't hung up on the names of James Cleveland or Billy Preston or Thurston Frazier. It was nice to work with them—we enjoyed working with them—but *they* were just as pleased and thrilled to work with *us*."[53]

On the other hand, the Reverend Doctor Stefanie Minatee, who grew up around the Angelic Choir, believed the troupe's newfound celebrity did have some impact on their daily lives. "The Angelic Choir was one of the best-dressed choirs of their time," Minatee said. "They were impeccably dressed every time they went out, and they knew it! They went out with the flair and style that was comparable to the way they sounded. They were trendsetters for the choirs of their day."[54] Brenda O'Neal agreed: "We were very stylish back in those days, with those robes."[55] But O'Neal also remembered how being fashionable could mean sacrificing comfort. Though the Angelic Choir's appearance at New York's Madison Square Garden was one of her greatest experiences, she said, "We had on lavender dresses with silver trim. I'll never forget the silver shoes because my feet killed me that night—wearing those silver shoes!"[56]

Lorraine Stancil was especially impressed by the Angelic Choir's soprano section. "Reverend Roberts had this thing where if there was a little pause anywhere in any song, he would point his finger at those sopranos, and they would have to hit [a high] note."[57] If only one soprano was needed to hit the high note, Roberts pointed to Bernadine Hankerson for the stave-topping note. Choirs still adopt that technique for dramatic emphasis.

By now, other church choirs, such as the one that sang "Peace Be Still" at the program they shared with the Angelic Choir, were paying attention to the ensemble from Nutley. As gospel promoter George Hudson put it in his liner notes, the Angelic Choir was now "the most imitated choir in America. The song arrangements that they have introduced are copied by Church choirs all over the country." Lorraine Stancil believed it was because "Reverend Lawrence Roberts and the Angelic Choir set the standard for church choirs to do music that was simple but had a lasting impact on our lives. They were consistent no matter where they went. The songs they sang were just as effective years later. That's the kind of choir they were; that's the kind of leader he was."[58]

The Angelic Choir's runaway success with "Peace Be Still" even prompted Thurston Frazier and the Voices of Hope to finally commit their version of Gwendolyn Lightner's arrangement to vinyl. Recorded November 20, 1965, the Voices of Hope's "Peace Be Still," featuring Lightner on piano and future Cleveland musician Alexander Hamilton also in the band, was released on a Capitol Records LP titled *Walk on by Faith*.[59] That same year, veteran record producer Richard Simpson captured the Harold Smith Majestics gospel choir singing "Peace Be Still" live in Detroit's Ford Auditorium. Simpson released the Simco single, like the Savoy single, as a two-sided 45. In December 1967, the Soul Stirrers gospel quartet joined the Majestics for a go at the song on Checker Records.[60] Not only does the Stirrers-Majestics arrangement on Checker follow the Angelic Choir's recorded version with fidelity, but Stirrers lead singer Martin Jacox borrows Cleveland's interjection, "Wake up, Jesus!" As several "Peace Be Still" singles were now in circulation, Savoy was justified in titling the Angelic Choir's version "(The Original) Peace Be Still" on its 45-rpm singles.

In 1965 Joe Peay watched as Savoy Records' Herman Lubinsky stepped onto the stage of the Olympic Auditorium in Los Angeles. In front of an estimated six to eight thousand attendees enjoying a gospel program featuring James Cleveland and the Cleveland Singers, he handed James a framed gold record of *Peace Be Still*.[61] In March 1966, Fred Mendelsohn reported to one hundred retail record dealers gathered in New Orleans for the Delta Dealers Convention that *Peace Be Still* had already sold more than three hundred thousand copies.[62] He told *Ebony* in 1968 that while "everything [James] records will sell[,] . . . the album that's our biggest seller right now? It's *Peace Be Still*."[63] By decade's end, *Peace Be Still* was cited as James Cleveland's biggest record to date, with annual sales of fifty thousand.[64] The accuracy of record sales reports is often as suspect as the heights and weights of football players in a college gridiron program. But if Mendelsohn's numbers are even close to accurate, the estimated number of units sold by 1969 was somewhere between four hundred fifty and five hundred thousand. Although half a million sold was, at the time, sufficient to be certified gold by the Recording Industry Association of America (RIAA), when gold status was conferred on albums with five hundred thousand units or more sold, there is no listing of the album or single in the RIAA database. In his seminal work *The Gospel Sound*, Anthony Heilbut put the sales figure even higher, at eight hundred thousand. "No record ever," Heilbut wrote, "neither Bing Crosby's 'White Christmas' nor the Beatles' 'Abbey Road,' has so blanketed its market. With 'Peace Be Still,' Cleveland became the most important gospel figure since Mahalia Jackson."[65]

10

I Stood on the Banks of Jordan

In 1964 Savoy sought to capitalize on the runaway success of "Peace Be Still," still dominating gospel radio and record sales, by producing a fourth volume of the Sunday Service series. Since First Baptist Church was still under construction and the popularity of *Peace Be Still* suggested that a larger crowd might be present for the next recording, Roberts scouted out an area church with sufficient accommodations. He selected St. John's Baptist Church in Scotch Plains, New Jersey, where he was friends with the pastor, the Reverend Sterling E. Glover.

Founded in 1907, St. John's Baptist Church was rebuilt and reopened in 1960 in an African-inspired circular shape to evoke "the Oneness of God."[1] Although the church was a hearty drive from Nutley and Newark, it was worth the trip because of its size and newness. Besides, on February 13, 1964, Roberts and Savoy had recorded an album by the church's Inspirational Choir. Recorded live in the church, the Inspirational Choir was remarkably gifted for an amateur church ensemble.[2] The choir's Savoy single, "It Is Well with My Soul" / "Sometimes My Burdens Are Hard to Bear," culled from the album, demonstrated vocal and emotional depth. Satisfied with St. John's acoustics, Roberts received permission from Glover to record the next Cleveland–Angelic Choir album there.[3] Recognizing the visibility that the recording would lend his church, Pastor Glover was undoubtedly all too eager to assist.

Caught up in Angelic Choir fever, George Hudson joined the live audience for volume four, *I Stood on the Banks of Jordan*. He described the scene at St. John's that Thursday evening, May 14, 1964:

> That night the Church was filled, and an air of expectancy hung over the audience. After about a ten-minute wait, the crowd burst into applause as the members of the Angelic Choir began filing into the choir loft. Rev. Roberts then took up his position in front of the choir, and James Cleveland removed his coat and seated himself at the piano. There was a hush throughout the Church, then James Cleveland began to sing "*I Stood on the Banks of Jordan*," joined by the choir singing "*To See the Ships Go Sailing Over*." From that point on, I was a witness to (and a part of) the most electrifying service I have ever experienced.[4]

Apparently the service was electrifying for more than just Hudson. In 1990 Fred Mendelsohn shared a recollection of the recording session with the Gospel Music Workshop of America newsletter, *The Score*:

> Due to the success of *Peace Be Still*, there was a tremendous crowd of people [at the session]. We had a drummer there, he wasn't our regular drummer, but he was very "spirit filled." Everytime [*sic*] James would turn around (James would be directing and arranging as he was singing), he would look at the drummer—who was seated on a pedestal. The drummer got so full of the spirit, he forgot what he was supposed to be playing, and actually fell off the stand! When that happened, the crowd went up![5]

Volume four was scheduled for release in September 1964,[6] producing two singles, both written by Cleveland: "No Cross, No Crown" and the elegiac two-part "I Stood on the Banks of Jordan," which provided the album its subtitle.[7] "Stood on the Banks" is based on a spiritual arranged in 1918 by Harry T. Burleigh as "I Stood on de Ribber ob Jerden" and in 1941 by Southernaires radio quartet singer William Henry Smith as "I Stood on the River of Jordan." Bootsy revealed that it was her husband, not Cleveland, who arranged the spiritual for the Angelic Choir: "Another song was needed for the album. James was hesitant in doing the song. That is why the intro was played so long. On the album, James took credit for writing the song. Being that Roberts wrote last minute, he didn't have time to copyright it."[8]

By the time the singers and musicians got to "Banks of Jordan," the fifth song on the program, the choir was fully caught in the spirit, their shouts punctuating the air as Cleveland reacted with his own "Lord, help us." His raspy-voiced and tear-stained solo on "Jordan," especially as he raised the title line, "I stood on the banks of Jordan," and the Angelic Choir responded with "to see the ships go sailing over," its members sounding emotionally spent at first but gaining in energy, was a fitting complement to "Peace Be Still." In fact, many similarities exist between "Jordan" and "Peace Be Still." For example, both use ships and water as metaphors. Both are extended theatrical epics, both feature Cleveland as lead singer and chief storyteller, and both rise and fall in dynamic intensity before arriving at a peaceful conclusion. Cleveland's commentary prompts encouragement from choristers such as "Sing it from your heart," and "Go 'head, James!" and hair-raising squalls from one female voice, possibly Gertrude Hicks. (Soprano Bernadine Hankerson's top notes are easily distinguishable.) This time, however, the struggle is not with a raging storm but with the heartache caused by a permanent separation from loved ones. The Jordan River serves as the metaphorical boundary between earth and heaven, where ships ferry passengers across from the earthly to the heavenly realm. Cleveland sings mournfully about his mother being on board a ship headed for the Promised Land. He wrenches as much melodrama as he can out of the narrative as, once again, the Angelic Choir represents a congregation of correspondents.

By the January 30, 1965, publication of the *Billboard* Hot Spiritual LPs chart, *Peace Be Still* was number one and *I Stood on the Banks of Jordan* was number two. By March, the LPs swapped positions on the album chart.[9] But if *Peace Be Still* was the lead sales generator, *I Stood on the Banks of Jordan* was the album that provided James Cleveland and the Angelic Choir with their first Grammy Award nomination in 1965, in the Best Gospel or Other Religious Recording category (Tennessee Ernie Ford took home the statuette for his album, *Great Gospel Songs*).[10] Cleveland and the Angelic Choir would receive another Grammy nomination in 1968, when "Bread of Heaven" from volume seven (*Miracle Worker*) of the Sunday Service series made the Best Gospel Soul Performance category. Nevertheless, the honor remained elusive: that year, Dottie Rambo, the sole Caucasian in the Soul Gospel category, took home the honor for "The Soul of Me."[11]

A Grammy may have eluded the Angelic Choir, but in 1967, when *Billboard* published its "Cream of the Catalogs" list, a special feature that recommended twelve hundred LP titles of all genres for record dealers to restock, *Peace Be Still* was one of only a handful of African American gospel albums, and one of only two Savoy releases, on the list.[12]

The Church That the Choir Built

By early February 1965, volumes three and four were battling one another on the national record charts; enough money seemed to have been raised at last to ready the new First Baptist Church building for occupancy. But one week before the membership was to march into its new church, one section caught fire. "The church was electric—the baseboard had electric coils," Bootsy said. "One of the carpenters, his cord fell down into the coils and caught on fire. It burned one side of the church. So we had to redo that section."[13] Years later, Roberts confided in Angelic Choir member Yvonne Walls that just before the fire occurred, he had been gloating over what *he* had accomplished. It was a humbling and expensive reminder that the building was not his doing alone. Pride goeth before a fall. Nevertheless, with his characteristic humor, Roberts told Walls that the portion to survive the fire was God's portion of the project; his portion was the charred section that needed rebuilding.[14]

A frenetic but ultimately successful effort to fix the fire-damaged area followed, and the new First Baptist Church opened for Sunday morning worship on Valentine's Day, February 14, 1965.[15] The modern A-frame edifice with colorful stained-glass windows and three cascading arches commanded the corner of Harrison and Memphis, on the footprint of the original structure.

Volume five, *Give Me My Flowers*, was the first James Cleveland and Angelic Choir Sunday Service album to be recorded in the new First Baptist Church. Fittingly, the album opens with Cleveland surveying the beautiful church from his position in the pulpit and congratulating Roberts and his congregation on its completion.

A bigger church edifice couldn't have come at a better time. The nationwide popularity of the Angelic Choir was resulting in overflow attendance at First Baptist Church's Sunday services. Church membership grew from twelve in 1960, when Roberts became pastor, to more than twenty-five hundred by his retirement from the pulpit in 1995. In addition to registered members, visitors from Newark and elsewhere would drop in on the Sunday morning service just to hear Roberts preach and the Angelic Choir sing.[16] Phyllis Morris wanted to be in the Angelic Choir so badly that she joined First Baptist for that reason: "Everybody knew the Angelic Choir, and the Sundays that they sang, you couldn't get in the door. If you were not [there] by 10:30 [a.m. for the 11:00 a.m. service], you couldn't get in! You couldn't find a parking space, you couldn't sit upstairs. Wasn't enough seats; you had to go downstairs. They would pull down a [video] screen."[17] Bernice Paschal, another church member, concurred, telling Birdie Wilson Johnson that the church was so packed on many Sundays that she and her family had to listen to the service from outside the building.[18] Thus, during the 1980s, the church built an extension to include more seats to accommodate the growing membership and visitors. Isaac Brown said they sold pavers inscribed with donors' names to pay for the extension.[19]

A frequently quoted aphorism about church membership is that good music brings people in the sanctuary and good preaching keeps them there. But for many First Baptist members like Morris, it was the other way around: "Reverend Roberts was such a dynamic minister, such a dynamic speaker. Adding the choir, it was like putting icing on a cake."[20]

In accordance with Roberts's initial intentions, First Baptist Church served as a live recording studio. Besides the Angelic Choir's own offerings, Evangelist Rosie Wallace and the choir from her First Church of Love, Faith and Deliverance recorded their 1966 Savoy album *No One but Jesus* in the new edifice.[21] And on Sunday, March 24, 1968, not only did James Cleveland and the Angelic Choir record volume eight of their Sunday Service series in the new church, but the now *Reverend* James Cleveland delivered his first recorded sermon, *God's Promise*, from the Nutley pulpit.

Not only did Roberts's reputation in the gospel music industry draw national artists to sing at First Baptist, but tobacco fortune heiress, socialite, and philanthropist Doris Duke (1912–93) hired Roberts to be her voice teacher. Recognizing Roberts's talent from listening to Angelic Choir recordings, and securing an introduction through the Reverend James Cleveland, whom she had initially approached about voice lessons, Duke sought out the First Baptist pastor. Roberts agreed to teach her and she joined the Angelic Choir in 1968. Curiosity seekers began attending First Baptist services just to catch a glimpse of the famous heiress. By the mid-1970s, the incessant swarm of media attention and gapers overwhelmed the seating capacity of the church and threatened the dignity of Sunday morning worship. Recognizing the toll her presence was taking on First Baptist, Duke politely resigned her spot in the Angelic Choir. Until her death on October 28, 1993, Duke's affection for the Roberts family never wavered.[22]

The Sunday Service recordings by James Cleveland and the Angelic Choir continued throughout the remainder of the 1960s. Between 1962 and 1969, the team recorded nine live albums and one studio album in 1968 of Christmas carols and hymns. "The Angelic Choir sang with everybody that was anybody," Roberts said. "We went to Radio City Music Hall. We went to the Shrine Auditorium in California. We went to Madison Square Garden with Duke Ellington, Sammy Davis Jr., and Roberta Flack, for Duke Ellington's birthday party. We were just a part of everything that was major during those years."[23] "We took gospel where it hadn't been before," Freeman Johnson added.[24]

The Angelic Choir also appeared at New York's famous Carnegie Hall and the Apollo Theater. Robert Logan remembered the Apollo booking in particular. "When we were at the Apollo with 'Peace Be Still,' the line went around the block. I remember one week we did four different services on Saturday night. It started with a matinee and lunch, and afternoon and then late at night. That's how big ['Peace Be Still'] was."[25] One Apollo show was memorable for more than the size of the audience. Etta Jean Nunnally recalled that Roberts got so excited during a portion of that program that he leaped off the stage, unaware that he was headed not for the main floor but into the gaping chasm of the orchestra pit. Nunnally laughed and commented, "He didn't realize how deep the floor was, but the crowd caught him!"[26]

Isaac Brown joined the Angelic Choir in the 1970s. Although many original members were still part of the ensemble, Brown remembered that they were "low on men" and that several men joined the same day he joined. His full-time job in law enforcement in nearby Montclair, New Jersey, made it difficult for him to make all the rehearsals and recordings ("I worked crazy hours," he said), and to be on a recording, a member had to make all the rehearsals. Nevertheless, what caught Brown's fancy was that the Angelic Choir was "one large family" and, trumpeter though he was who played in local bands, he enjoyed singing with the group as often as he could. He recalled that when they traveled to appear on gospel programs in the 1970s and 1980s, they sang their old hits, such as "Peace Be Still" and "Christ Is the Answer," but Roberts would alter the arrangements from time to time, including accelerating the tempo. Slow or fast, the songs made Brown "feel great inside" to sing them "and to be around those who sang them for many, many years.

You got pleasure from watching the people enjoy themselves. And to watch the members who had been there for many years receive the response from the people. I felt like it was somewhere I was supposed to be."[27]

One of Roberts's own treasured memories of touring with the choir was a program at Detroit's Cobo Hall after the 1972 release of the choir's double album, *Sunday Song Service*. The album, reminiscent of the earlier live in-service recordings but without James Cleveland, included "Hold the Light." This remake of the Roberta Martin Singers' 1959 hit was about nine minutes long, more than half of it a sermonette, with Roberts taking Cleveland's role in setting the stage for the song's message. Roberts's recollection is yet another indication of just how popular the Angelic Choir had become in little more than a decade: Detroit promoter and radio announcer Martha Jean (the Queen) Steinberg

> had us in Detroit at Cobo Hall. I saw this long line of people standing out at Cobo Hall because we were staying at a hotel across the street. My choir and I thought it was a basketball game or something going on over there, and my organist [probably Robert Logan] and I went downstairs and across the street to find out what was happening. We said, "What's going on, all these people here?" And they said, "We're trying to get last-minute tickets to hear that man do 'Hold the Light.'" Oh, I was floored![28]

In 1969 Roberts and the Angelic Choir received the Mahalia Jackson Memorial Award from the National Gospel Symposium of Music "for making the most substantial contribution to gospel music since Wings over Jordan," a reference to the landmark radio choir from Cleveland, Ohio, whose national broadcasts over CBS radio were a Sunday-morning staple in African American households during the 1930s and 1940s. "We believe that music keeps the gospel alive," Roberts remarked about the honor.[29]

As the 1960s and the Sunday Service series concluded, the relationship between Lawrence Roberts and James Cleveland remained solid. Isaac Brown remembers Cleveland joining the Angelic Choir on a multiartist gospel program during the 1970s or 1980s, held at what is now the Meadowlands Arena in East Rutherford, New Jersey.[30] But the two ministers' relationship was heading into new territory. In 1967 Cleveland invited Roberts and other friends and associates to Detroit to share his vision for a national gospel music convention. The concept was based on the structure of the longstanding National Convention of Gospel Choirs and Choruses but aimed at a younger generation and stressed music training and education. The Gospel Music Workshop of America (GMWA), Cleveland explained, would be a week-long convention with ample opportunities for gospel artists, choirs, musicians, and industry people to fellowship, take courses in such topics as vocal performance and—for the choirs—learn new songs to take home to their respective churches. Detroit hosted the first GMWA convention in 1968, but future confabs would move to various cities throughout the country. Roberts was named to the first GMWA board of directors and was its president in 1969.[31]

Roberts maintained his production responsibilities at Savoy Records until 1974, when he left to spend more time on his ministerial duties at First Baptist and with the Angelic Choir. A primary task was to train John Daniels to be his successor at Savoy. Bringing Daniels on board, Dennis Bines noted, likely could not have been done while Herman Lubinsky, who had died in Newark on March 16, 1974, was in charge. He would have fought against Roberts leaving and bringing someone in to take his place. But Daniels was far from a rookie in the gospel music world. Born October 14, 1936, in Red Level, Alabama, Daniels cut his musical teeth as a member of a family gospel group called the Daniels Singers (not the Apollo recording artists). He also sang with the Charles Taylor Singers and became music minister, choir director, and piano accompanist for the Cornerstone Church of Christ in Jersey City, New Jersey. Daniels established Glori Records in Jersey City in 1969. Living up to its motto, "The New Gospel Sound," Glori gave a national platform to an ever-expanding circle of contemporary gospel groups and choirs formed in the immediate wake of the profound success of the Edwin Hawkins Singers. Artists who recorded for Glori included Bishop Kenneth Moales, Reverend Timothy Wright, Lloyd Reese, Robert Fryson and the Voices Supreme, saxophonist Vernard Johnson, and the Helen Hollins Singers. The second gospel album on Glori was by the First Baptist Church's children's choir, called the Little Angel Choir, accompanied by Gertrude Hicks and Robert Logan.

Roberts, who shared his record production expertise with Daniels during the early days of Glori, knew Daniels was the right person to take his place at Savoy. "Reverend Roberts never left John out there by himself with Savoy," remembered Bines, Daniels's godson. "He always helped John and

Savoy, whatever they needed."[32] Daniels even produced the final Angelic Choir album for Savoy, 1977's *The Missionary and the President—When I Get Home*.

When Daniels formed Tomato Records, his next label endeavor, Roberts was there to assist again. In late 1978, the Angelic Choir recorded a double album, *Unchanging Hand*, for Tomato and *From Us to You* for Daniels's New Birth imprint in 1980. *From Us to You* featured Lorraine Stancil on the Raymond Rasberry composition "Touch Somebody's Life," with David Cole accompanying on piano. Cole went on to success as one of the two Cs (along with Robert Clivilles) in the dance music troupe C + C Music Factory. Their 1990 single "(Gonna Make You Sweat) Everybody Dance Now" was a massive dance hit, landing at the top spot of *Billboard*'s Hot 100 singles list two weeks in a row. "Reverend Roberts would get so irritated with [Cole], 'David stop doing that, don't do that run no more!'" Lorraine Stancil laughed. David "would do it just to ruffle his feathers! But he was phenomenal and Reverend Roberts loved him dearly."[33] Pop songstress Mariah Carey wrote her hit, "One Sweet Day," in memory of Cole after his untimely passing in 1995 at age thirty-two. And sadly, Daniels's new enterprise was short-lived. "John had gotten himself tied up with some unscrupulous people who took advantage of him," Roberts recalled.[34]

Outside of David Cole, the only other Angelic Choir member to venture into the popular music arena was Connie Pitts. Her "Working People," recorded for HOB Records in 1974, is a funk-infused message song with strings and background vocalists that evoked in lyric, melody, and arrangement the Temptations' "Papa Was a Rolling Stone."

Perhaps the greatest legacy left to gospel music by *Peace Be Still* and the Sunday Service series was how it altered the way albums of African American gospel music were recorded. Although gospel music is still produced in professional studios, a large percentage of new releases are recorded live in a church or a large auditorium. As Angelic Choir member Jacqui Watts-Greadington put it, the Angelic Choir's live albums "paved the way for the Kirk Franklins, the Winans, and the people that are in front of audiences and doing it now. We were actually recording during church. It's wonderful to go back and hear some of those voices, some of the older soldiers that have gone on. They were feeling the moment."[35] "In the church," said Brenda

O'Neal, "people could really express themselves—as opposed to the studio, where when we ended the song we had to be still. We couldn't say anything. It was a big difference."[36]

For Savoy Records, live-in service recordings became its key differentiator in the music marketplace. In fact, nearly as soon as the Sunday Service series had run its course, the company kicked off the *James Cleveland Presents* series. Savoy, on this series of albums, which debuted in 1970 with the first full-length recording by Helen Stephens and the Voices of Christ of Berkeley, California, gave Cleveland free rein to offer a record deal on Savoy to talented church choirs, groups, and singers he discovered at the GMWA and while traveling the country. They were often recorded live each in its own church. Fred Mendelsohn explained the whole process to Arnold Shaw: "On the album [Cleveland] sings one of the songs, and the artist takes it from there. The fact that he is on the album sells it and introduces a new artist. The follow-up is an album by the new artist alone. There's no promotion. You send the new releases to the jockeys and wait. At times, a record will not take off until six months after it's released, but then it will go on selling for sixty years."[37]

Alexander Hamilton, director of Cleveland's Southern California Community Choir on Aretha Franklin's 1972 *Amazing Grace*, explained the process to author Aaron Cohen: James Cleveland

> had a contract on Savoy and it worked great. I think he had eight, ten albums a year he had to do. Way it worked was all he had to do was have his name on it and one song to get paid. Real smart of him—he would look around to the good groups and say, "I'm James Cleveland and will get you on Savoy." We'd do one marathon, six, seven hour session and the album would be done. It would be 'James Cleveland Presents . . .'" and he became known as the Star Maker.[38]

James Cleveland Presents provided national exposure to a young generation of directors, songwriters, soloists, and choirs, many of whom were already active in Cleveland's GMWA or would soon be. Several live in-service albums in the series became national best sellers at the level of a *Peace Be Still*. For example, in 1975 the Charles Fold Singers of Cincinnati's first *James Cleveland Presents* album, recorded live, became a best seller largely on the popularity of a selection called "Jesus Is the Best Thing That Ever Happened to Me." Featuring Cleveland on lead vocal, this gospelized version of Jim

Weatherly's "You Are the Best Thing," a charter for Gladys Knight, pro-
pelled the album to the top of the *Billboard* Top Gospel Albums chart and
to gospel album of the year status on *Billboard*'s 1976 *Talent in Action* list.
It remained on the magazine's Top Gospel Albums chart four years after
its release. Cleveland and Fold became two of the top-selling gospel artists
of the 1970s. Successive albums with the Charles Fold Singers were part
of Cleveland's next multivolume live in-service album series. "Best Thing"
remains a standard in the gospel choir repertory. Whenever it is sung, the
song evokes exclamations of emotion similar to those on "Peace Be Still."

In addition to being the biggest star in gospel music, Cleveland had
become a pastor, organizing his own church, Cornerstone Institutional Baptist Church in Los Angeles, in November 1970. Cleveland built his church's
famous Voices of Cornerstone choir from teenagers and young adults. He
also assembled the Southern California Community Choir from members
of his and other Los Angeles churches, with Annette May Thomas as its
first president and one of its principal soloists.[39] Later, in 1982, Cleveland
organized the Los Angeles Gospel Messengers, a young adult choir created
specifically to present songs by up-and-coming composers such as Quincy
Fielding Jr., Calvin Bernard Rhone, Kurt Carr, and B. J. Fears.

In January 1972 Cleveland, having gone from being skeptical about the
live in-church recording process to being its premier spokesperson, brought
the Southern California Community Choir and one of its directors, Alexander Hamilton, to New Temple Missionary Baptist Church in the Watts
neighborhood of Los Angeles. Over two days that month, Cleveland and
the Southern California Community Choir supported Aretha Franklin on
her gospel album, *Amazing Grace*. The double album was certified Gold by
the Recording Industry Association of America (RIAA) on July 14, 1972,
a little more than a month after its release. Surpassing *Peace Be Still* as
the best-selling gospel record of all time, *Amazing Grace* went on to win a
Grammy Award and on August 26, 1992, it was certified Double Platinum
by the RIAA, signaling sales of two million units.[40] A CD recording of the
entire two-day session is available, as is the long-awaited documentary film
accompanying the album.

Peace Be Still and the Angelic Choir even went to college. Jacqui Watts-
Greadington, a music major studying with Professor Omar Robinson at
Langston University in Oklahoma, introduced the Angelic Choir to her
class. "My Aunt Bernadine [Hankerson] was an example for those of us

majoring in opera," Watts-Greadington said. "She was an example of the type of voice you should have if you were trying to be a coloratura soprano. It really meant a lot to me to be the only person from New Jersey and have the Angelic Choir, that I'd grown up with, be a part of our vocal music program."[41] Watts-Greadington would go on to join her aunt in the Angelic Choir.

Although it was not nominated for a Grammy, *Peace Be Still* was nonetheless inducted into the Grammy Hall of Fame in 1999. Five years later, it entered the Library of Congress National Recording Registry. Organized in 2002 and originally inducting fifty songs per year, the registry now inducts twenty-five recordings per year that showcase "the range and diversity of American recorded sound heritage in order to increase preservation awareness." About the selection's inclusion in the National Recording Registry, the Library of Congress said, "This enormously successful gospel recording influenced many later groups and remains an excellent example of gospel performance."[42] Iconic recordings inducted alongside *Peace Be Still* in the Registry's third year included James Brown's *Live at the Apollo*, the Beach Boys' *Pet Sounds*, Public Enemy's *Fear of a Black Planet*, Hoagy Carmichael's inaugural recording of "Stardust," and Rosetta Tharpe's 1944 recording of "Down by the Riverside."[43]

11

Doxology

On August 10, 1990, one day before the opening of the twenty-third annual Gospel Music Workshop of America convention, held that year in Washington, DC, James Cleveland was hospitalized. *Billboard*'s Lisa Collins reported that he was treated for "cardiac irregularities, possible pneumonia, and extreme exhaustion." It was the first of the annual confabs he missed, as acute an indication as any that the King of Gospel's health was failing. Released from the hospital on August 27, Cleveland participated in his church's Labor Day services. Toward the end of 1990, Cleveland's friends and associates put together a musical celebration honoring his fifty years as a gospel recording artist. Among those participating were the Hawkins Family, Andraé Crouch, Stephanie Mills, Billy Preston, and members of the original Caravans. The most poignant moment, however, came at the conclusion, when Cleveland mustered up what little energy and voice he had to say "thank you" to the assembly. He had apparently been practicing all day just to say two words to his adoring public. This heartrending moment—hearing an instantly recognizable voice depleted to a whisper—sent shivers through the attendees.

The Reverend James Cleveland passed away at Brotman Medical Center in Culver City, California, on Saturday, February 9, 1991. Mourners traveled from across the nation to attend the funeral services while musicians rehearsed the music that would adorn these celebrations of life. An intimate memorial took place at Cornerstone on Friday night, February 15, and a much larger service the following day at the Los Angeles Shrine Auditorium. Some four thousand attendees began lining up outside the Shrine as early as 6:00 a.m. for the 11:00 a.m. service. Cleveland lay atop his coffin, clad in white and bathed in red velvet—what the King of Gospel himself would have called "happy colors." The Shrine service lasted more than four hours, as artist after artist, celebrity after celebrity, came bearing gifts of music and testimonials, Lawrence Roberts among them. In his preacher's cadence, Roberts called Cleveland a "genius stylist," a "prolific songwriter," and a "master choir director." He added that "It goes without saying that Reverend James Cleveland was a legend in his own time."[1] "Peace Be Still" was among the songs performed at the service.

"James gave me my first mink stole," Bootsy said, imitating Cleveland's gruff and straightforward mannerism: "'You need some fur, girl, you need some fur.' My husband said, 'That's my wife!' [James] said, 'Bootsy needs some fur!' When [James] got sick, we would go visit him. He would say, "Lawrence, of all the people I know, you and Bootsy are the only ones to come see about me."[2]

When Doris Duke died in 1993, she acknowledged her friends Lawrence and Dolores Roberts by leaving them a portion of her estimable estate. The bequest afforded the couple an opportunity to retire to Stone Mountain, Georgia, where Roberts spent his days attending Victory for the World Church, pastored by its founder, Doctor Kenneth Samuel. "I love it," Roberts exclaimed, "and when I'm not doing that, I'm out on my dock fishing, taking life easy, and enjoying life."[3] At peace.

In 2005, with Roberts in Georgia and First Baptist Church in new hands, the Angelic Choir decided to formally retire, but not before holding one final reunion at the church. The June 19, 2005, program was the last time the original choir and its longstanding director sang together. They held emotional rehearsals for days prior to the performance, which itself resulted in shouts of joy, tears of memory, and, for Freeman Johnson, a roof-raising "hallelujah time."[4] To Roberts, working with the Angelic Choir was "thirty-eight of the most golden years of my life."[5]

Three years later, Roberts, too, was gone. He took his last breath on Monday, July 14, 2008. The funeral service was held at Victory for the World

Church in Stone Mountain, Georgia. It is intriguing to note that, of all the songs Roberts could have chosen to accompany the procession of his coffin out of the church and into the hearse, he wanted the Silver Convention's 1975 disco hit "Fly Robin Fly." It was his wish from the moment he first heard it, Yvonne Walls remembered.[6] His sense of humor intact even unto death, the Reverend Lawrence Curtis Roberts was buried in Melwood Cemetery in Stone Mountain. Dolores, the Roberts children, and their families still reside in Stone Mountain.

A tribute program took place at Greater Abyssinian Baptist Church in Newark on Saturday afternoon, September 13, 2008. Members of the Angelic Choir sang "One of These Days I'll Cross That River" as the family processed into the church. Guest artists included Cissy Houston and the Reverend Doctor Stefanie Minatee and her Jubilation choir. "Peace Be Still" and "I Shall Wear a Crown" were among the musical selections. Toward the end, Raymond Murphy led a group of singers, including Pearl and Stefanie Minatee and Freeman Johnson, in a musical tribute to Bootsy. Donnie Harper of the New Jersey Mass Choir and the Reverend Charles Banks were among a litany of speakers who paid their respects publicly to their colleague and friend.[7]

Reverend Roberts "was all things to all people," recalled Angelic Choir member Lorraine Stancil. "He was Godly proud of his abilities to do what he did, what he was called to do, but never boastful. Confident in his giftedness. He was full of wisdom and could turn any conversation into something you would be so engrossed in, you could burn your dinner. That's who he was. And whatever challenges he had, he didn't wear them. [That's] not to say that he was never angry or disappointed or hurt. Some of those things I did see, but they never overshadowed the phenomenal man he was."[8] Added Phyllis Morris, "I think that most people felt our music because it meant something to them. We recorded in the church during the church services so you know it was real, you could feel it. As Reverend Roberts would say, it will give you a lift that will last."[9]

Although many of the original Angelic Choir members have passed on as of this writing, seven or eight still attend First Baptist Church with fidelity, including Phyllis Morris and Inez Reid. "We don't have quite as many people in the congregation as we had years ago," Reid said, "but we still have a nice congregation. We have a wonderful preacher now, Reverend Brian Evans. He directs the choir like Reverend Roberts did and he's a good singer and a very good speaker."[10]

In 2009 Roberts was inducted into the Nutley (NJ) Hall of Fame.[11] And until her death on March 1, 2019, Roberts's longtime friend, the musician Gertrude Deadwyler Hicks, could be found on Sundays in Newark, back where it all started, accompanying the Zion Hill Baptist Church choir on piano. "I don't try to sing though," she said in October 2017. "Only if the spirit of the Lord comes in will I sing. And I can't get up and get my shout in. All I can do is tap my feet." She added with a sly grin: "But I'm still bringin' it."[12]

Notes

Introduction

1. The six hundred thousand calculation is mine and is based on figures cited in the trade press by Fred Mendelsohn. Anthony Heilbut puts the sales figure at more than eight hundred thousand units. The sales figures were reported, and the difference may not be inconsistent in fact. In any event, gauging record sales is an imprecise science. See Heilbut, *Gospel Sound*, 214.

2. Tom Fisher, "James Cleveland," in McNeil, *Encyclopedia of American Gospel Music*, 84.

3. bell hooks quoted by Jeff Nelson in "I Was Pulled Over This Week Too," LinkedIn, July 8, 2016, https://www.linkedin.com/pulse/i-pulled-over-week-too -jeff-nelson.

4. Kelley Hoskins, "Community Organizations Band Together to Host "Peace Be Still" Week against Violence," *Fox2Now*, February 23, 2020, https://fox2now .com/news/community-organizations-band-together-to-host-peace-be-still-week -against-violence/.

5. Yolanda DeBerry interview, October 12, 2020.

Chapter 1. The Reverend Lawrence C. Roberts and the First Baptist Church of Nutley

1. *Nutley Sun*, February 17, 1917, 1.

2. Birdie Johnson, *Gospel Music*, 19.

3. Clark, *Dark Ghetto*, 176.

4. Ancestry.com, 1920 United States Federal Census [database on-line], Provo, UT.

5. Much of the First Baptist Church of Nutley history comes from Hattie Black and Bettye Timmons, "History of the First Baptist Church of Nutley, NJ," First Baptist Church of Nutley Anniversary Booklet (Nutley, NJ: First Baptist Church, 2014). A *Nutley Sun* article dated April 8, 1965, states that the original mission at Chestnut Street was founded in 1905, a date that appears to be incongruent with the church's own history. It is more likely that the 1905 date refers to the church membership's securing of the Passaic Street facility.

6. *Nutley Sun*, January 13, 2000, A15.

7. Anonymous obituary, Rev. Dr. Lawrence C. Roberts (Paterson, NJ: Carnie P. Bragg Funeral Home, 2008, accessed January 26, 2021, https://www.braggfuneral home.com/obituary/Rev.-Lawrence-C.-Roberts/Stone-Mountain-GA/561059.

8. Lawrence Roberts, video interview with Eric Majette Jr. of the Living Testimony Foundation, loaned by Majette to author, September 19, 2019.

9. Johnson, *Gospel Music*, 8; Ancestry.com, *1940 United States Federal Census* [database on-line]. Provo, UT, USA. Year: 1940; Census Place: Newark, Essex, New Jersey; Roll: m-t0627–02425; Page: 4A; Enumeration District: 25–457.

10. Ancestry.com, *U.S., World War I Draft Registration Cards, 1917–1918* [database on-line], Registration State: Georgia, Registration County: Lee County 0157 (Provo, UT: Ancestry.com).

11. Ancestry.com, 1930 United States Federal Census [database on-line], Year: 1930; Census Place: Newark, Essex, New Jersey; Page: 15A; Enumeration District: 01570157 (Provo, UT: Ancestry.com); FHL microfilm: 2341073.

12. Mumford, *Newark*, 20–23, 27–28.

13. Houston, *How Sweet*, 35.

14. Mumford, *Newark*, 20.

15. Ancestry.com, 1930 United States Federal Census [database on-line], Year: 1930; Census Place: Newark, Essex, New Jersey; Page: 15A; Enumeration District: 0157 (Provo, UT: Ancestry.com); FHL microfilm: 2341073; 1940 United States Federal Census [database on-line], Year: 1940; Census Place: Newark, Essex, New Jersey; Roll: m-t0627–02425; Page: 4A; Enumeration District: 25–457.

16. "'We Patch Anything': WPA Sewing Rooms in Fort Worth, Texas," *Living New Deal*, May 27, 2013, https://livingnewdeal.org/we-patch-anything-wpa-sewing-rooms-in-fort-worth-texas/; Ancestry.com, 1940 United States Federal Census [database on-line] (Provo, UT, USA: Ancestry.com Operations, 2012).

17. Stancil interview.

18. Johnson, *Gospel Music*, 8.

19. Arts High School website, www.nps.k12.nj.us/ART/our-school/our-history/, accessed October 29, 2015.

20. Johnson, *Gospel Music*, 9–10.

21. Ancestry.com, *U.S., School Yearbooks, 1900–1999* [database on-line], "U.S., School Yearbooks, 1880–2012," School Name: Arts High School; Year: 1954 (Lehi, UT: Ancestry.com).

22. Lawrence Roberts interview.

23. Ibid.

24. Johnson, *Gospel Music*, 10; "Our History," Metropolitan Baptist Church website, www.mbcnewarknj.org/aboutus/whatwebelieve/history.php, accessed August 26, 2016.

25. Logan interview.

26. Johnson, *Gospel Music*, 11; Krupnick's location personally confirmed in 1940 Newark City Directory by Glenn G. Geisheimer, webmaster of www.oldnewark .com.

27. Johnson, *Gospel Music*, 11.

28. Ibid., 11.

29. Ibid., 24. Johnson identifies "L & N" as signifying the Lincoln and Nash Railroad, but no such railroad company existed; I suspect she meant the Louisville & Nashville Railroad, commonly known as the L&N Railroad. It does not appear that this group is in any way connected to the L&N Gospel Singers that recorded for Federal Records in 1950.

30. Johnson, *Gospel Music*, 12.

31. Dolores Roberts interview.

32. Ibid.

33. Ibid.

34. Ibid.

35. Roberts, *Gospel Truth*, 1.

36. Logan interview.

37. Ibid.

38. Dolores Roberts interview.

39. Roberts anonymous obituary, 2008.

Chapter 2. Gospel Music in Newark

1. Funk album notes.

2. Ibid.

3. Biographical information on the Coleman Hotel, Coleman Records, and the Coleman Brothers comes from Tony Cummings, "The Coleman Brothers: The Newark Gospel Music Pioneers," *Cross Rhythms*, http://www.crossrhythms.co.uk/articles/music/The_Coleman_Brothers_The_Newark_Gospel_music_pioneers/42801/p1/, accessed January 24, 2016; Houston, *How Sweet*, 38.

4. Houston, *Remembering Whitney*, 12.

5. Ibid., 14–16.

6. Houston, *How Sweet*, 66.

7. Houston, *Remembering Whitney*, 16–17.

8. "Our Church," New Hope Baptist Church website, https://www.newhope newark.org/our-church, accessed October 6, 2019.

9. Houston, *How Sweet*, 126; Freeman Johnson interview conducted by Dennis Bines, June 18, 2005, on *Angelic Choir Reunion and Retirement Celebration*, DVD, Interfaith TV Ministries, 2005.

10. Johnson, *Gospel Music*, 21.

11. Roberts, *Gospel Truth*, 2.

12. Lawrence Roberts, video interview with Eric Majette Jr. of the Living Testimony Foundation, date unknown; video clip from larger interview loaned to author by Majette, September 19, 2019.

13. Roberts, *Gospel Truth*, 2; Johnson, *Gospel Music*, 26.

14. Roberts, *Gospel Truth*, 2.

15. Pruter, *Chicago Soul*, 15.

16. Hayes and Laughton, *Gospel Discography*, 371; according to the discography, each of the two recording sessions left two songs unissued: "Lord, What about Me" and "Lord We Trust in You" (1954) and "A Space for Me" and "Bless Us" (1958). The 1958 single was not released on Savoy but on the company's new Gospel subsidiary.

17. Minatee interview.

18. Bostic album notes.

19. Dolores Roberts interview.

20. Shaw, *Honkers and Shouters*, 343–44.

21. Ibid., 351; *Billboard*, November 14, 1942, 60.

22. Broven, *Record Makers*, 57.

23. *Radio Dealer*, January 1923, 37, 56.

24. Ibid.; Jaker, Sulek, and Kanze, *Airwaves*, 140.

25. Shaw, *Honkers and Shouters*, 238, 343; Broven, *Record Makers*, 58; Kukla, *Swing City*, 242.

26. Shaw, *Honkers and Shouters*, 345.

27. Broven, *Record Makers*, 14.

28. *Billboard*, January 30, 1943, 64.

29. *Billboard*, November 14, 1942, 20, 60.

30. Although Savoy was formed in 1942, the company's single record jackets announced it was organized in 1939. This recording is likely the rationale behind the assertion of a 1939 start. "Rhythm and Bugs," on Savoy 100, concludes with a quickly-edited snippet of audience applause, suggesting that the audition discs are really recordings of live performances.

31. Savoy Records Discography, https://www.jazzdisco.org/savoy-records/catalog-78-rpm-100–5500-series/, accessed April 16, 2020.

32. Shaw, *Honkers and Shouters*, 344.

33. Shaw, *Honkers and Shouters*, 344; *Billboard*, January 30, 1943, 24.

34. Cherry and Griffith. "Down to Business," 5n17.

35. Shaw, *Honkers and Shouters*, 356; *Billboard*, October 16, 1943, 65.

36. Jay Bruder, e-mail communication, July 15, 2018.

37. Shaw, *Honkers and Shouters*, 345.

38. Ibid., 356.

39. Fox, *King of the Queen City*, 87.

40. Broven, *Record Makers*, 56–57; Shaw, *Honkers and Shouters*, 345.

41. Fox, *King of the Queen City*, 88.

42. Shaw, *Honkers and Shouters*, 353.

43. *Billboard 1944 Music Year Book*, 95.

44. *Billboard*, June 19, 1948, 13.

45. Broven, *Record Makers*, 56.

46. Shaw, *Honkers and Shouters*, 345.

47. Ben Ratliff, "Ozzie Cadena, 83, Producer for Jazz Musicians, Dies," *New York Times*, April 21, 2008, http://www.nytimes.com/2008/04/21/arts/music/21cadena .html?_r=0.

48. Peter Keepnews, "Rudy Van Gelder, Audio Engineer Who Helped Define Sound of Jazz on Record, Dies at 91," *New York Times*, August 25, 2016, https:// www.nytimes.com/2016/08/26/arts/music/rudy-van-gelder-audio-engineer-who -helped-define-sound-of-jazz-on-record-dies-at-91.html?_r=0.

49. *Billboard*, February 2, 1957, 24.

50. Shaw, *Honkers and Shouters*, 353.

51. Lawrence Roberts interview 2006; Roberts, *Gospel Truth*, 2.

52. Lawrence Roberts Singers biography and list of singers from unknown gospel program, courtesy of Dennis Bines.

53. Osborne interview. The family still owns the piano.

54. Hankerson and Hicks interview.

55. Examples of 1950s novelty records about outer space include sampling pioneers Buchanan and Goodman's "Flying Saucer" (Luniverse, 1956) and Sheb Wooley's "Purple People Eater" (MGM, 1958).

56. The concern over *Sputnik* moved beyond questions of espionage. As Mark Thompson argues in his 2007 master's thesis, *Space Race*, *Sputnik* also forced the United States to come to terms with having fallen behind the Soviet Union in science education. For African Americans, many of whom attended schools without science classes, the ultimate culprit of the country's shortcomings in the space race was its obsession with segregation. Thompson quotes Charles H. Loeb, whose pointed question in the November 16, 1957, issue of the African American newsweekly, the *Cleveland Call and Post*, was telling: "Who can say that it was not the institution of the Jim-Crow school that has deprived this nation of the black scientist who might have solved the technological kinks delaying our satellite launching?" (Thompson, *Space Race*, 29).

57. Roberts, *Gospel Truth*, 2–3.

58. Ibid.; Lawrence Roberts interview.

59. Hayes and Laughton, *Gospel Discography*, 140.

60. *Billboard*, March 24, 1958, 66. It is likely that radio listeners unfamiliar with the song's formal title simply requested "the Sputnik Song."

61. *Billboard*, March 31, 1958, 48–49.

62. Vocal harmony group authority Marv Goldberg provides details of the Apollo Theater appearance in his show-by-show list of programs at the historic theater, from its opening in January 1934 through 1960. www.uncamarvy.com/

ApolloTheaterShows/apollo.html, accessed March 15, 2019; Lawrence Roberts Singers bio from unknown gospel program, courtesy of Dennis Bines.

63. Hicks interview.

64. Hayes and Laughton, *Gospel Discography*, 283.

65. The Chordettes were a female barbershop quartet from Sheboygan, Wisconsin. Their 1958 pop hit, "Lollipop," released on Archie Bleyer's Cadence Records, was topping the pop charts at the time.

66. Lawrence Roberts interview.

67. Roberts, *Gospel Truth*, 3.

68. It is possible that the group Roberts accompanied on organ was the Davis Sisters, who recorded six sides in New York City on May 6, 1958 (Hayes and Laughton, *Gospel Discography*, 84), with their longtime pianist, Curtis Dublin. The May session date falls squarely between the Gospel Chordettes/Lawrence Roberts Singers' two recording sessions and allows for sufficient time to have passed after the release of "I Can't Believe It" for the record to have become popular and set in motion the successive events in Roberts's narrative.

69. In multiple accounts, including the one on page three of his autobiography, *The Gospel Truth*, and his 2005 interview with the author, Lawrence Roberts noted that he began working for Savoy Records in 1954. This date is inconsistent with the 1958 recording date of the Gospel Chordettes disk, which first brought him to the company's attention. He also claims to have left Savoy in 1978 (*Gospel Truth*, 8) and has referred to a twenty-year career with Savoy. This would make 1958 the more likely date of his hire by Lubinsky. Also, the Lawrence Roberts Singers' 1958 single, "If You Make It to the Moon" and "Softly and Tenderly" (Savoy 4102), shows Roberts in the songwriting credits.

70. Roberts, *Gospel Truth*, 3.

71. Johnson, *Gospel Music*, 42–43.

72. Ibid., 44–45.

73. Lawrence Roberts interview.

74. Roberts, *Gospel Truth*, 4.

75. Johnson, *Gospel Music*, 45.

76. *Billboard*, February 16, 1959, 57.

77. *Billboard*, October 19, 1959, 10.

Chapter 3. The Birth of the Angelic Choir

1. Roberts, *Gospel Truth*, 5.

2. Ibid., 5.

3. Black and Timmons, "History of the First Baptist Church of Nutley, NJ"; Angelic Choir, *It's the Holy Ghost*, uncredited album notes, Savoy MG 14049, 1961.

4. *Nutley Sun*, April 8, 1965, 20.

5. Anonymous obituary, Rev. Dr. Lawrence C. Roberts (Paterson, NJ: Carnie P. Bragg Funeral Home, 2008, accessed January 26, 2021, https://www.braggfuneral home.com/obituary/Rev.-Lawrence-C.-Roberts/Stone-Mountain-GA/561059.

6. Logan telephone interview, August 14, 2019.

7. Dolores Roberts interview.

8. Hicks interview.

9. Ibid.

10. Dolores Roberts interview.

11. Ancestry.com. *U.S., Social Security Applications and Claims Index, 1936–2007* [database on-line], Provo, UT. Original data: Social Security Applications and Claims, 1936–2007, https://www.ancestry.com/discoveryui-content/view/33853346: 60901.

12. Nunnally interview.

13. Ibid.

14. Logan interview.

15. Ibid. Inez Reid, who came to First Baptist as part of the Voices of Faith, in her interview also remembered the church having only a piano and organ initially.

16. Murphy interview.

17. Dolores Roberts interview.

18. Hayes and Laughton, *Gospel Discography*, 404.

19. Johnson, *Gospel Music*, 40.

20. Murphy interview. Roberts may have changed the choir's name to avoid confusion with Thurston Frazier's Voices of Hope Choir, a Capitol recording artist. The last thing Roberts needed was another Gospel Chordettes conflict.

21. Hayes and Laughton, *Gospel Discography*, 15.

22. The song would inspire other covers, most notably by the Barrett Sisters. As recently as 2012, Chicago's Anita Wilson gave the song, retitled "Jesus Will," a contemporary bounce. The following year, Wilson's version reached number 13 on *Billboard*'s Top Gospel Charts (Jim Asker, "Big Daddy Weave Makes Big Move; Anita Wilson's 'Best of My Love' Remake Hits Gospel Chart Top 10," *Billboard*, November 6, 2015, https://www.billboard.com/index.php/articles/business/chart-beat/6753902/big-daddy-weave-anita-wilson-best-of-my-love.

23. *Billboard*, "The Hot 100," July 24, 1961, 40.

24. Johnson, *Gospel Music*, 41.

25. Hayes and Laughton, *Gospel Discography*, 385–86. It wasn't Sam Windham's first recorded solo on slide guitar. He took an extended solo on the Ward Singers' "Didn't It Rain," recorded live at a 1958 program at New York's Town Hall. Sam Windham also appeared with the Ward Singers on a September 1959 program at the Apollo Theater. Dot Records recorded the Town Hall event and Forum Circle released an LP of the Apollo program.

26. *Billboard*, May 19, 1962, 26.

27. Murphy interview.

28. Dolores Roberts interview.

29. Murphy interview.

30. Stancil interview.

31. Minatee interview.

32. Morris interview, March 14, 2017.

33. JaVan Hicks interview, March 14, 2017.

34. *Billboard*, April 14, 1962, 6.

Chapter 4. The Arrival of James Cleveland

1. Shaw, *Honkers and Shouters*, 353.

2. *Billboard*, May 23, 1960, 4.

3. Marv Goldberg's R&B Notebooks—Apollo Theater Shows, www.uncamarvy.com/ApolloTheaterShows/apollo.html, accessed March 15, 2019.

4. The author is grateful to Rebecca "Betty" Brooks, Cleveland's youngest sister, for providing this information.

5. Bil Carpenter, *Uncloudy Days: The Gospel Music Encyclopedia* (San Francisco: Backbeat, 2005), 87–88.

6. Heilbut, *Gospel Sound*, 207.

7. Ibid.; Heilbut, *Fan Who Knew Too Much*, 34.

8. *Chicago Defender*, December 19, 1942, 5.

9. Cleveland quote in Carpenter, *Uncloudy Days*, 87–88; "The Rev. James Cleveland, 59; Pastor Hailed as 'King of Gospel,'" *New York Times*, February 11, 1991, http://www.nytimes.com/1991/02/11/obituaries/the-rev-james-cleveland-59-pastor-hailed-as-king-of-gospel.html?mcubz=0.

10. Heilbut, *Gospel Sound*, 207.

11. Willis interview.

12. Evans interview.

13. Folk e-mail.

14. Hayes and Laughton, *Gospel Discography*, 155.

15. Hayes and Laughton suggest that Cleveland may have accompanied the Roberta Martin Singers on some of their Apollo sessions (*Gospel Discography*, 229). Cleveland quote in Carpenter, *Uncloudy Days*, 88.

16. "Gospel's James Cleveland's Dead at 59," *Toronto Star*, February 11, 1991, Entertainment D8, quoted in Darden, *People Get Ready*, 270.

17. Lorenza Brown Porter, December 2005 interview with author for Gospel Memories radio broadcast, aired on WLUW-FM, January 1, 2006.

18. Robert Sacre, "Meditation Singers," *Encyclopedia of American Gospel Music*, 254.

19. Hayes and Laughton, *Gospel Discography*, 236.

20. Ibid., 137.

21. Daniels Smith interview; Hayes and Laughton, *Gospel Discography*, 51; Harrington, "Shirley Caesar," 61.

22. *The GMWA Score* 1, no. 2 (February 1990): 3.

23. Heilbut, *Fan Who Knew Too Much*, 118.

24. *Ebony*, October 1967, 48.

25. Marovich, *City Called Heaven*, 261–62.

26. The Voices of Tabernacle, *The Love of God*, uncredited liner notes, HOB Records, LP-233, 1959.

27. *Billboard*, July 25, 1960, 38.

28. Hayes and Laughton, *Gospel Discography*, 236, 287. It is likely Cleveland also produced the Meditations' sides because he was back at Universal a week later to produce Chicago's Helen Robinson Youth Choir for Specialty.

29. Unreleased Specialty cuts of Meditations and Helen Robinson Youth Chorus were later issued on *Good News* SPCD-7032–2, 1993, and *Golden Age Gospel Choirs (1954–1963)*, Specialty SPCD-7068–2, 1997, respectively.

30. *Billboard*, October 26, 1959, 50.

31. *Billboard*, August 31, 1974, 18.

32. Hayes and Laughton, *Gospel Discography*, 65.

33. *Billboard*, June 20, 1960, 67.

34. Thomas interview.

35. Later, James Cleveland would remedy this by using recording studios in Los Angeles, including Ray Charles's RPM Studio.

36. Lawrence Roberts interview.

37. "Rev. Lawrence Roberts interview," from the Malaco Music Group DVD *Gospel Legends*, 2007, interview available as Malaco Music Group Gospel Legends, "Rev. Lawrence Roberts interview," on YouTube, May 13, 2014, https://www.youtube.com/watch?v=qs_XaXBsu44.

Chapter 5. In Search of the Authentic: The Live In-Service Recording

1. Martin, *Preaching on Wax*, 2, 6.

2. Ibid., 98–100.

3. Ibid., 20.

4. Ibid., 60, 73.

5. Ibid., 89.

6. Ibid., 112–15.

7. "Sin-Killing Sanders: The Legacy of Bishop Oscar Haywood Sanders," *The Old Landmark: Celebrating Our Apostolic Heritage*, February 14, 2007, https://oldlandmark.wordpress.com/category/people/oneness-pentecostals/oscar-sanders/.

8. Available on *Negro Religious Field Recordings*, vol. 1, Document DOCD-5312, 1994. Album notes by Ken Romanowski.

9. Ibid.

10. Braxton D. Shelley, "'This Must Be the Single': Valuing the Live Recording in Contemporary Gospel Performance," in *Living the Life I Sing: Gospel Music from the Dorsey Era to the Millennium*, ed. Alphonso Simpson Jr. and Thomas A. Dorsey III (San Diego, CA: Cognella, 2017), 140.

11. Martin, *Preaching on Wax*, 172.

12. Hayes and Laughton, *Gospel Discography*, 293–94.

13. Hildebrand and Nations liner notes.

14. The Jaxyson test pressing of "Get Back Jordan," from the collection of Chris Strachwitz, can be heard on King Louis H. Narcisse, *It's So Nice to Be Nice*, Gospel Friend OLN-2001, 2003.

15. Hayes and Laughton, *Gospel Discography*, 73.

16. *Billboard*, July 14, 1951, 12; Wald, *Shout, Sister, Shout!*, 123.

17. *Billboard*, July 14, 1951, 12.

18. Hayes and Laughton, *Gospel Discography*, 380.

19. *Billboard*, July 3, 1954, 27.

20. Hayes and Laughton, *Gospel Discography*, 334.

21. Joe Richman and Samara Freemark, producers, "A Nephew's Quest: Who Was Brother Claude Ely?" NPR's *Radio Diaries*, May 5, 2011, https://www.npr.org/2011/05/05/136019632/a-nephews-quest-who-was-brother-claude-ely.

22. Hayes and Laughton, *Gospel Discography*, 159.

23. Hildebrand and Nations liner notes.

24. Ibid.

25. Special thanks to Eli Husock for sharing this rare recording with the author.

26. *Night with Daddy Grace*, uncredited liner notes.

27. Several singers and musicians on "Great Day," including Charles Craig, Hulah Gene Dunklin Hurley, and organist Francis Chandler, became part of the Voices of Tabernacle. "Great Day" would be licensed and distributed nationally by Vee Jay Records.

28. Growing up, popular vocalist and actor Ronnie Dyson ("Why Can't I Touch You?," 1970) was a member of the Washington Temple Celestial Choir.

29. Hayes and Laughton, *Gospel Discography*, 385.

30. Pierce liner notes.

31. Mahalia Jackson's Newport Jazz Festival performance appears on *Moving On Up a Little Higher*, Shanachie Entertainment / Spirit Feel 6066, 2016.

32. Heilbut, *Fan Who Knew Too Much*, 258.

33. Ibid., 15.

34. Marovich, *City Called Heaven*, 184.

35. Prial, *Producer*, 208.

36. Ibid., 210.

37. Ibid., 211.

38. Ibid.

39. *Billboard*, November 7, 1960, 39.

40. *Billboard*, May 16, 1960, 3.

41. Greater Abyssinian Baptist Church, "Our History," http://www.greaterabyssinian.org/about-gabc.html, accessed December 18, 2019.

42. Hayes and Laughton, *Gospel Discography*, 30; Bible Way Church of God Choir, *Let the Church Roll On*, King LP 736, 1960.

43. Hayes and Laughton, *Gospel Discography*, 262.

Chapter 6. This Sunday—In Person

1. Hayes and Laughton, *Gospel Discography*, 76.

2. *Billboard*, May 19, 1962, 26.

3. Hayes and Laughton, *Gospel Discography*, 239.

4. Dolores Roberts interview.

5. Hicks interview.

6. Logan interview.

7. Broughton, *Black Gospel*, 112.

8. Hayes and Laughton, *Gospel Discography*, 65; Cleveland, *This Sunday,* uncredited album notes; Marshall is the session drummer on Del Shannon's 1960 pop hit "Runaway." Information on Joe Marshall comes from Eugene Chadbourne, "Joseph Marshall," Allmusic.com, http://www.allmusic.com/artist/joseph-marshall -mn0001757823, accessed March 20, 2016; and Howard Rye, "Marshall, Joe [Joseph, Jr.]," Grove Music Online, https://doi.org/10.1093/gmo/9781561592630 article.J633400, accessed May 13, 2020.

9. Despite the "Reverend" honorific, Cleveland was not yet ordained at the time of this recording.

10. Hayes and Laughton, *Gospel Discography*, 65.

11. *Billboard*, November 3, 1962, 1.

12. Roberts, *Gospel Truth*, 6.

13. Richard Harrington, "Inspiring the Multitudes: The Reverend James Cleveland and His Gospel Legacy," *Washington Post*, February 17, 1991, Sunday Show G1, quoted in Darden, *People Get Ready*, 272.

14. *Billboard*, September 8, 1962, 14.

15. Hayes and Laughton, *Gospel Discography*, 66. The December 12 album was released as Savoy LP 14068, *The Soul of James Cleveland*. In addition to Billy Preston on organ, Joe Marshall was on drums.

16. Cleveland, *How Great Thou Art*, uncredited album notes.

17. Hayes and Laughton, *Gospel Discography*, 66.

18. Ibid.

19. *Billboard*, March 16, 1963, 68.

20. *Billboard*, August 19, 1989, 61.

21. Greer, *Only a Look*, 151.

22. Hayes and Laughton, *Gospel Discography*, 230.

23. Reid interview.

24. Hicks interview.

25. Greer, *Only a Look*, 153.

26. *Billboard*, May 11, 1963, 26; October 19, 1963, 30.

27. Black and Timmons, "History of the First Baptist Church of Nutley, NJ."

28. Logan interview, August 14, 2019.

29. Hicks interview.

30. *Angelic Choir*, uncredited liner notes; Hayes and Laughton, *Gospel Discography*, 15.

31. *Angelic Choir*, uncredited liner notes.

32. Bines interview.

33. Dolores Roberts interview.

34. Logan interview, June 13, 2018.

Chapter 7. Peace Be Still

1. Dolores Roberts interview.

2. Logan interview.

3. Reid interview.

4. Gospel choirs do not employ a bass section.

5. Reid interview.

6. Although he was not at Trinity Temple in 1963, the church's current pastor, Dr. Norman Kenneth Miles Sr, told me that unless another event was taking place, he couldn't see any reason the church would have declined a request from First Baptist to use its sanctuary on a Thursday evening (Miles interview). The Thursday, September 19, 1963, date used by Hayes and Laughton, *Gospel Discography*, comes from Ruppli and Porter, *Savoy*, 196.

7. Broughton, *Black Gospel*, 112.

8. Porter e-mail.

9. Logan telephone conversation.

10. Ruppli and Porter, *Savoy*, 196.

11. Thomas interview.

12. Reid interview.

13. Murphy interview.

14. Broughton, *Black Gospel*, 112.

15. Bernadine Hankerson interview.

16. Murphy interview.

17. Johnson, *Gospel Music*, 43–44. A visual example of this technique can be seen in the 1972 film *Amazing Grace*, directed by Alan Elliott and Sydney Pollack. In the film, which documents the recording of Aretha Franklin's Atlantic album *Amazing Grace*, a heavy blanket of the type movers use to protect furniture during transport is draped over the top of the piano.

18. Hicks interview.

19. Pickard interview. Pickard did play piano on volume 7 of the James Cleveland and Angelic Choir Sunday Service series (Savoy MG 14171), as well as on James Cleveland's first recorded sermon, captured live in 1968 at First Baptist Church (Savoy MG 14220). Hayes and Laughton, *Gospel Discography*, 67–68.

20. Hayes and Laughton, *Gospel Discography*, 168.

21. Ancestry.com, New York, New York, U.S., Birth Index, 1910–1965 [database on line], https://www.ancestry.com/imageviewer/collections/61457/images/

47769_b353821–00131. Original data: New York City Department of Health, courtesy of VitalSearch Worldwide, www.vitalsearch-worldwide.com digital images.

22. From a musical program dated Sunday, October 17, 1993, location unknown. Photo available on Discogs.com: https://www.discogs.com/artist/807441-Solomon-Herriott-Jr. The program spells his name "Heriott," though the URL has it as "Herriott."

23. Hayes and Laughton, *Gospel Discography*, 169.

24. New York City Chapter of the American Guild of Organists, "Pipe Organs of NYC: Mother A.M.E. Zion Church," accessed October 14, 2018, http://www.nycago.org/Organs/NYC/html/MotherAMEZion.html.

25. Rev. Dr. Malcolm Byrd interview.

26. Byrd interview.

27. Dr. Shelley listened to the *Peace Be Still* album and on October 28, 2018, emailed the author a document titled "James Cleveland and the Angelic Choir: *Peace Be Still,* Analytic Observations," a selection-by-selection musicological evaluation.

28. Hayes and Laughton, *Gospel Discography*, 66.

29. All biblical references come from the King James Version.

30. Shelley, "James Cleveland and the Angelic Choir."

31. Ibid.

32. Hicks interview.

33. Shelley, "James Cleveland and the Angelic Choir."

34. Little Cedric and the Hailey Singers was a family quartet that took inspiration from contemporary gospel groups such as the Winans. Brothers Cedric and Joel went on to become half of the bestselling R&B vocal group Jodeci and later worked as the R&B duo K-Ci and JoJo.

35. Karen Lynn Davidson, *Our Latter-day Hymns: The Stories and the Messages*, quoted in the Tabernacle Choir blog in "'Master, the Tempest Is Raging': A Hymn about the Storms of Life," July 6, 2018, https://www.thetabernaclechoir.org/articles/the-history-of-master-the-tempest-is-raging.html.

36. C. W. S., "Horatio R. Palmer," Conjubilant with Song blogspot, Monday, April 26, 2010, http://conjubilant.blogspot.com/2010/04/horatio-r-palmer.html; Mary Ann Baker, "Master, the Tempest Is Raging!," Cyber Hymnal, https://hymnary.org/text/master_the_tempest_is_raging.

37. Cyber Hymnal, "Master, the Tempest Is Raging," accessed January 22, 2021, http://www.hymntime.com/tch/htm/m/a/s/t/mastertt.htm, and Cyber Hymnal, "Mary Ann Baker," accessed January 22, 2021, http://www.hymntime.com/tch/bio/b/a/k/e/baker_ma.htm.

38. "Edison Artists." *Edison Phonograph Monthly* 11, no. 2 (March 1913): 9, 10; *Edison Amberola Monthly* 11 (1913), 15l; USCB Cylinder Audio Archive, accessed April 9, 2020, http://www.library.ucsb.edu/OBJID/Cylinder0707.

39. The author is grateful to the Reverend Ewell's daughter, Melodi Ewell Lovely, for providing biographical details on her father.

40. Jon Thurber, "Obituary: Gwendolyn Lightner; Choir Director Gave Gospel Music on West Coast a Modern Beat," *Los Angeles Times*, September 6, 1999, http://articles.latimes.com/1999/sep/06/news/mn-7389.

41. Thurber, "Obituary: Gwendolyn Lightner."

42. Dje Dje and Cogdell, "California Black Gospel," 133, 141.

43. Lovely interview.

44. Joe Peay e-mail.

45. Dje Dje and Cogdell, "California Black Gospel," 195–96, 53n.

46. No known recordings exist of "Peace Be Still" by the Voices of Victory.

47. Thomas interview.

48. Lovely interview.

49. It is interesting to note that even the Edison Mixed Quartet's 1912 arrangement was recorded in 9/8.

50. Heilbut e-mail.

51. Nunnally interview.

52. Peay interview.

53. Vocal and instrumental techniques designed to engage and stimulate reactions of surprised delight from listeners are mainstays in African American music performance generally and gospel in particular.

54. Shelley, "James Cleveland and the Angelic Choir."

55. The crescendo and decrescendo can be heard on the Edison Mixed Quartette's 1912 version, though not with the intensity of the Angelic Choir's rendition.

56. Boone, "James Cleveland's 'Peace Be Still.'"

57. Dolores Roberts interview.

58. Minatee interview.

59. Heath interview.

60. Jabir, "'Peace Be Still,'" 1.

61. Shelley, "This Must Be the Single," 141, 144.

62. Unless otherwise noted, biographical information on Geraldine Griffin and Anna Quick comes from the Watlington interview.

63. "Only 11 and Eyeing Her Future," *New York Amsterdam News*, March 14, 1964, 18. The author thanks Will Boone for providing this article.

64. "Only 11," 18.

65. Hayes and Laughton, *Gospel Discography*, 66.

66. Shelley, "James Cleveland and the Angelic Choir."

67. Boone, "James Cleveland's 'Peace Be Still.'"

68. Watlington interview.

69. Pruter, *Chicago Soul*, 103.

70. *Cash Box*, October 3, 1964, 24.

71. Pruter, *Chicago Soul*, 103–4. Collier has since entered the ministry and, as Pastor Mitty Collier, has gone back to gospel. Now when she sings "I Had a Talk," she uses Cleveland's original lyrics.

72. Watlington interview.

73. Cyber Hymnal, "Where He Leads Me," accessed February 21, 2016, http://www.hymntime.com/tch/htm/w/h/e/r/wherehlm.htm; Cyber Hymnal, "John Samuel Norris," accessed February 21, 2016, http://www.hymntime.com/tch/bio/n/o/r/r/norris_js.htm.

74. Dixon, Godrich, and Rye, *Blues and Gospel Records*, 362, 845.

75. The French Vogue label released selections from *Mahalia Jackson Sings* on a series of LPs (Hayes and Laughton, *Gospel Discography*, 190).

76. Southern Gospel History, "Where He Leads Me," accessed March 4, 2019, http://www.sghistory.com/index.php?n=W.WhereHeLeadsMe.

77. Southern Gospel History, "Where He Leads Me."

78. Shelley, "James Cleveland and the Angelic Choir."

79. Hayes and Laughton, *Gospel Discography*, 15.

80. In April 2018, the author and Malaco Music Group's longtime producer and archivist Wolf Stevenson searched the Malaco vault in Jackson, Mississippi. Although we came upon a few tapes of *Peace Be Still*, they were reproductions of the tape created to record the final album and presumably made for reissue purposes or to have extras on hand. None included the two unreleased matrices.

81. Dixon et al., *Blues and Gospel Records*, 226.

82. *Billboard*, July 29, 1950, 13.

83. Hayes and Laughton, *Gospel Discography*, 343.

84. It is interesting to note that the original composition of "The Twist" was written by Jo Jo Wallace, guitarist and member of the gospel quartet the Sensational Nightingales.

85. Shelley, "James Cleveland and the Angelic Choir."

86. Ibid.

87. *I Shall Wear a Crown*, vol. 3, uncredited album notes (Miracle Valley, AZ: Miracle Revival Recordings 171, undated).

88. Thomas A. Whitfield and the Thomas Whitfield Company, *Hallelujah Anyhow* (Detroit, MI: Sound of Gospel 2D 140, 1983).

89. Spencer, *Protest and Praise*, 203, 217.

90. Shelley, "James Cleveland and the Angelic Choir."

91. Dixon et al., *Blues and Gospel Records*, 482. On the Wiseman side, the narrator explains that the song was sung by "the Negro soldiers, both in this country and over in France, during the war."

92. Shelley, "James Cleveland and the Angelic Choir."

93. See Greene, *Passion for Polka*, esp. 88–89.

94. Woods interview.

95. Warren, *Ev'ry Time*, 135–39; Library of Congress, *Catalog of Copyright Entries*, 3rd series (1961), 231.

96. Hayes and Laughton, *Gospel Discography*, 20.

97. Bessie Griffin and the Gospel Pearls recorded "Caught Up to Meet Him" for Liberty Records in a live program at Chicago's "The Bear" club in May 1963. Other than its similar focus on happiness in the hereafter, the song bears little

resemblance to either the Back Home Choir or Cleveland–Angelic Choir version. See Hayes and Laughton, *Gospel Discography*, 149.

98. Choirs of the Metropolitan Baptist Church, *In Service* (Atlanta: Faith LP 1001, ca. 1963).

99. Shelley, "James Cleveland and the Angelic Choir."

100. William Hunt, "Ken, Thomas," *Dictionary of National Biography*.

101. One could argue, however, that the Lord's Prayer and the pastoral sermon are also essential parts of the order of worship service and have been recorded.

102. Shelley, "James Cleveland and the Angelic Choir."

Chapter 8. The Performativity of "Peace Be Still"

1. Darden, *Nothing but Love*, vol. 2, 107–8.

2. Castellini, "Sit In," 25.

3. Ibid., 5.

4. Ibid., 6–7.

5. Ibid., 105.

6. Walker, *Somebody's Calling My Name*, 17.

7. "Aretha and Her Father—the Reverend C. L. Franklin," Jerry the Jazz Musician, August 17, 2018," https://jerryjazzmusician.com/2018/08/aretha-and-her-father-the-reverend-c-l-franklin/.

8. Quoted in Castellini, "Sit In," 70.

9. Walker, *Somebody's Calling My Name*, 128.

10. Jabir, "Peace Be Still," 2.

11. Boone, "James Cleveland's 'Peace Be Still.'"

12. Quoted in Darden, *People Get Ready*, 249.

13. Emily J. Lordi, *The Meaning of Soul: Black Music and Resilience Since the 1960s* (Durham, NC: Duke University Press, 2020), 5.

14. Chekhov, "Sea Gull," 168.

15. Lordi, *The Meaning of Soul*, 8.

16. Alain Locke, "Negro Youth Speaks," in *The New Negro: Voices of the Harlem Renaissance*, ed. Locke (New York: Touchstone, 1997), 47.

17. *Wall Street Journal*, May 18–19, 2019, C11.

18. Jabir, "Peace Be Still," 2.

19. Locke, "Negro Youth Speaks," 53.

20. Van Rijn, *Roosevelt's Blues*, xv–xvi.

21. Ibid., xvi.

22. Independent record labels as producers of gospel songs with more explicit protest or freedom language is the crux of Castellini's thesis, "Sit In."

23. Hayes and Laughton, *Gospel Discography*, 123.

24. There are rare exceptions, such as "I'm Grateful to the NAACP" by the Gospel Pilgrims, released in 1951 by Atlantic Records. Then again, in 1951, the now-behemoth Atlantic had yet to realize its biggest hits by the Clovers, the

Drifters, Ruth Brown, and Ray Charles and therefore functioned more like an independent label.

25. Billingsley, *Mighty like a River*, 185.

26. Ibid., xxi, 10.

27. Ibid., 10.

28. Lincoln and Mamiya, *Black Church*, 347.

29. Ibid.

30. Schnable, "Singing the Gospel," 1.

31. Castellini, "Sit In," 27.

32. Drake and Cayton, *Black Metropolis*, 12.

33. Mumford. *Newark*, 34, 50, 52.

34. Ibid., 32.

35. Ibid., 38.

36. Ibid., 31, 36.

37. Ibid., 20, 23.

38. Ibid., 53, 54, 64.

39. Ibid., 37–38.

40. Ibid., 27.

41. Ibid., 64–65.

42. Ibid., 70–71.

43. Ibid., 60–61.

44. Ibid., 103; Boskin, *Urban Racial Violence*, 118.

45. Mumford. *Newark*, 78.

46. Ibid., 103.

47. Ibid., 80–82, 88–89, 94.

48. *New Jersey Afro American*, August 17, 1963, 1.

49. Dolores Roberts interview.

50. Stancil interview.

51. Cohodas, *Spinning Blues into Gold*, 196–97.

52. *Billboard*, October 12, 1968, 19, 88.

53. Checker 5048, 1968.

54. Ibid.

55. Checker 5046, 1968.

56. Checker 5043, 1967.

57. Nikki Giovanni and the New York Community Choir, *Truth Is on Its Way*, Right-On Records, 1971. Many thanks to Doctor Johari Jabir for introducing me to this selection.

58. The entire performance was captured on the album soundtrack, but only portions were included in the film.

59. Mel Stuart, dir., *Wattstax* (Culver City, CA: Columbia, 1973).

60. Heaven Dee-Etts, Designer DLP 7256.

61. Marovich album notes, 46, 50.

62. *Billboard,* July 11, 1992, 30.

63. *James Cleveland and the Cleveland Singers with the New Jersey Mass Choir* (Newark, NJ: Savoy SL-14761, 1984). It is probable that Gertrude Deadwyler Hicks, a member of the New Jersey Mass Choir, participated on this recording.

64. Minatee interview.

65. *Billboard,* February 1, 2020, 41.

Chapter 9. The Release of Peace Be Still

1. *Cash Box,* October 12, 1963, 42.

2. Hudson album notes.

3. Ruppli and Porter, *Savoy,* 196; Hayes and Laughton, *Gospel Discography,* 66.

4. SJC stands for Savoy, James Cleveland; 63 represents the year of recording (1963), and the number after the dash is the assigned matrix number.

5. Shaw, *Honkers and Shouters,* 353.

6. Lawrence Roberts interview.

7. Biographical information on Harvey Williams comes from the Williams interview and from Williams, "Harvey Scott Williams," *Personal Prologue: Family Roots and Personal Branches,* July 30, 2018, https://margoleewilliamsbooks.com/tag/harvey-scott-williams/.

8. Phil Thomson, "Harvey: The Mysterious, Cult-Following Designer of Gospel Album Sleeves." Cross Rhythms UK, http://www.crossrhythms.co.uk/articles/music/Harvey_The_mysterious_cultfollowing_designer_of_gospel_album _sleeves/37762/p1/, accessed December 2, 2009; comments by Harvey Williams's half-sister, Margo Lee Williams, and son Keith Williams, posted in reply to Thomson on December 10 and December 9, 2014, respectively. See also http://www.cvinyl.com/coverart/harvey.php, accessed September 10, 2018.

9. Lawrence Roberts interview.

10. John Glassburner's website, Harvey, July 2010, www.harveyalbums.com, contains nearly a full list of Harvey-designed covers for Savoy.

11. Williams interview.

12. David Peterkofsky, prod. and host, "31. Robbie Rogers and the Mysterious Artist Harvey," *For Keeps: A Podcast about Collections and Connections,* forkeeps podcast.com/s6e1-robbie-rogers-and-the-mysterious-artist-harvey, February 1, 2019.

13. Williams interview.

14. Peterkofsky, "Robbie Rogers."

15. Margo Lee Williams, Facebook message to author, March 23, 2020.

16. Williams interview.

17. Williams Facebook message.

18. Peterkofsky, "Robbie Rogers."

19. Williams interview.

20. Peterkofsky, "Robbie Rogers."

21. Heath interview.

22. A. Jeffrey LaValley, Facebook message to author, July 7, 2016.

23. Smallwood interview.

24. Ibid.

25. Ibid.

26. Smallwood, *Total Praise*, 104–5.

27. Johnson, *Gospel Music*, 50.

28. Peay interview.

29. *Billboard,* August 22, 1964, 14.

30. *Billboard*, September 12, 1964, 12.

31. *Billboard*, July 10, 1965, 40.

32. Hayes and Laughton, *Gospel Discography*, 332.

33. *Billboard*, February 27, 1965, 34, 44.

34. Robert M. Marovich, "Walter Hawkins," Malaco Music Group, www.malaco.com/artists/gospel/walter-hawkins, accessed March 8, 2019.

35. *Billboard*, May 10, 1969, 34.

36. Dolores Roberts interview.

37. Logan interview.

38. Murphy interview.

39. Carroll interview.

40. Johnson, *Gospel Music*, 53.

41. Johnson, *Gospel Music*, 55–56. Dolores Roberts repeated the story during her interview.

42. Johnson, *Gospel Music*, 55.

43. "History of the First Baptist Church of Nutley, NJ." 125th Anniversary Program; Johnson, *Gospel Music*, 20.

44. Logan telephone conversation with author, August 14, 2019.

45. O'Neal interview.

46. Johnson, *Gospel Music*, 51.

47. Hudson liner notes.

48. Logan, August 14, 2019, telephone conversation.

49. Reid interview.

50. Logan, August 14, 2019, telephone conversation.

51. Heath interview.

52. Viale, *I Remember Gospel*, 91.

53. Hicks and Murphy interviews.

54. Minatee interviews.

55. Brenda O'Neal, interview with author, March 14, 2017.

56. Ibid.

57. Stancil interview.

58. Ibid.

59. Hayes and Laughton, *Gospel Discography*, 378.

60. Ibid., 325–26.

61. Peay interview; *New Jersey Afro-American*, April 14, 1979, 18. Such gold awards are for publicity and not the same as the certified Gold Records awarded by the Recording Industry Association of America, which are based on confirmed sales of five hundred thousand or more copies of albums or singles.

62. *Billboard*, March 5, 1966, 40, 42.

63. *Ebony*, November 1968, 80.

64. *Billboard*, August 16, 1969, S-16.

65. Heilbut, *Gospel Sound*, 214.

Chapter 10. I Stood on the Banks of Jordan

1. Glover album notes.

2. Hayes and Laughton, *Gospel Discography*, 293.

3. Much gratitude to Nellie Suggs and Sylvia Hicks for information on St. John's Baptist Church.

4. Hudson album notes to *James Cleveland and the Angelic Choir*, vol. 7 (Savoy MG 14171, 1968).

5. *GMWA Score* 1, no. 2 (February 1990): 3.

6. *Cash Box*, August 29, 1964, 7.

7. Hayes and Laughton, *Gospel Discography*, 66.

8. Dolores Roberts, personal communication to author, May 2020.

9. *Billboard*, March 6, 1965, 50.

10. *Billboard*, March 20, 1965, 6. The list refers to the album erroneously as *Standin' on the Banks of the River*.

11. Eleventh Annual Grammy Awards (1968): https://www.grammy.com/grammys/awards/11th-annual-grammy-awards-1968, accessed January 15, 2021.

12. *Billboard*, January 28, 1967, 46, 50.

13. Dolores Roberts interview.

14. Walls interview.

15. *Nutley Sun*, April 8, 1965, 20.

16. Johnson, *Gospel Music*, 28–29.

17. Morris, October 13, 2013, interview.

18. Johnson, *Gospel Music*, 28.

19. Brown interview.

20. Morris, March 21, 2017, interview.

21. *Gospel News Journal* 2, no. 6 (March 1966): 3.

22. Anonymous obituary, Rev. Dr. Lawrence C. Roberts (Paterson, NJ: Carnie P. Bragg Funeral Home, 2008, accessed January 26, 2021, https://www.braggfuneralhome.com/obituary/Rev.-Lawrence-C.-Roberts/Stone-Mountain-GA/561059.

23. Lawrence Roberts interview.

24. Interview of Freeman Johnson from the DVD *Angelic Choir Reunion and Retirement Celebration* (Newark, NJ: Interfaith TV Ministries, 2005).

25. Logan interview.

26. Nunnally interview.

27. Brown interview.

28. Lawrence Roberts interview.

29. *Nutley Sun*, July 3, 1969, 5.

30. Brown interview.

31. Reese, *Gospel Music Workshop*, 10–13.

32. Bines interview.

33. Stancil interview.

34. Roberts, *Gospel Truth*, 8.

35. Watts-Greadington, March 21, 2017, interview.

36. O'Neal, March 21, 2017, interview.

37. Shaw, *Honkers and Shouters*, 356–57.

38. Cohen, *Amazing Grace*, 53–54.

39. Thomas interview.

40. Cohen, *Amazing Grace*, 9, 132; https://www.riaa.com/gold-platinum/?tab _active=default-award&se=aretha+franklin#search_section, accessed March 25, 2019.

41. Watts-Greadington, March 21, 2017, interview.

42. Library of Congress National Recording Preservation Board, "Registry Titles with Descriptions and Expanded Essays," www.loc.gov/programs/national -recording-preservation-board/recording-registry/descriptions-and-essays/, accessed March 8, 2019.

43. Library of Congress National Recording Preservation Board, 2004 additions, https://www.loc.gov/programs/national-recording-preservation-board/ recording-registry/registry-by-induction-years/2004/, accessed March 6, 2016.

Chapter 11. Doxology

1. Elaine Woo, "4,000 Give Cleveland a Gospel Farewell," *Los Angeles Times*, February 17, 1991, http://articles.latimes.com/print/1991–02–17/local/me-2205 _1_gospel-music.

2. Dolores Roberts interview.

3. Lawrence Roberts interview.

4. Freeman Johnson interview for *Angelic Choir Reunion and Retirement Celebration*, Interfaith TV Ministries, DVD, 2005.

5. Lawrence Roberts interview.

6. Walls interview.

7. "Celebrating the Life and Legacy of Rev. Dr. Lawrence Curtis Roberts," memorial service program, Barbara J. Kukla Papers, Newark Public Library, https://digital.npl.org/islandora/object/kukla%3A919877e4–631d-427e-9d86 -6cc88d00bcb4#page/2/mode/2up, accessed January 16, 2021.

8. Stancil interview.

9. Morris interview.

10. Reid interview.

11. Nutley Public Library, "2009 Hall of Fame Inductee, Lawrence Curtis Roberts," Nutley Hall of Fame, http://nutleyhalloffame.nutleypubliclibrary.org/2009-roberts/, accessed April 28, 2020.

12. Hicks interview.

Bibliography

Interviews

Dennis Bines, telephone interview, December 20, 2018.

Isaac Brown, telephone interview, December 6, 2017.

Jay Bruder, e-mail communication, July 15, 2018.

Rev. Dr. Malcolm Byrd, telephone interview, February 4, 2021.

Vivian Carroll, interview, October 13, 2013, Nutley, New Jersey.

Yolanda DeBerry, telephone interview, October 12, 2020.

Rev. Dr. Clay Evans, interview, January 18, 2007, Chicago, Illinois.

Eugene Folk, e-mail communication, December 13, 2016.

Gloria Logan Givens, interview, October 13, 2013, Nutley, New Jersey.

Bernadine Hankerson, interview, October 13, 2013, Nutley, New Jersey.

Linwood Heath, telephone interview, May 5, 2016.

Anthony Heilbut, e-mail correspondence, March 2, 2016.

Gertrude Deadwyler Hicks, interview, October 13, 2013, Nutley, New Jersey.

Gertrude Deadwyler Hicks, telephone interview, March 14, 2017.

Gertrude Deadwyler Hicks, telephone interview, October 9, 2017.

JaVan Hicks, telephone interview, March 14, 2017.

Robert Logan, telephone interview, June 13, 2018.

Robert Logan, telephone interview, August 14, 2019.

Robert Logan, telephone interview, April 20, 2020.

Melodi Ewell Lovely, telephone interview, May 12, 2020.

Norman Kenneth Miles Sr., telephone interview, July 31, 2019.

Rev. Dr. Stefanie Minatee interview, October 13, 2013, Nutley, New Jersey.

Rev. Dr. Stefanie Minatee, telephone interview, April 26, 2016.

Phyllis Morris, interview, October 13, 2013, Nutley, New Jersey.
Phyllis Morris, telephone interview, March 14, 2017.
Raymond Murphy, interview, October 13, 2013, Nutley, New Jersey.
Etta Jean Nunnally, telephone interview, September 6, 2017.
Brenda O'Neal, interview, October 13, 2013, Nutley, New Jersey.
Brenda O'Neal, telephone interview, March 14, 2017.
Sandra Osborne, interview, February 23, 2018, Newark, New Jersey.
Joe Peay, e-mail correspondence, October 19, 2015.
Joe Peay, telephone interview, November 24, 2015.
Herbert Pickard, telephone interview, ca. January 2016.
Bob Porter, e-mail correspondence, April 19, 2020.
Lorenza Brown Porter, telephone interview, December 2005.
Inez Reid, telephone interview, May 23, 2018.
Dolores "Bootsy" Roberts, telephone interview, March 9, 2016.
Rev. Dr. Lawrence C. Roberts, telephone interview, August 2006.
Richard Smallwood, telephone interview, March 6, 2018.
Nellie Grace Daniels Smith, interview, July 12, 2012, Decatur, Georgia.
Lorraine Stancil, telephone interview, July 12, 2016.
Annette May Thomas, telephone interview, December 2, 2016.
Yvonne Walls Winslow, interview, October 13, 2013, Nutley, New Jersey.
Yvonne Walls Winslow, telephone interview, March 14, 2017.
Yvonne Walls Winslow, interview, February 23, 2018, Newark, New Jersey.
Geraldine Griffin Watlington, telephone interview, August 20, 2016.
Margo Lee Williams, telephone interview, April 12, 2019.
Floriene Watson Willis, telephone interview, July 5, 2013.
Jacqui Watts-Greadington, interview, October 13, 2013, Nutley, New Jersey.
Jacqui Watts-Greadington, telephone interview, March 14, 2017.
Kenneth Woods Jr., interview, February 19, 2007, Chicago, Illinois.

Primary Sources

Billboard
The Cash Box
Chicago Defender
Ebony
Edison Amberola Monthly
Edison Phonograph Monthly
The GMWA Score
Gospel News Journal
Los Angeles Times
New Jersey Afro American
New York Amsterdam News
New York Times
Nutley Sun

Radio Dealer
Toronto Star
Wall Street Journal

Secondary Sources

Absher, Amy. *The Black Musician and the White City: Race and Music in Chicago, 1900–1967*. Ann Arbor: University of Michigan Press, 2014.

Billboard magazine. *Billboard 1944 Music Year Book*. New York: Billboard, 1944.

Billingsley, Andrew. *Mighty like a River: The Black Church and Social Reform*. New York: Oxford University Press, 1999.

Black, Hattie, and Bettye Timmons. *First Baptist Church of Nutley Anniversary Booklet*. Nutley, NJ: First Baptist Church, 2014.

Boone, Will. "James Cleveland's 'Peace Be Still' in the Midst of the Civil Rights-Era Tempest." Paper presented at the Society for Ethnomusicology Conference, Pittsburgh, Pennsylvania, November 16, 2014.

Boskin, Joseph. *Urban Racial Violence in the Twentieth Century*. Beverly Hills, CA: Glencoe, 1969.

Broughton, Viv. *Black Gospel: An Illustrated History of the Gospel Sound*. Dorset, UK: Blandford, 1985.

Broven, John. *Record Makers and Breakers: Voices of the Independent Rock 'n' Roll Pioneers*. Urbana: University of Illinois Press, 2009.

Carpenter, Bil. *Uncloudy Days: The Gospel Music Encyclopedia*. San Francisco: Backbeat, 2005.

Castellini, Michael. "Sit In, Stand Up and Sing Out!: Black Gospel Music and the Civil Rights Movement." MA thesis. Georgia State University, 2013.

Chekhov, Anton. "The Sea Gull," in *Chekhov: The Major Plays*. New York: Signet Classics, 1964.

Cherry, Robert, and Jennifer Griffith. "Down to Business: Herman Lubinsky and the Postwar Music Industry." *Journal of Jazz Studies* 10, no. 1 (Summer 2014): 1–24.

Clark, Kenneth P. *Dark Ghetto: Dilemmas of Social Power*. Middletown, CT: Wesleyan University Press, 1989.

Cohen, Aaron. *Amazing Grace*. New York: Continuum, 2011.

Cohodas, Nadine. *Spinning Blues into Gold: The Chess Brothers and the Legendary Chess Records*. New York: St. Martin's, 2000.

Darden, Robert. *Nothing but Love in God's Water*. Vol. 2, *Black Sacred Music from Sit-Ins to Resurrection City*. University Park: Pennsylvania State University Press, 2016.

———. *People Get Ready! A New History of Gospel Music*. New York: Continuum, 2004.

Davidson, Karen Lynn. *Our Latter-day Hymns*, quoted in the Tabernacle Choir blog in "'Master, the Tempest Is Raging': A Hymn about the Storms of Life," July 6, 2018, https://www.thetabernaclechoir.org/articles/the-history-of-master -the-tempest-is-raging.html.

Dixon, Robert M. W., John Godrich, and Howard W. Rye. *Blues and Gospel Records, 1890–1943,* 4th ed. Oxford, UK: Clarendon, 1997.

DjeDje, Jacqueline Cogdell. "The California Black Gospel Tradition: A Confluence of Musical Styles and Cultures." In DjeDje and Eddie S. Meadows, eds. *California Soul: Music of African Americans in the West,* 124–75. Berkeley: University of California Press, 1998.

Drake, St. Clair, and Horace R. Cayton. *Black Metropolis: A Study of Negro Life in a Northern City.* New York: Harcourt, Brace, 1945.

Fox, Jon Hartley. *King of the Queen City: The Story of King Records.* Urbana: University of Illinois Press, 2009.

Greene, Victor. *A Passion for Polka.* Berkeley: University of California Press, 1992.

Greer, Ronald L. *Only a Look.* Bloomington, IN: Westbow, 2015.

Harrington, Brooksie Eugene. "Shirley Caesar: A Woman of Words." Ph.D. diss., Ohio State University, 1992.

Hayes, Cedric J., and Robert Laughton. *The Gospel Discography, 1943–1970.* West Vancouver, BC: Eyeball Productions, 2007.

Heilbut, Anthony. *The Fan Who Knew Too Much.* New York: Alfred A. Knopf, 2012.

———. *The Gospel Sound,* 4th ed. New York: Limelight, 1992.

Houston, Cissy. *How Sweet the Sound: My Life with God and Gospel.* New York: Doubleday, 1998.

———. *Remembering Whitney.* New York: Harper, 2013.

Hunt, William. "Ken, Thomas." *Dictionary of National Biography.* Edited by Sir Sidney Lee. New York: Macmillan, 1892.

Jabir, Johari. "'Peace Be Still': Rev. James Cleveland and the Paradox of Peace in the Civil Rights Movement." Unpublished paper, 2019.

Jaker, Bill, Frank Sulek, and Peter Kanze. *The Airwaves of New York: Illustrated Histories of 156 AM Stations in the Metropolitan Area, 1921–1996.* Jefferson, NC: McFarland, 1998.

Johnson, Birdie Wilson. *Gospel Music in Newark and North Jersey through the Eyes of Reverend Dr. Lawrence C. Roberts.* Self-published, 2001.

Kukla, Barbara J. *Swing City: Newark Nightlife, 1925–50.* New Brunswick, NJ: Rutgers University Press, 2002.

Lincoln, C. Eric, and Lawrence H. Mamiya. *The Black Church in the African American Experience.* Durham, NC: Duke University Press, 1990.

Locke, Alain, ed. *The New Negro: Voices of the Harlem Renaissance.* New York: Touchstone, 1997.

Lordi, Emily J. *The Meaning of Soul: Black Music and Resilience Since the 1960s.* Durham, NC: Duke University Press, 2020.

Marovich, Robert M. *A City Called Heaven: Chicago and the Birth of Gospel Music.* Urbana: University of Illinois Press, 2015.

———. *The Gospel according to Malaco.* Jackson, MI: Malaco Music Group, 2019.

Martin, Lerone. *Preaching on Wax: The Phonograph and the Shaping of Modern African American Religion.* New York: New York University Press, 2014.

Mumford, Kevin. *Newark: A History of Race, Rights, and Riots in America*. New York: New York University Press, 2007.

Prial, Dunstan. *The Producer: John Hammond and the Soul of American Music*. New York: Farrar, Straus and Giroux, 2006.

Pruter, Robert. *Chicago Soul*. Urbana: University of Illinois Press, 1992.

Reese, Charles F. *The Gospel Music Workshop of America*. Dayton, OH: Gospel Music Workshop of America, 2004.

Roberts, Lawrence C. *The Gospel Truth*. Pittsburgh, PA: Dorrance, 1993.

Ruppli, Michel, and Bob Porter. *The Savoy Label: A Discography*. Westport, CT: Greenwood, 1980.

Schnable, Allison. "Singing the Gospel, Forging the Ties That Bind? Ethnographic Study of a Youth Gospel Choir." Working Paper 43. Princeton, NJ: Princeton University Center for Arts and Cultural Policy Studies, 2011.

Shaw, Arnold. *Honkers and Shouters: The Golden Years of Rhythm and Blues*. New York: Collier, 1978.

Shelley, Braxton D. "'This Must Be the Single': Valuing the Live Recording in Contemporary Gospel Performance." In *Living the Life I Sing: Gospel Music from the Dorsey Era to the Millennium*. Edited by Alphonso Simpson Jr. and Thomas A. Dorsey III, 139–47. San Diego, CA: Cognella, 2017.

Smallwood, Richard. *Total Praise: The Autobiography*. Newark, NJ: Godzchild, 2019.

Spencer, Jon Michael. *Protest and Praise: Sacred Music of Black Religion*. Minneapolis, MN: Fortress, 1990.

Thompson, Mark A. *Space Race: African American Newspapers Respond to Sputnik and Apollo 11*. Master's Thesis, University of North Texas, December 2007.

Van Rijn, Guido. *Roosevelt's Blues: African-American Blues and Gospel Songs on FDR*. Jackson: University Press of Mississippi, 1997.

Viale, Gene. *I Remember Gospel and I Keep on Singing*. Bloomington, IN: Author House, 2010.

Wald, Gayle F. *Shout, Sister, Shout! The Untold Story of Rock-and-Roll Trailblazer Sister Rosetta Tharpe*. Boston: Beacon, 2007.

Walker, Wyatt Tee. *Somebody's Calling My Name: Black Sacred Music and Social Change*. Valley Forge, PA: Judson, 1992.

Warren, Gwendolyn Sims. *Ev'ry Time I Feel the Spirit*. New York: Henry Holt, 1997.

Young, Alan. *Woke Me Up This Morning: Black Gospel Singers and the Gospel Life*. Jackson: University Press of Mississippi, 1997.

Album Notes

Angelic Choir. *It's the Holy Ghost*. Uncredited album notes, Savoy MG 14049, 1961. 33¹/₃ rpm phonograph disc.

Angelic Choir. *The Angelic Choir*. Uncredited album notes. Savoy MG 14075, 1963. 33¹/₃ rpm phonograph disc.

Bostic, Joe. Album notes to *Gospel Singing at Newport with the Back Home Choir and the Drinkard Singers*. RCA Victor MG V-8245, 1958. 33 1/3 rpm phonograph disc.

Cleveland, James, with the Angelic Choir. *This Sunday—in Person: James Cleveland with the Angelic Choir*. Volume 1. Uncredited album notes. Savoy MG 14059, 1962. 33¹/₃ rpm phonograph disc.

Cleveland, James, with the Angelic Choir. *How Great Thou Art*. Volume 2. Uncredited album notes. Savoy MG 14063, 1962. 33¹/₃ rpm phonograph disc.

Funk, Ray. Album notes to *Newark Gospel Quartets*. Gospel Heritage HT 324, 1990. 33¹/₃ rpm phonograph disc.

Glover, Anna L. Album notes to *The Saint John's Inspirational Choir of Scotch Plains, NJ*. Savoy MG 14088, 1964. 33¹/₃ rpm phonograph disc.

Hildebrand, Lee, and Opal Nations. Album notes to *The Great 1955 Shrine Concert*. Specialty SPCD-7045–2, 1993. Compact disc.

Hudson, George. Album notes to Volume 7: *James Cleveland and the Angelic Choir*. Savoy MG 14171, 1968. 33¹/₃ rpm phonograph disc.

I Shall Wear a Crown, vol. 3. Uncredited album notes. Miracle Valley, AZ: Miracle Revival Recordings 171, undated. 33¹/₃ rpm phonograph disc.

A Night with Daddy Grace. Uncredited album notes. Harlequin HQ 702, 1955. 33¹/₃ rpm phonograph disc.

Pierce, Don. Album notes to *Wally Fowler's All Nite Singing Concert*. Starday SLP-112, 1959. 33¹/₃ rpm phonograph disc.

The Voices of Tabernacle. *The Love of God*. Uncredited album notes. HOB Records, LP-233, 1959. 33¹/₃ rpm phonograph disc.

Online Resources

All Music: www.allmusic.com.

Ancestry.com: www.ancestry.com.

Arts High School, New Jersey. "Our History." www.nps.k12.nj.us/ART/our-school/our-history/.

Billboard: www.billboard.com.

"Celebrating the Life and Legacy of Rev. Dr. Lawrence Curtis Roberts," memorial service program, Barbara J. Kukla Papers, Newark Public Library, https://digital.npl.org/islandora/object/kukla%3A919877e4–631d-427e-9d86-6cc88d00bcb4#page/2/mode/2up.

Cummings, Tony. "The Coleman Brothers: The Newark Gospel Music Pioneers." Cross Rhythms. www.crossrhythms.co.uk/articles/music/The_Coleman_Brothers_The_Newark_Gospel_music_pioneers/42801/p1/.

CVinyl.com.

Discogs.com.

Glassburner, John. Harvey website. www.harveyalbums.com.

Goldberg, Marv. R&B Notebooks. www.uncamarvy.com/ApolloTheaterShows/apollo.html.

Greater Abyssinian Baptist Church, Newark, NJ. "Our History." http://www.greaterabyssinian.org/about-gabc.html.

Grammy.com.

Hymntime.com.

JazzDisco. Savoy Records Discography Project. www.jazzdisco.org/savoy-records.

Jerry Jazz Musician. https://jerryjazzmusician.com.

Keepnews, Peter. "Rudy Van Gelder, Audio Engineer Who Helped Define Sound of Jazz on Record, Dies at 91." *New York Times*, August 26, 2016. https://www.nytimes.com/2016/08/26/arts/music/rudy-van-gelder-audio-engineer-who-helped-define-sound-of-jazz-on-record-dies-at-91.html?_r=0.

Library of Congress National Recording Registry. www.loc.gov/programs/national-recording-preservation-board/recording-registry/descriptions-and-essays/.

The Living New Deal. "We Patch Anything": WPA Sewing Rooms in Fort Worth, Texas. livingnewdeal.org/we-patch-anything-wpa-sewing-rooms-in-fort-worth-texas/.

Malaco Music Group: www.malaco.com.

Metropolitan Baptist Church, Newark, NJ. "Our History." www.mbcnewarknj.org/aboutus/whatwebelieve/history.php.

National Public Radio. www.npr.org.

Nelson, Jeff. "I Was Pulled Over This Week Too." LinkedIn, July 8, 2016. www.linkedin.com/pulse/i-pulled-over-week-too-jeff-nelson.

New Hope Baptist Church, Newark, NJ. www.newhopenewark.org.

New York City Chapter of the American Guild of Organists. www.nycago.org.

Nutley Hall of Fame, Nutley (NJ) Public Library. "2009 Hall of Fame Inductee Lawrence Curtis Roberts." http://nutleyhalloffame.nutleypubliclibrary.org/2009-roberts/.

Obituary, Rev. Dr. Lawrence C. Roberts, author unknown, 2008.

The Old Landmark: Celebrating Our Apostolic Heritage. "Sin-Killing Sanders: The Legacy of Bishop Oscar Haywood Sanders." oldlandmark.wordpress.com/category/people/oneness-pentecostals/oscar-sanders/.

Old Newark (NJ) website. www.oldnewark.com.

Peterkofsky, David, producer and host. *For Keeps: A Podcast about Collections and Connections*. https://forkeepspodcast.com/s6e1-robbie-rogers-and-the-mysterious-artist-harvey.

Recording Industry Association of America. Gold and Platinum Awards. www.riaa.com/gold-platinum.

Roberts, Rev. Lawrence interview. From the Malaco Music Group DVD *Gospel Legends*, 2007. Interview also available as Malaco Music Group Gospel Legends, "Rev. Lawrence Roberts Interview," on YouTube: May 13, 2014. https://www.youtube.com/watch?v=qs_XaXBsu44.

Southern Gospel History. www.sghistory.com.

Thomson, Phil. "Harvey: The Mysterious, Cult-Following Designer of Gospel Album Sleeves." Cross Rhythms. www.crossrhythms.co.uk/articles/music/Harvey_The_mysterious_cultfollowing_designer_of_gospel_album_sleeves/37762/p1/.

University of California at Santa Barbara Cylinder Archive. http://cylinders
.library.ucsb.edu/.

Williams, Margo Lee. "Harvey Scott Williams." *Personal Prologue: Family Roots
and Personal Branches,* July 30, 2018. https://margoleewilliamsbooks.com/tag/
harvey-scott-williams/.

Videos

Angelic Choir Reunion and Retirement Celebration. Interfaith TV Ministries, 2005.
DVD.

Majette, Eric Jr. Video interview of Rev. Lawrence Roberts. Living Testimony
Foundation, 2005.

Stuart, Mel, dir. *Wattstax.* Culver City, CA: Columbia, 1973. Film.

Index

Index

ROBERT M. MAROVICH hosts *Gospel Memories* on Chicago's WLUW 88.7 FM and is founder and editor-in-chief of *The Journal of Gospel Music*, http://www.journalofgospelmusic.com. In 2019, he was nominated for a GRAMMY Award, Best Album Notes, for *The Gospel According to Malaco*. He is the author of *A City Called Heaven: Chicago and the Birth of Gospel Music*.

Music in American Life

"Susanna," "Jeanie," and "The Old Folks at Home": The Songs of Stephen C. Foster
from His Time to Ours (2d ed.)   *William W. Austin*

Songprints: The Musical Experience of Five Shoshone Women   *Judith Vander*

"Happy in the Service of the Lord": Afro-American Gospel Quartets in
Memphis   *Kip Lornell*

Paul Hindemith in the United States   *Luther Noss*

"My Song Is My Weapon": People's Songs, American Communism, and the Politics
of Culture, 1930–50   *Robbie Lieberman*

Chosen Voices: The Story of the American Cantorate   *Mark Slobin*

Theodore Thomas: America's Conductor and Builder of Orchestras,
1835–1905   *Ezra Schabas*

"The Whorehouse Bells Were Ringing" and Other Songs Cowboys Sing
Collected and Edited by Guy Logsdon

Crazeology: The Autobiography of a Chicago Jazzman   *Bud Freeman,
as Told to Robert Wolf*

Discoursing Sweet Music: Brass Bands and Community Life in Turn-of-the-Century
Pennsylvania   *Kenneth Kreitner*

Mormonism and Music: A History   *Michael Hicks*

Voices of the Jazz Age: Profiles of Eight Vintage Jazzmen   *Chip Deffaa*

Pickin' on Peachtree: A History of Country Music in Atlanta, Georgia
Wayne W. Daniel

Bitter Music: Collected Journals, Essays, Introductions, and Librettos
Harry Partch; edited by Thomas McGeary

Ethnic Music on Records: A Discography of Ethnic Recordings Produced in the
United States, 1893 to 1942   *Richard K. Spottswood*

Downhome Blues Lyrics: An Anthology from the Post–World War II Era
Jeff Todd Titon

Ellington: The Early Years   *Mark Tucker*

Chicago Soul   *Robert Pruter*

That Half-Barbaric Twang: The Banjo in American Popular Culture   *Karen Linn*

Hot Man: The Life of Art Hodes   *Art Hodes and Chadwick Hansen*

The Erotic Muse: American Bawdy Songs (2d ed.)   *Ed Cray*

Barrio Rhythm: Mexican American Music in Los Angeles   *Steven Loza*

The Creation of Jazz: Music, Race, and Culture in Urban America
Burton W. Peretti

Charles Martin Loeffler: A Life Apart in Music   *Ellen Knight*

Club Date Musicians: Playing the New York Party Circuit   *Bruce A. MacLeod*

Opera on the Road: Traveling Opera Troupes in the United States,
1825–60   *Katherine K. Preston*

The Stonemans: An Appalachian Family and the Music That Shaped Their
Lives   *Ivan M. Tribe*

Transforming Tradition: Folk Music Revivals Examined   *Edited by Neil V. Rosenberg*

The Crooked Stovepipe: Athapaskan Fiddle Music and Square Dancing in Northeast
Alaska and Northwest Canada   *Craig Mishler*

The University of Illinois Press
is a founding member of the
Association of University Presses.

———————————————————

Composed in 10.25/14 Chaparral Pro
with ITC Garamond Std display
by Lisa Connery
at the University of Illinois Press
Manufactured by Sheridan Books, Inc.

University of Illinois Press
1325 South Oak Street
Champaign, IL 61820-6903
www.press.uillinois.edu